WordPerfect®
Workbook
for IBM Personal Computers

Version 5.0
©WordPerfect Corporation 1988
All Rights Reserved
Printed in U.S.A.

WKXXENWPIXX50—8/88
ISBN 1-55692-200-0

WordPerfect Corporation • 1555 N. Technology Way • Orem, Utah 84057 U.S.A.
Telephone: (801) 225-5000 • Telex: 820618 • FAX: (801) 227-4477

Contents

Introduction

The WordPerfect Workbook is designed to help you understand how to create and format a variety of documents. Along the way you are introduced to many of the features of WordPerfect and some ideas for automating word processing tasks.

Because of the power and flexibility of WordPerfect, not all features or applications of the program can be covered in the workbook. However, by turning to the WordPerfect reference manual, you can find many of the answers you need when using WordPerfect to create your own documents.

Computers

By the time you are ready to start using the Workbook, you (or someone else) should already have installed WordPerfect and your printer, and know how to start the WordPerfect program. All these details can be found in the Getting Started section of the WordPerfect reference manual.

Hard Disk

If you are running WordPerfect from a hard disk, then make sure that your default directory is C:\WP50\LEARN before starting the lessons.

1 Press **List Files** (F5) and check the name of the directory at the bottom of your screen.

If you do not see "Dir C:\WP50\LEARN*.*" displayed, then you need to change to the C:\WP50\LEARN directory, or WordPerfect will not be able to find the workbook files.

2 Type an equal sign (=) to change directories, and then type **c:\wp50\learn** for the name of the new default directory.

If you have your workbook files copied to another directory, then type the name of that directory instead of C:\WP50\LEARN.

3 Press **Enter** (←) to change to the C:\WP50\LEARN directory, and then press **Cancel** (F1) to return to the normal WordPerfect screen.

You should now be ready to start the lessons in the workbook.

Two Disk Drives

If you are running WordPerfect from a two disk drive system, you need to create a Workbook diskette from your Learning diskette, or there will not be enough room to save the files you create in the lessons.

You can create a Workbook diskette by following the steps below.

1 Place the Learning diskette in drive A, and a blank, formatted diskette in drive B.

If you do not know how to format a diskette, turn to the Two Disk Drives heading in the Special Techniques lesson of Fundamentals.

2 From the DOS prompt, type **copy a:*.wkb b:** and then press **Enter** (↵) to copy the first group of workbook files to the formatted diskette in drive B.

3 When the copying is completed, enter the following commands (one at a time) to copy the rest of the files to the formatted diskette in drive B:

```
copy  a:*.wpm  b:
copy  a:*.sty  b:
copy  a:*.wpg  b:
```

When you finish copying the files, the diskette in drive B is ready to be used for the lessons. After starting WordPerfect, make sure your Workbook diskette is in drive B, and then start the lessons.

Lessons

The lessons begin by covering the fundamentals of word processing, and then branch out into three areas of special emphasis.

While you can start at Lesson 1 and go straight through the lessons, you may want to skip *Fundamentals* if you are familiar with WordPerfect and select the lessons you want to do from the other three sections. Except for *Fundamentals* and the first two lessons of *Merging Documents*, the lessons do not need to be done in any particular order.

Keystrokes

Keystrokes are included in the steps of each lesson to guide you through accomplishing a task. The names of features (**Center**, **Format**, **Style**, etc.) are bolded, while menu options are capitalized (Advance, Margins, Page, etc.).

All are followed by the key(s) you need to press to select the feature or option, except for the following standard word processing keys.

Most of the features in WordPerfect are selected by pressing a Function key on your keyboard (F1, F2, F3, etc.). Often you will need to hold down **Shift**, **Alt**, or **Ctrl** and then tap a function key to select the feature.

Whenever you need to hold down one key and then tap another, the two keys are separated by a hyphen (e.g., Ctrl-F1). If there are any additional keys to press, they are separated by a comma from the first two keystrokes (Shift-F8,1).

Menu Options

You can select an option from a menu in WordPerfect by typing the option number or by typing the letter that is bolded in the option name.

A OPTION NUMBER
B OPTION LETTER

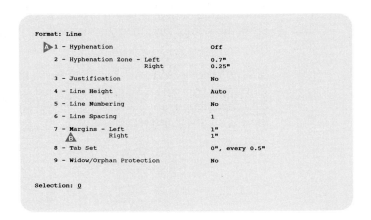

```
Format: Line

 A  1 - Hyphenation                        Off

    2 - Hyphenation Zone - Left            0.7"
                          Right            0.25"

    3 - Justification                      No

    4 - Line Height                        Auto

    5 - Line Numbering                     No

    6 - Line Spacing                       1

    7 - Margins - Left                     1"
     B            Right                    1"

    8 - Tab Set                            0", every 0.5"

    9 - Widow/Orphan Protection            No


Selection: 0
```

While the numbered options are used in the workbook lessons, you may want to try using the bolded letters to select options.

Printers and Settings

The first time you save a document created in WordPerfect, the document is assigned to the printer that is currently selected. Because the Standard Printer is sent with each copy of WordPerfect, the workbook files on your Learning diskette were created with the Standard Printer selected.

As soon as you retrieve a workbook file, WordPerfect automatically selects the Standard Printer for you. However, you need to select your own printer before printing. Steps are included in the lessons (when needed) to help you select your printer.

The workbook files were also created using the standard feature settings (initial settings) that come with your original copy of WordPerfect. Because the initial settings of the program can be changed with Setup (Shift-F1), your copy of WordPerfect may have a different set of initial settings.

If a step is not working correctly, or an option on a menu shows a setting that does not match that on an illustrated screen, it may be that Setup has been used to change a setting.

Tutorial

A tutorial is included on the Learning diskette (or in your C:\WP50\LEARN directory) that provides an alternative to working through *Fundamentals* in the workbook.

If you are unfamiliar with computers and word processing, or are having difficulties with the first few lessons, you may want to start with the tutorial instead of the workbook. The tutorial guides you *on screen* through an introduction to the keyboard and the basic skills of word processing. If you press the wrong key, then the tutorial lets you know which keystroke to use.

Several other lessons are also included in the tutorial that introduce individual features of WordPerfect (Text Columns, Table of Authorities, etc.) Instructions for starting the tutorial are included in Getting Started in the WordPerfect reference manual.

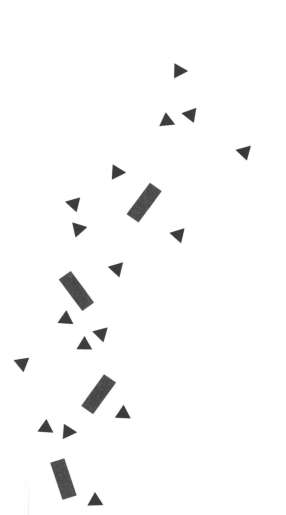

Lesson 1: Personal Note

At times you may want to attach a personal note to a letter or form. Instead of trying to locate a pen and piece of paper, you can use WordPerfect to quickly type and print the note.

Typing the Note

1 Type the following note *without* pressing Enter (↵) when you reach the end of a line:

The enclosed form needs to be filled out before receiving medical benefits through the company. You should complete sections A through D and return the form by Friday for your benefits to start at the beginning of next month.

Press Shift to type capital (uppercase) letters. If you type an incorrect letter or word, press Backspace until the mistake is erased, and then begin typing again.

There are three things that you may have noticed while typing the note.

A CURSOR
B WORD WRAPPING
C STATUS LINE

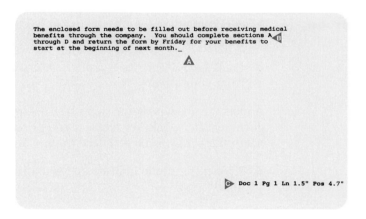

First, a cursor (usually a blinking "-") moves ahead of the text as you type, or backward if you are using Backspace to erase a mistake. The cursor indicates the place where the next character will be typed or erased.

Second, when a line fills with text, the cursor returns to the left margin in a new line. This automatic return is often referred to as word wrapping.

The screens in the workbook lessons were created with the Standard Printer selected. Because you selected your own printer when installing WordPerfect, the words may wrap in a different place on the screen.

Third, the bottom line of the screen (the status line) lets you know if you are editing a second document (Doc), on which page (Pg) and line (Ln) the cursor is located, and the current position of the cursor in the line (Pos).

Because the status line is used by WordPerfect to display the cursor position (and other messages), it remains at the bottom of the screen and cannot be used for typing or editing text.

Printing the Note

Now that you have typed the note, it can be sent to the printer.

2 Press **Print** (Shift-F7) to display the print menu.

3 Select Full Document (1) from the Print menu to send the note to the printer.

If your printer does not print, check to make sure it is turned on, on line, and that the printer cable is attached securely to your computer and printer. If you did not select a printer when installing WordPerfect, then the printer may have problems printing.

For details on selecting a printer, turn to the Appendix in the WordPerfect reference manual.

Clearing the Screen

After printing the note, the screen can be cleared to begin creating or editing another document.

4 Press **Exit** (F7) to let WordPerfect know you want to remove the note from your screen.

A message appears on the status line, asking if you want to save the document (to a disk) for future use. For some documents, like personal notes, there may be no real need to store the document once it is printed.

5 Type **n** (for no) to indicate that you do not want to save the personal note.

A second message appears on the status line, asking if you want to exit (leave) WordPerfect.

6 Type **n** to clear the screen and stay in WordPerfect.

Because you chose to stay, WordPerfect clears the screen for you.

Doc 1 Pg 1 Ln 1" Pos 1"

By using Exit to clear the screen, you do not need to use Backspace to erase all the characters before starting a new document.

Summary

During this lesson, you were introduced to the following tasks:

- Clearing the screen (without saving).
- Printing a document.

For a complete listing of all tasks introduced in the lessons, turn to *Feature Summary* at the end of the workbook.

Lesson 2: Letter 1 – First Draft

One of the documents most frequently created with WordPerfect is a letter. Because a letter may go through several drafts before it is ready to send, the first draft of a business letter is typed and printed in this lesson, and then revised in a later lesson.

Typing the Inside Address

Most business letters begin with an inside address.

1 Type the first line of the inside address:

Reservations Manager

At this point, the cursor needs to be returned to the left margin at the beginning of a new line.

2 Press **Enter** to wrap the cursor to the left margin and start a new line.

By pressing Enter, you can start your own new line *before* the cursor reaches the right margin. Now, finish typing the inside address using Enter to end each line of the address.

3 Type the rest of the address:

Parkway Inn
1780 Delaware Ave.
Buffalo, NY 14209

Enter can also be used to add blank lines for extra spacing between blocks of text on the page.

4 Press **Enter** twice to add two blank lines for extra spacing.

Typing the Subject Line

The subject line in a letter briefly states the purpose of the letter. Because the reservations manager should immediately understand the purpose of the letter, the subject line can be emphasized by typing the words in capital (uppercase) letters.

However, instead of holding down Shift, try using Caps Lock to lock all the letters into uppercase.

5 Press **Caps Lock** to type uppercase letters. Notice that the "Pos" on the status line switches to uppercase letters.

6 Type the subject line *without* using Shift:

corporate marketing conference reservations

7 Press **Enter** twice to add extra spacing.

Now, compare your letter to the one illustrated in the screen below.

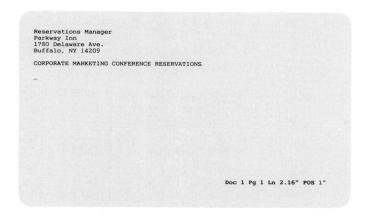

```
Reservations Manager
Parkway Inn
1780 Delaware Ave.
Buffalo, NY 14209

CORPORATE MARKETING CONFERENCE RESERVATIONS

-




                                          Doc 1 Pg 1 Ln 2.16" POS 1"
```

From time to time during the lessons, a screen or printed document will be illustrated to help you determine if you are on the right track.

If you are lost, you can always start the lesson over by using Exit to clear your screen.

8 Press **Caps Lock** to return to typing lowercase letters. Notice that the "Pos" on the status line switches to uppercase and lowercase letters again.

Typing the Message   **9** Type the message of the letter:

We would like to make reservations for a marketing conference to be held on December 1, 2, and 3 of this year. A minimum of 40 persons will be attending. Besides accommodations for those attending, we will also require your largest suite, a conference room, and an extra meeting room for smaller gatherings.

An early confirmation would be sincerely appreciated.

If you have not already been introduced to the arrow keys, they are usually located to the right of the typing keys on your keyboard. The arrow keys let you move the cursor up, down, to the left, or to the right through your document without disturbing the text.

Because the arrow keys are used to move the cursor through text on your screen, they are sometimes called the cursor keys.

10 Place the cursor on the space *after* the word "also" in the last sentence of the first paragraph (use the arrow keys).

11 Press **Backspace** until you erase the word "also" and the space before it.

The arrow keys can also be used to move to a place in your document where a word needs to be added. For example, the type of suite that needs to be reserved should be indicated.

12 Place the cursor on the first letter of the word "suite" in the same sentence.

13 Type **executive** and press the **Space Bar**.

Notice that the text in the line moves forward to make room for the new word. You can move the cursor anywhere you want in a document and add new text by simply typing.

14 Press **Down Arrow** (↓) once and watch how WordPerfect adjusts the words in each line to make room for the new text.

You may need to press Down Arrow more than once to adjust the paragraph.

This adjustment is called "rewriting" and WordPerfect does it for you automatically as you move down through your text.

Typing the Signature Block

After typing the message of the letter, space can be left for a signature by pressing Enter to add some empty lines.

15 Place the cursor at the end of the sentence "An early confirmation. . .".

16 Press **Enter** four times to leave room for a signature.

17 Type the following signature block:

Megan Sills
Marketing Director

The first draft of the letter is finished. Before printing, compare your letter to the one illustrated below.

```
Reservations Manager
Parkway Inn
1780 Delaware Ave.
Buffalo, NY 14209

CORPORATE MARKETING CONFERENCE RESERVATIONS

We would like to make reservations for a marketing conference to
be held on December 1, 2, and 3 of this year.  A minimum of 40
persons will be attending.  Besides accommodations for those
attending, we will require your largest executive suite, a
conference room, and an extra meeting room for smaller
gatherings.

An early confirmation would be sincerely appreciated.


Megan Sills
Marketing Director_



                                        Doc 1 Pg 1 Ln 4.16" Pos 2.8"
```

If the first paragraph on your screen does not look *exactly* the same as the one illustrated, Enter may have been pressed at the end of each line (instead of letting WordPerfect wrap the lines).

Also remember that the illustrations in the workbook were created using the Standard Printer. For details on how printer selection affects the lessons in the workbook, turn to the Printers and Settings heading in the workbook introduction.

Printing the Letter

The letter can be sent to the printer by using the Print menu.

18 Press **Print** (Shift-F7) and select Full Document (1) from the Print menu to send the letter to the printer.

Notice that the printed page looks similar to the text on your screen. As you type, WordPerfect makes sure that each line of text contains the same words on the screen as on the printed page.

You may have also noticed that the text at the right margin is lined up evenly. This feature is called right justification, and is on when you first start WordPerfect.

If you prefer to have justification off when a document is printed, turn to the Justification heading in the Special Techniques lesson at the end of Fundamentals *for details.*

Saving the Letter

With the document printed, you are ready to clear your screen with Exit. However, because the letter will be revised later on, it should be saved before clearing the screen.

19 Press **Exit** (F7) and type **y** (for yes) when you see the Save message.

The "Document to be saved:" message is displayed on the status line at the bottom of the screen. Saving a document means storing it as a file on a diskette or hard disk. Before a file can be created with WordPerfect, the file needs to be named.

20 Type **park** and then press **Enter** to name the file in which the letter will be saved.

A light (usually red) should light up on the diskette drive or hard disk to indicate that WordPerfect is saving the letter in a file on disk. After the letter has been saved, WordPerfect then displays the Exit message, asking if you want to exit the WordPerfect program.

21 Type **n** (for no) to stay in the program and have WordPerfect clear the screen.

Displaying the Filename

Before finishing the lesson, you may want to check to see if the file was actually saved by using WordPerfect's file management feature.

22 Press **List Files** (F5), and then press **Enter** to display a list of files on your disk.

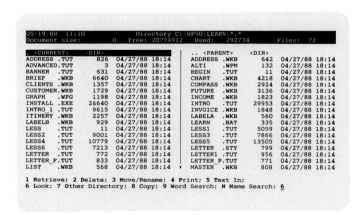

While all the filenames on your screen may not be displayed in the above illustration, you should be able to find the "Park" filename. If the filename is not listed, then you may need to press Down Arrow until the name scrolls on to the screen.

If you are in the wrong place, press Cancel (F1) until you return to the document screen, and then try repeating the lesson from step 22. You should not type anything or press any other key after pressing List Files (except Enter) to display the correct list of files.

After locating the file, notice that the size of the file (in bytes) and the date and time it was created are included with the filename. This information can be very important when trying to keep a large number of files organized.

23 Press **Exit** (F7) to leave the list of files and return to the WordPerfect screen.

You should now have a cleared screen and be ready to continue on to the next lesson.

Summary

During this lesson, you were introduced to the following tasks:

- Adding extra spacing.
- Displaying a list of filenames.
- Moving the cursor.
- Saving a document and clearing the screen.
- Typing upper-case letters.

For a complete listing of all tasks introduced in the lessons, turn to *Feature Summary* at the end of the workbook.

Lesson 3: Memo Form

One of the most frequently used forms in a business office is the memo. The memo heading usually includes a date, the name of the person receiving the memo (To), the name of the person sending the memo (From), and a brief description of the subject (Subject or RE). The area below the heading is then reserved for the contents of the memo.

One of the advantages of using a word processor is that you can create a memo form, save it as a file, and then retrieve the form any time you need to type a memo. You do not need to keep a supply of pre-printed memo forms in stock, as the same memo form file can be used over and over again.

Designing the Form

The first step in creating a memo form (or any form) is to design the form. For example, a simple design for a corporate memo might include the following titles and a line to separate the heading from the message.

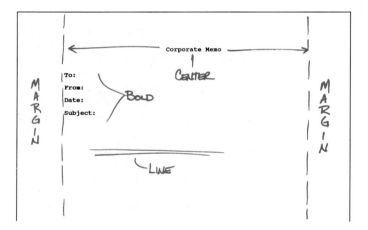

Notice that the "Corporate Memo" title is centered between the margins. The rest of the titles in the memo heading are bolded (highlighted) to help the reader quickly find information in the heading.

Centering the Memo Title

After deciding on a design, you can use WordPerfect's features to help you create the form.

1 Press **Center** (Shift-F6) to center the cursor between the left and right margins.

The cursor moves to the center position in line 1. You may want to glance down at the status line to see the exact position (Pos) of the cursor in the line.

2 Type **Corporate Memo** for the memo title.

As you type, WordPerfect automatically centers the title between the margins.

3 Press **Enter** to end centering and return the cursor to the left margin.

4 Press **Enter** three more times to add extra spacing between the memo title and the memo heading.

Highlighting the Other Titles

Now that the memo title has been created, you can type the rest of the titles by using Bold to highlight the text, and Tab and Enter to add extra spacing to the right and below the title.

5 Press **Bold** (F6) to begin bolding.

Check the status line and notice that the "Pos" number is now brighter (monochrome screens) or a different color (color screens) to show you that Bold is on.

6 Type **To:** and then press **Bold** (F6) again to end bolding.

7 Press **Tab** to add some space between the title and the text that will be filled in.

8 Press **Enter** twice to add double spacing after the "To:" title.

Now that you have created the "To:" title, type the "From:" and "Date:" titles using the same features.

9 Press **Bold** (F6), type **From:** for the title, and then press **Bold** again to end bolding.

10 Press **Tab** for extra spacing to the right of the title, and then press **Enter** twice for extra spacing after the title.

11 Press **Bold** (F6), type **Date:** for the title, and then press **Bold** again to end bolding.

12 Press **Tab** for extra spacing to the right of the title, and then press **Enter** twice for extra spacing after the title.

Now, try typing the "Subject:" title on your own, following the keystrokes in steps 11 and 12.

13 Type **Subject:** for the last title using **Bold**, **Tab**, and **Enter**.

Your memo form should now look similar to the one illustrated below.

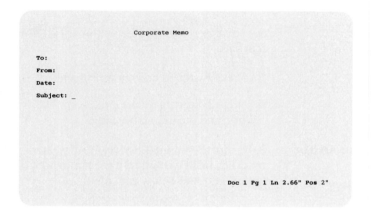

Creating a Line

Equal signs (=) can be used to draw a simple double line between the heading and the message area. However, instead of typing one character at a time, there are two ways that you can quickly create a line with equal signs.

The first way is to simply hold down the key.

14 Hold down the equal sign (=) until the line is filled with equal sign characters, then release the key.

You may need to press Backspace to erase any equal signs that wrapped to the next line.

Most of the keys on your keyboard are designed to repeat when you hold them down. This is a great feature if you want to repeat a character, or hold down an arrow key to move the cursor quickly through the text.

However, the function keys (F1 through F10, etc.) are also repeating keys. Holding down one of these keys turns a feature on and off continuously. When using a function key, simply tap the key lightly to select a feature.

Now that you have been introduced to repeating keys, there is a more precise way of repeating a character.

15 Hold down Backspace to quickly erase the line of equal signs.

While the repeating keys are a feature of your keyboard, WordPerfect also provides a way of repeating characters by entering a repeat value, and then typing a single character.

16 Press **Center** (Shift-F6) to center the line of equal signs.

17 Press **Escape** (Esc) to select the Repeat feature.

18 Type **40** for the repeating value, and then type an equal sign (=).

A centered line of 40 equal signs immediately appears. By using a repeat value, you can instantly create a line that is exactly the length you need.

19 Press **Enter** twice to end centering and add extra spacing.

Your memo form should now look similar to the one illustrated below.

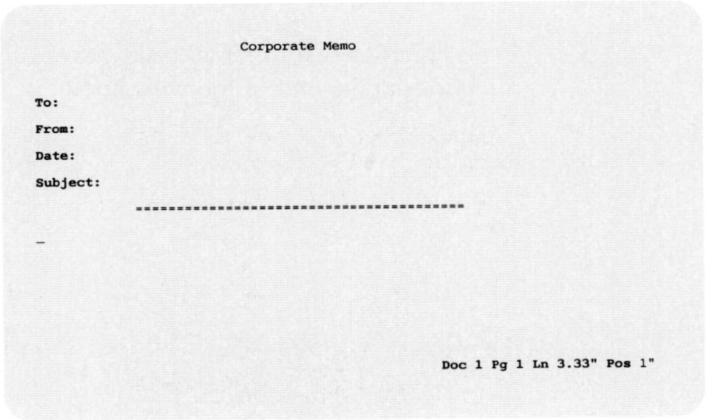

```
                          Corporate Memo


        To:

        From:

        Date:

        Subject:

                     ---------------------------------------

        _




                                       Doc 1 Pg 1 Ln 3.33" Pos 1"
```

Inserting a Date

Before saving the memo form, an extra item can be added to the design that will save you time when filling in the memo.

20 Place the cursor on the "Date:" title, and then press **End** to move the cursor to the end of the line.

21 Press **Date/Outline** (Shift-F5) and select Date Code (2).

The current date appears! And because you selected Date Code, the displayed date will always be current whenever you fill in or print the memo.

Saving the Form

With the date code added, the memo form is ready to save.

22 Press **Exit** (F7) and type **y** (for yes) to save the memo.

23 Type **memo** for the filename, and then press **Enter** to save the form.

24 Type **n** to stay in WordPerfect and clear the screen.

If you want to check and see if the file was actually saved on disk, go ahead and use List Files (F5) as you did in Lesson 2. Otherwise, you are ready to continue to the next lesson.

Summary

During this lesson, you were introduced to the following tasks:

- Adding extra spacing.
- Bolding text.
- Centering text between the left and right margins.
- Inserting a date.
- Repeating a character.

For a complete listing of all tasks introduced in the lessons, turn to *Feature Summary* at the end of the workbook.

Lesson 4: Letter 1 – Second Draft

The first draft of the reservation letter (Lesson 2) has been reviewed and contains a few editing remarks. Because the first draft has already been saved in a file on disk, all you need to do is retrieve the letter, make the necessary changes, print it for approval, and then save the edited letter.

Retrieving the Letter

List Files can be used to retrieve the letter from the file on your disk.

1 Press **List Files** (F5), and then press **Enter** to display a list of files on your disk.

2 Move the cursor to the "Park" filename, and then select Retrieve (1) from the menu at the bottom of the list.

A copy of the file is retrieved to the WordPerfect screen for editing. This is only a copy; the original contents stay in the file on disk in case you want to start over again. The name of the file is displayed in the left half of the status line for your convenience.

Typing Over the Dates

With a copy of the first draft on the screen, you are ready to begin making changes. Checking the edited letter, it appears that the conference has been moved to December 6, 7, and 8.

```
Reservations Manager
Parkway Inn
1780 Delaware Ave.
Buffalo, NY 14209

CORPORATE MARKETING CONFERENCE RESERVATIONS
                        6, 7, and 8
We would like to make reservations for a marketing conference to
held on December 1, 2, and 3 of this year.  A minimum of 40
persons will be attending.  Besides accommodations for those
attending, we will require your largest executive suite, a
conference room, and an extra meeting room for smaller
gatherings.

An early confirmation would be sincerely appreciated.


Megan Sills
Marketing Director
```

3 Place the cursor on the number "1" in the first paragraph.

Instead of erasing each date and then typing the new date, Typeover can be used to replace the numbers as you type. Typeover is turned on and off by pressing Insert in the lower-right corner of your keyboard.

4 Press **Insert** (Ins) to turn on Typeover.

When Typeover is on, a "Typeover" message appears in the left half of the status line.

5 Type **6, 7, and 8** to replace the old with the new dates.

6 Press **Insert** (Ins) again to turn off Typeover, and return to inserting text.

Moving the Sentence The sentence about the minimum number of persons attending the conference needs to be moved to the beginning of the second paragraph.

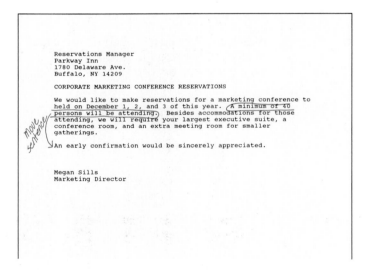

```
            Reservations Manager
            Parkway Inn
            1780 Delaware Ave.
            Buffalo, NY 14209

            CORPORATE MARKETING CONFERENCE RESERVATIONS

            We would like to make reservations for a marketing conference to
            held on December 1, 2, and 3 of this year.  A minimum of 40
            persons will be attending.  Besides accommodations for those
            attending, we will require your largest executive suite, a
            conference room, and an extra meeting room for smaller
            gatherings.

            An early confirmation would be sincerely appreciated.


            Megan Sills
            Marketing Director
```

One way of moving the sentence would be to erase it using Backspace, and then type it at the beginning of the second paragraph. However, WordPerfect provides a Move feature that performs the same task with just a few keystrokes.

7 Place the cursor anywhere in the "minimum persons" sentence.

8 Press **Move** (Ctrl-F4) and select Sentence (1) from the menu.

The entire sentence is immediately highlighted so you can see the text WordPerfect will be helping you to move. A menu on the status line lets you select a Move, Copy, Delete or Append option.

9 Select Move (1) to remove (cut) the sentence from the paragraph.

The sentence is removed from the screen and saved in a special file. Now all you need to do is to indicate where you want the sentence relocated, and then retrieve it with Enter (instead of Retrieve).

10 Place the cursor at the beginning of the second paragraph.

11 Press **Enter** to retrieve the sentence.

You have completed the move in just a few keystrokes. Now, check your screen to make sure that the sentence is in the correct place.

▲ SENTENCE AT BEGINNING OF SECOND PARAGRAPH

```
Reservations Manager
Parkway Inn
1780 Delaware Ave.
Buffalo, NY 14209

CORPORATE MARKETING CONFERENCE RESERVATIONS

We would like to make reservations for a marketing conference to
be held on December 6, 7, and 8 of this year.  Besides
accommodations for those attending, we will require your largest
executive suite, a conference room, and an extra meeting room for
smaller gatherings.
A minimum of 40 persons will be attending.  An early confirmation
would be sincerely appreciated.


Megan Sills
Marketing Director



C:\WP50\LEARN\PARK                        Doc 1 Pg 1 Ln 3.16" Pos 1"
```

Centering the Letter

Although it was not mentioned in the editing remarks, a short letter looks better on the page if it is centered between the top and bottom margins.

You could move to the beginning of the letter and add a few empty lines to force the text down the page. However, WordPerfect provides a Center Page Top to Bottom feature that does all the work for you.

12 Press **Page Up** (PgUp) to move the cursor to the very beginning of the letter.

13 Press **Format** (Shift-F8) and select Page (2) to display a menu of page formats.

14 Select Center Page Top to Bottom (1) from the menu, and then press **Exit** (F7) to return to the letter.

Previewing the Letter

While the letter is not centered on the document screen, you can see it centered on the preview screen. The preview screen is a special screen that lets you take a look at how your document will appear on the printed page.

15 Press **Print** (Shift-F7) and select View Document (6).

If you have a graphics card in your computer, you should see the full page displayed on the screen.

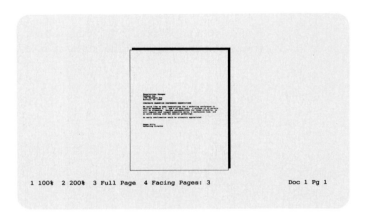

If you do not have a graphics card in your computer, then WordPerfect does its best to represent the printed page on your screen. You will not be able to see a full page on your screen; however, you should be able to see the added space above the text that indicates the letter will be centered.

In the preview screen, as in the document screen, the length and number of lines in the letter will depend on which printer you selected when installing WordPerfect. The above preview screen displays the letter with the Standard Printer selected.

Printing the Letter

After previewing the letter, you can return to the Print menu to send it to the printer.

16 Press **Cancel** (F1) to return to the Print menu.

17 Select Full Document (1) to send the second draft of the letter to the printer.

While you cannot make any corrections to the document from the preview screen, you can return to the document screen, make the necessary changes, and then preview the document again before printing.

Looking into the File

At the beginning of the lesson it was noted that the letter on your screen is only a copy of the file contents on disk. If that is true, then you have been making changes to the copy while the original has remained untouched.

18 With the printed letter in hand, press **List Files** (F5), and then press **Enter** to display the list of files.

19 Move to the "Park" filename and select Look (6) from the menu at the bottom of the screen.

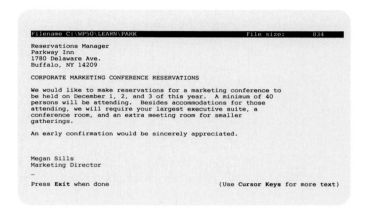

```
Filename C:\WP50\LEARN\PARK                        File size:      834

Reservations Manager
Parkway Inn
1780 Delaware Ave.
Buffalo, NY 14209

CORPORATE MARKETING CONFERENCE RESERVATIONS

We would like to make reservations for a marketing conference to
be held on December 1, 2, and 3 of this year.  A minimum of 40
persons will be attending.  Besides accommodations for those
attending, we will require your largest executive suite, a
conference room, and an extra meeting room for smaller
gatherings.

An early confirmation would be sincerely appreciated.


Megan Sills
Marketing Director
_

Press Exit when done                       (Use Cursor Keys for more text)
```

What you are now seeing is the actual contents of the "Park" file on disk. Compare the file contents to the printed letter, and you can immediately see that the document in the file has not been changed at all.

20 Press **Exit** (F7) once to leave the Look screen, and then press **Exit** again to return to the edited letter.

Replacing the File

Although the letter on file and the edited copy on your screen are now different, they both have the same filename. Because the letter in the file on disk is no longer needed, it can be replaced with the edited version.

21 Press **Exit** (F7) and type **y** to save the edited letter.

The name "Park" appears next to the "Document to be saved:" message at the bottom of the screen. WordPerfect always displays the name of the copy in case you want to use the same name when saving.

The name of the directory or diskette from which the document was retrieved is also included with the name of the document. When the directory or diskette name is included with the filename, it is called the "pathname" of the file.

22 Press **Enter** to use the "Park" name.

WordPerfect checks to see if there is another file on disk with the same name. Because the "Park" filename already exists, WordPerfect asks if you want to replace the original letter with the edited copy on the screen.

23 Type **y** to replace the original letter with the edited version, and then type **n** to stay in WordPerfect and clear the screen.

Was the original letter replaced by the edited copy? Before finishing the lesson, you can check again by using Look.

24 Press **List Files** (F5), and then press **Enter** to display the list of files.

25 Move the cursor to the "Park" file and press **Enter** to select the Look option.

You can select Look by typing a "6" or by pressing Enter.

Compare the printed letter to the file contents. As you can see, the first draft of the letter is gone and the edited version is now in the "Park" file.

26 Press **Exit** (F7) once to leave the Look screen, and then press **Exit** again to return to the document screen.

The advantages of being able to work on a copy while keeping the original safely stored are important. And, once you are satisfied with the changes, it only takes a few keystrokes to replace the original version with the edited copy.

Summary

During this lesson, you were introduced to the following tasks:

- Centering text between the top and bottom margins.
- Looking into a file on disk.
- Moving a sentence.
- Moving the cursor a page at a time.
- Previewing a document.
- Replacing a document on disk and clearing the screen.
- Retrieving a file (List Files).
- Typing over existing text.

For a complete listing of all tasks introduced in the lessons, turn to *Feature Summary* at the end of the workbook.

Lesson 5: Memo Fill-in

A memo needs to be sent to all department managers, informing them of the tentative plans for the regional marketing conference. Because you have already created and saved a memo form (Lesson 3), you can retrieve it, fill it in, and then print the memo.

1 Press **List Files** (F5), and then press **Enter** to display the list of files.

2 Place the cursor on the "Memo" file, and then select Retrieve (1) to retrieve the file.

Filling In the Heading

With the memo form on the screen, you can start filling in the heading information.

3 Place the cursor on the "To:" title and then press **End** to move to the end of the line.

4 Type **All Marketing Managers** for the "To" information.

End is convenient to use when filling in a line of text in the memo because it places the cursor in the exact position needed to type the information.

Editing in Reveal Codes

Before continuing to fill in the memo, it may be useful to introduce you to a special editing screen that lets you see what really happens when you press End.

5 Place the cursor at the beginning of the "From:" title.

6 Press **Reveal Codes** (Alt-F3) to see the WordPerfect codes in the memo.

Your screen should now look similar to the one illustrated below, with the top half of the screen displaying the memo the way it normally looks, and bottom half of the screen displaying the memo with all the WordPerfect codes.

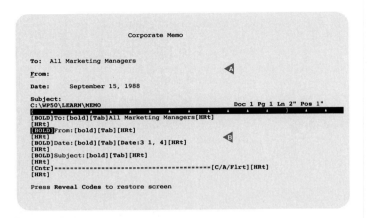

A reverse video bar divides the screen in half, and indicates the position of each tab stop setting with a triangle (▲).

Below the bar is the Reveal Codes screen, which displays the codes that WordPerfect places in a document whenever you press a key such as Tab, Enter, or Bold. Each code tells WordPerfect exactly what to do when displaying or printing the memo.

The [Bold] and [bold] codes around the "From:" title tell WordPerfect to begin and end printing bolded characters.

7 Press **Right Arrow** (→) to place the cursor between the [Bold] and [bold] codes surrounding the "From:" title.

Notice that the cursor in the Reveal Codes screen is a solid block that is placed directly on each code or character as you move the cursor.

When the cursor is between the Bold codes, the Pos number on the status line is bolded (top half of the screen).

8 Press **Right Arrow** (→) until the cursor is on the [Tab] code.

When the cursor moves past the [bold] code, WordPerfect ends bolding and returns to displaying (and printing) normal text, and the Pos number returns to a normal display.

▲ UNBOLDED POS NUMBER

▲ CURSOR ON TAB CODE

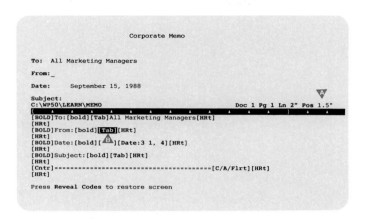

The tab is shown as a [Tab] code, and moves the cursor to the next tab stop setting.

9 Press **Right Arrow** (→) to move the cursor past the [Tab] code.

Once you insert a tab, it can be quickly adjusted by resetting the tab stops instead of adding or erasing spaces. In addition, text will line up on a tab, but may not always line up if you have used spaces.

While you're in the Reveal Codes screen, you may want to try filling in the rest of the memo heading.

10 Make sure that the cursor is to the right of the [Tab] code in the Reveal Codes screen, and then type **Megan Sills** for the "From:" information.

As you make changes in the bottom half of the screen, you can see the effect they are having on the memo in the upper half of the screen.

11 Place the cursor at the beginning of the "Subject:" line, and then press **End** to move the cursor to the end of the line.

When you press End, the cursor moves past all of the codes in the line to the exact place you need to enter the information for the subject. This is especially helpful when you are in the document screen, and cannot see the WordPerfect codes.

12 Type **Corporate Marketing Conference** for the subject information.

Before leaving the Reveal Codes screen, notice the [HRt] and [Date:3 1, 4] codes.

A [HRt] CODE
B [DATE:3 1, 4] CODE

The [HRt] codes are inserted each time you press Enter, and they tell WordPerfect to end the current line and return to the left margin to start a new line. The [Date:3 1, 4] code tells WordPerfect to display and print the current date in the memo.

WordPerfect depends on the computer for the current date. Whatever date is set when you turn on your computer is the date that WordPerfect uses.

You are probably beginning to realize that codes are very similar to text. You insert them by pressing a key, and you can erase them with Backspace or Delete.

13 Place the cursor on the [Tab] code next to "Corporate Marketing Conference."

14 Press **Delete** (Del) to erase the code, and then press **Tab** to insert another [Tab] code into the memo.

As you can see, a code is simply an instruction telling WordPerfect exactly what you want done with the text.

15 Press **Reveal Codes** (Alt-F3) to return to the document screen.

16 Press **Page Down** (PgDn) to move the cursor to the very end of the memo form.

Typing the Message

You can now finish filling out the memo by typing the message in the area below the line of equal signs.

17 Type **We have arranged** for the beginning of the message.

Underlining a Word

Because the reservations at the Parkway Inn have not been confirmed, the word "tentatively" should be included before "arranged." It would also be a good idea to emphasize the word by underlining it.

18 Place the cursor on the "a" at the beginning of the word "arranged."

19 Press **Underline** (F8), and type **tentatively** in the memo.

Notice that the word is underlined as you type, and that the Pos number on the status line is underlined to indicate that Underline is on.

```
                        Corporate Memo


     To:  All Marketing Managers
     From:    Megan Sills
     Date:    September 15, 1988
     Subject:  Corporate Marketing Conference
              -------------------------------------------

     We have tentativelyarranged




     C:\WP50\LEARN\MEMO                    Doc 1 Pg 1 Ln 3.33" Pos 2.9"
```

Underlining on the screen depends on the type of monitor you are using. Color monitors may display underlining in a different color, while some monochrome monitors cannot display underlining at all.

20 Press **Underline** (F8) to turn off the feature, and then press the **Space Bar**.

Now you can continue typing the rest of the memo for the marketing supervisors.

21 Press **End** to move to the end of the line, press the **Space Bar** and then type:

a Corporate Marketing Conference for December 6, 7, and 8 to be held at the Parkway Inn in Buffalo, New York. All marketing managers and representatives are required to attend. If you wish to bring a spouse or friend, please let Beverly know by the end of the month so that arrangements can be made.

I will let you know as soon as possible when final approval has been given for the time and place.

Your filled in memo should now look similar to the one illustrated in the screen below.

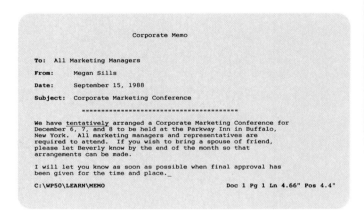

Setting a Tab Stop

The information in the heading may not be lined up on the same tab stop, or may be too close to the titles. You could adjust the alignment of the information by adding one or more extra tabs. However, the problem can also be corrected by setting a single tab stop for the entire memo.

22 Press **Page Up** (PgUp) to move the cursor to the very beginning of the memo.

23 Press **Format** (Shift-F8), select Line (1) to display the menu of line formats, and then select Tab Set (8).

A tab ruler appears at the bottom of the screen with an "L" marking the position of each current tab stop.

TAB STOP

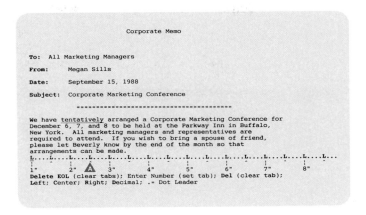

You can erase all the tab stops by using Delete to End of Line, and then set a single tab stop at 2 inches.

24 Press **Home** and then **Left Arrow** (←) to move to the beginning of the ruler.

25 Press **Delete to End of Line** (Ctrl-End) to erase all the preset tab stops.

26 Press **Right Arrow** (→) until the cursor stops at 2" (or any place you want) on the tab ruler, and then type **L** to set a left-justified tab stop.

27 Press **Exit** (F7) twice to save the new tab setting and return to the memo.

Now all the information in the memo heading is lined up at 2 inches (or whatever setting you selected).

28 Press **Reveal Codes** (Alt-F3) to display the tab setting code.

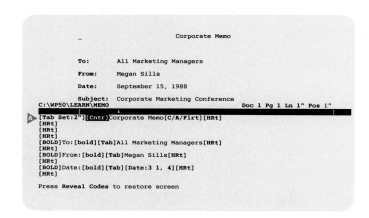

29 Press **Reveal Codes** (Alt-F3) to return to the document screen.

Printing the Memo

With the memo finished, you can send it to the printer.

30 Press **Print** (Shift-F7), and then select Full Document (1) to send the memo to the printer.

The printed memo should look like the version you created on your screen, with the tab setting at exactly 2 inches (or whatever setting you selected) from the left margin.

Saving the Memo

With the memo printed, you are ready to save the memo for future reference. However, because you will use the same memo form again, you need to create a new file for the filled in memo.

31 Press **Exit** (F7) and type **y** to save the filled in memo.

Even though the original memo form filename appears next to the "Document to be saved:" message, you can type a new filename to have WordPerfect create a new file for the filled-in memo.

32 Type **parkmemo** and press **Enter** to create the "parkmemo" file.

33 Type **n** to clear the screen and stay in WordPerfect.

The memo is now ready to send to the marketing managers, and you have your own copy on disk in case you ever need to refer to it again.

Before finishing the lesson, you may want to practice setting a tab stop by retrieving the memo form ("Memo") and setting a tab stop at 2 inches. This will save you the time of inserting a new tab setting code each time you use the memo form.

Summary

During this lesson, you were introduced to the following tasks:

- Editing in the Reveal Codes screen.
- Moving the cursor.
- Setting a tab stop.
- Underlining text.

For a complete listing of all tasks introduced in the lessons, turn to *Feature Summary* at the end of the workbook.

Lesson 6: Letter 1 – Final Draft

The second draft of the reservation letter has returned with no additional editing marks. However, the date at the top of the letter and initials below the signature block still need to be included.

Retrieving the Letter

By now you should be familiar with the filename of the letter, so try using Retrieve (instead of List Files) to retrieve a copy of the second draft to the screen.

1 Press **Retrieve** (Shift-F10) and notice that a "Document to be retrieved:" message appears on the status line.

2 Type **park** and then press **Enter** to retrieve a copy of the letter from the file.

Inserting a Date

The date of the reservation letter should be the date the letter is signed. Assuming the letter needs to go out today, you can use Date (as you did in the memo) to insert the current date. However, instead of inserting a code, you can insert the date as text.

3 Press **Reveal Codes** (Alt-F3), and then place the cursor to the right of the Center Page code (if it is not already there).

The Center Page code should always be at the very beginning of the document.

4 Press **Date/Outline** (Shift-F5) and select Date Text (1).

5 Press **Enter** four times to add extra spacing between the date and the inside address.

6 Press **Up Arrow** (↑) until the cursor is at the beginning of the date.

Unlike inserting the date code in the memo, when you select Date Text, the date is inserted as text.

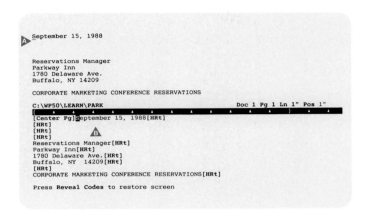

```
▲ September 15, 1988


  Reservations Manager
  Parkway Inn
  1780 Delaware Ave.
  Buffalo, NY 14209

  CORPORATE MARKETING CONFERENCE RESERVATIONS

  C:\WP50\LEARN\PARK                              Doc 1 Pg 1 Ln 1" Pos 1"
[                                                             ]
  [Center Pg]September 15, 1988[HRt]
  [HRt]
  [HRt]       ▲
  [HRt]
  Reservations Manager[HRt]
  Parkway Inn[HRt]
  1780 Delaware Ave.[HRt]
  Buffalo, NY  14209[HRt]
  [HRt]
  CORPORATE MARKETING CONFERENCE RESERVATIONS[HRt]

  Press Reveal Codes to restore screen
```

Because the date appears as text in the Reveal Codes screen, there are no instructions for WordPerfect to keep the date current.

7 Press **Reveal Codes** (Alt-F3) to return to the document screen.

Typing the Initials

Now that the date is set, you can move to the bottom of the letter and add the initials.

8 Press **Page Down** (PgDn) to move the cursor to the end of the signature block, and then press **Enter** twice to double space.

9 Type **cjg** to add the typist's initials to the letter.

Spell-checking the Letter

As a final step in the editing process, you can use WordPerfect's spelling checker to make sure there are no spelling errors, double words, or words that mistakenly contain numbers.

The spelling checker compares each word in a document to a dictionary list of over 120,000 words to make sure that every word is spelled correctly. Whenever WordPerfect can't match a word against the list, then the spelling checker stops and displays suggested spellings for the word.

A SUGGESTED SPELLING

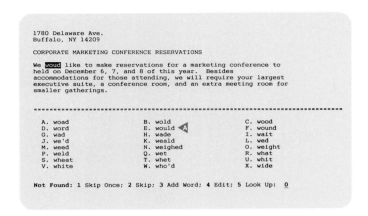

```
1780 Delaware Ave.
Buffalo, NY 14209

CORPORATE MARKETING CONFERENCE RESERVATIONS

We woud like to make reservations for a marketing conference to
held on December 6, 7, and 8 of this year.  Besides
accommodations for those attending, we will require your largest
executive suite, a conference room, and an extra meeting room for
smaller gatherings.

---------------------------------------------------------------

      A. woad              B. wold              C. wood
      D. word              E. would  ◄A         F. wound
      G. wad               H. wade              I. wait
      J. we'd              K. weald             L. wed
      M. weed              N. weighed           O. weight
      P. weld              Q. wet               R. what
      S. wheat             T. whet              U. whit
      V. white             W. who'd             X. wide

Not Found: 1 Skip Once; 2 Skip; 3 Add Word; 4 Edit; 5 Look Up: 0
```

You can correct the spelling by typing the letter next to a suggested word, or by selecting Edit from the menu, making the correction yourself, and then pressing Exit (F7) to continue spell checking.

Sometimes WordPerfect stops on the proper name of a person or street because the word is not found in the dictionary.

A NO SUGGESTED SPELLINGS
B WORD NOT FOUND MENU

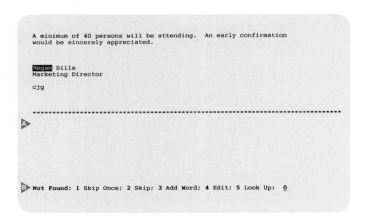

```
A minimum of 40 persons will be attending.  An early confirmation
would be sincerely appreciated.


Megan Sills
Marketing Director

cjg


A ---------------------------------------------------------------




B Not Found: 1 Skip Once; 2 Skip; 3 Add Word; 4 Edit; 5 Look Up: 0
```

If the spelling is correct, then you can select Skip from the menu to have the speller skip over that word for the rest of the document.

If you are running WordPerfect from two disk drives, insert your Speller diskette in drive B before continuing the lesson.

With this brief introduction to the speller, try spell-checking the reservation letter on your own. Most individuals seem to agree that the spelling checker is quite easy to use.

10 Press **Spell** (Ctrl-F2) to display the Spell menu.

11 Select Document (3) from the menu to begin spell-checking the reservation letter.

Remember that when the spelling checker stops on a proper name, simply select Skip to continue. If you get lost, you can always press Cancel (F1) one or two times to stop the spell-checking and return to the document screen.

12 Spell-check the letter.

After spell-checking is finished, WordPerfect displays a count of the number of words in the letter and a message telling you to press any key to continue.

13 Press any key to return to the document screen.

Printing and Saving

Now that the final draft of the letter is finished, you can send it to the printer, and then save it on disk.

If you are running WordPerfect from two disk drives, you need to replace the Speller diskette with your Workbook diskette before continuing the lesson.

14 Press **Print** (Shift-F7) and select Full Document (1).

15 Press **Exit** (F7) and type **y** to save the letter.

16 Press **Enter** to use the "Park" filename, type **y** to replace the original file with the edited letter on the screen, and then type **n** to clear the screen and stay in WordPerfect.

The final draft is stored on disk, and you are ready to continue on to the next lesson.

Summary

During this lesson, you were introduced to the following tasks:

- Inserting a date.
- Retrieving a file (Retrieve).
- Spell-checking a document.

For a complete listing of all tasks introduced in the lessons, turn to *Feature Summary* at the end of the workbook.

Lesson 7: Getting Help

Now that you have been introduced to a few basic features of WordPerfect, it would be a good idea to explore the resources available for getting the help you may need to solve a problem, answer a question, or find out more about WordPerfect.

Cancel

One of the most valuable tools for helping you out of an immediate problem is the Cancel key. By pressing Cancel one or more times, you can back out of menus or messages.

For example, suppose you have retrieved a letter and are making some editing changes.

1 Press **Retrieve** (Shift-F10), type **musicbox.wkb** for the filename, and then press **Enter** to retrieve a copy of the letter.

After making the necessary corrections, you are ready to save the document and clear the screen.

2 Press **Exit** (F7), type **y** to save the letter, press **Enter** to use the same filename, and then type **y** to replace the letter.

You are now faced with the question "Exit WP? (Y/N) No". All of a sudden, you remember that the left and right margins need to be changed to 2 inches.

If you type "y", you will exit WordPerfect. If you type "n", the screen will be cleared, and you will need to retrieve the letter again. However, you can also press Cancel to keep the letter on the screen.

3 Press **Cancel** (F1) to return to the letter.

You are returned to the same place in the letter to continue editing. You are now ready to change the margin settings.

4 Press **Format** (Shift-F8), select Line (1), and then select Margins Left/Right (7).

As you are about to enter the new margin settings, you remember that you forgot to make sure that the cursor was at the beginning of the document.

5 Press **Cancel** (F1) three times to return to the letter.

6 Press **Reveal Codes** (Alt-F3) and notice that a margin setting code was not placed in the letter.

7 Press **Page Up** (PgUp) to make sure you are at the beginning of the letter.

8 Press **Format** (Shift-F8), select Line (1), and then select Margins Left/Right (7).

9 Type **2** and press **Enter** for the left margin, and then type **2** and press **Enter** for the right margin.

10 Press **Exit** (F7) to return to the letter.

Notice that a margin setting code is now inserted into the letter, and the Pos number on the status line indicates the new left margin.

Exit is designed to save the setting and return you to the document, while Cancel is designed to return you to the document without saving the setting (whenever possible).

11 Press **Reveal Codes** (Alt-F3) to return to the document screen.

12 Press **Exit** (F7), and then type **n** twice to clear the screen (you do not need to save the letter for the exercise).

Remember to use Cancel as your first "line of defense" when trying to back out of a problem situation.

Help

Many people do not realize that WordPerfect provides a method of getting information that is as close as their keyboard. Help is like having a quick reference manual at your fingertips. You can turn to Help for a list of features and keystrokes, a brief explanation of each feature, or even a keyboard template.

If you are running WordPerfect from two disk drives, you need to make sure that the WordPerfect 1 diskette is in drive B before continuing the lesson. The Help files are located on the WordPerfect 1 diskette.

For example, you may have forgotten where Justification is located in WordPerfect.

1 Press **Help** (F3), and then type **j** to display a list of all the features that start with the letter "J".

A list immediately appears with Justification and the keystrokes you need to press to use the feature.

2 Press **Enter** (or the **Space Bar**) to exit Help.

If you have forgotten what Justification does, a page of reference information is just a keystroke away.

3 Press **Help** (F3), press **Format** (Shift-F8), type **2**, and then type **3** to display a page explaining the Justification feature.

4 Press **Enter** (or the Space Bar) to exit Help.

Where can you find a keyboard template? Try using Help.

5 Press **Help** (F3) twice to display a keyboard template.

When you do find the keystrokes for a feature by displaying the template (or the alphabetical list), you can immediately display the reference page from the template or list by simply pressing the keystrokes.

6 Find Move on the displayed keyboard template, and then press the appropriate key (Ctrl-F4).

While on one reference page, you can turn to another by pressing the appropriate keystrokes for the feature, or by returning to the list (or template), finding the keystrokes, and then pressing them.

7 Press **Bold** (F6) to turn to the page on bolding.

8 Type **d** to display a list of all features that start with "D".

9 Find Date, and then press the appropriate keystrokes to display the reference page.

10 Press **Help** (F3) to return to the keyboard template, and then press **Enter** (or the **Space Bar**) to exit Help.

As you can see, Help is quite flexible and provides a variety of information. If you want a reminder as to how Help works, simply press the Help key.

11 Press **Help** (F3) to display instructions for using Help.

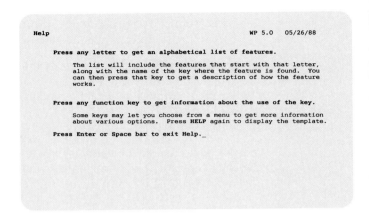

Notice that the version number and date of the program are listed in the upper right corner of the screen. This information is useful to customer support when referring to problems you are having with the program.

12 Press **Enter** (or the Space Bar) to exit Help.

Help is a way of quickly finding the keystrokes for a particular feature, and some summary reference material. However, if you want detailed information about a feature, you should turn to your WordPerfect reference manual for an in-depth explanation.

If you are running WordPerfect from two disk drives, replace the WordPerfect 1 diskette with the workbook diskette before continuing.

Quick Reference

A handy, quick reference card is provided in your WordPerfect package that lists all the features in alphabetical order, along with the appropriate keystrokes. Also included are the keystrokes for some basic word processing tasks such as saving, retrieving, and printing.

You may want to keep the Quick Reference card at your computer if you find it easier to use than Help for quickly locating keystrokes. It is also small enough to take with you on the road, home, or wherever you may be using WordPerfect.

Feature Summary

If you are looking for the keystrokes to accomplish a task in WordPerfect (clearing the screen, erasing files, etc.), the WordPerfect workbook includes an extensive *Feature Summary* at the end of the book with keystrokes included for all the features introduced in the workbook.

You may want to turn to *Feature Summary* right now to discover the kind of information you can expect to find. However, if detailed explanation is what you need, the best place to turn is to the WordPerfect reference manual.

Reference Manual

The greatest amount of information available on any single WordPerfect feature can be found in the WordPerfect reference manual. The manual is divided into the following basic sections:

- Getting Started
- Reference
- Appendix
- Glossary/Index

While the *Getting Started* section provides some interesting information about the WordPerfect package, try turning to the *Reference* first to find the information you need. Topics are listed alphabetically with subheadings in the left margin that point you to specific details.

If you are having trouble locating the subject, then the *Index* provides a more direct access to the information. Simply look for the topic and then turn to the referenced page.

The *Appendix* provides technical information for those who are doing special installations of WordPerfect. You can also find details on some advanced features of WordPerfect, such as the macro programming language.

The primary purpose of the reference manual is to provide detailed, technical information on individual features. If you are looking for information on how to perform special tasks (printing envelopes) or create specialized documents (newsletters), then turn to the WordPerfect workbook.

Customer Support

For most people, it is comforting to know help is as close as the nearest telephone. And WordPerfect's customer support department is the best available in the software industry.

However, because the support is given over the telephone, you need to be able to describe the problem as clearly as possible to the person at the other end of the line. So, before picking up the receiver to call customer support, take a moment to collect your thoughts and any information that might be valuable.

For example, try duplicating the problem, and then write down the keys you pressed that caused the error. It is also important that you know the type of computer, monitor, and printer you are using, and some basic features of the equipment (amount of memory, serial or parallel printer, etc.).

The better the information, the quicker customer support can respond with a solution that will help you be successful in using WordPerfect for your personal or business needs.

Getting Started in the WordPerfect reference manual provides all the information you need to contact customer support.

Supplemental Materials

WordPerfect is the most powerful word processor available. While the package contains detailed information on the individual features of WordPerfect, it would take volumes to write about all the things you can do with the program.

A newsletter is automatically sent to all registered WordPerfect users keeping them updated on new features and applications. You may also want to check your local bookstore for other publications that deal with WordPerfect applications.

Summary

During this lesson, you were introduced to the following tasks:

- Canceling a message or menu and returning to your document.
- Displaying a keyboard template.
- Displaying a list of features and keystrokes.
- Displaying a page of reference information for a feature.

For a complete listing of all tasks introduced in the lessons, turn to *Feature Summary* at the end of the workbook.

Lesson 8: Letter 2 – First Draft

The majority of business letters are only one page in length. However, there are times when a letter may require two, three, or even more typed pages. Whatever the length, WordPerfect provides the features to make editing a quick and easy task.

Retrieving the Letter

For example, the first draft of a three-page letter needs some editing changes to prepare the letter for final approval.

1 Press **Retrieve** (Shift-F10) and enter **musicbox.wkb** to retrieve a copy of the rough draft.

From now on, the word "enter" will be used whenever you need to press Enter after typing the bolded text. For example, after typing the "musicbox" filename, you need to press Enter to retrieve a copy of the letter.

You may have noticed that the filename of the letter included a ".wkb" at the end of the name. If you want to know more about how files are named, turn to the Special Techniques lesson at the end of Fundamentals.

Using the Home Key

The first correction is several lines down the page.

```
Ms. Heather Wilson
Director of Sales
Swiss America, Inc.
1030 Harrington Blvd.
Newark, NJ 07112

Dear Ms. Wilson,

After recently visiting the Sundheim booth at the WURLD trade
exposition in Amsterdam, I was very impressed with both the
quality and variety of hand-crafted music boxes displayed.  After
speaking with the Sundheim marketing director, he indicated that
distribution of the music boxes in the United States is handled
directly through your company.

As you know, HALVA International has retailed an exclusive line
of jewelry from Europe for over 50 years.  Until recently, we
have handled the majority of our business through a mail order
service.

We are now planning to expand our business by opening several
retail outlets in major cities through the United States.  At the
same time, we would also like to include a complete line of
Sundheim music boxes.

We would like to order a selection of music boxes from the
following list for the conference:

Fairies
Pan's Pipes
Gondolier
Silver Harmonies
```

In fact, it is close to (or at) the bottom of the screen. You could use Down Arrow to move to the correction, but a faster way is to use Home.

The Home key is usually located on the right side of your keyboard.

2 Press **Home** and then press **Down Arrow** (↓).

Notice that the cursor *jumped* down to the last line on your screen. Pressing Home once and then Up Arrow or Down Arrow moves you quickly backward or forward through your document a screen at a time. Home is important for moving through larger areas of text.

3 Place the cursor on the "c" in the word "complete" in the last sentence of the third paragraph.

Using the Delete Key

Instead of using Backspace to erase the word, try using Delete. Like Backspace, Delete erases both text and codes. However, it erases the character *at* the cursor instead of the character to the *left* of the cursor.

4 Press **Delete** (Del) until the word "complete" is erased.

Restoring Deleted Text

Once you erase a word (or any length of text) with WordPerfect, you can always bring it back by using Undelete.

5 Press **Cancel** (F1) to bring back the erased word.

After pressing Cancel, the erased word is displayed as it appeared in the text (if you did not move the cursor).

▲ ERASED WORD

```
Ms. Heather Wilson
Director of Sales
Swiss America, Inc.
1030 Harrington Blvd.
Newark, NJ 07112

Dear Ms. Wilson,

After recently visiting the Sundheim booth at the WURLD trade
exposition in Amsterdam, I was very impressed with both the
quality and variety of hand-crafted music boxes displayed.  After
speaking with the Sundheim marketing director, he indicated that
distribution of the music boxes in the United States is handled
directly through your company.

As you know, HALVA International has retailed an exclusive line
of jewelry from Europe for over 50 years.  Until recently, we
have handled the majority of our business through a mail order
service.

We are now planning to expand our business by opening several
retail outlets in major cities through the United States.  At the
same time, we would also like to include a complete line of
Sundheim music boxes.                              ▲
Undelete: 1 Restore; 2 Previous Deletion: 0
```

WordPerfect saves up to the last three deletions. The saved deletions can be seen one at a time by selecting the Show Previous Deletion option. However, all you need to do now is restore the most recent deletion.

6 Select Restore (1) to place the word "complete" back into the letter.

Now that you have seen how easy it is to restore deleted text, keep the Undelete feature in mind whenever you make a mistake and erase the wrong character, word, or phrase while doing the lessons.

Erase the word "complete" again before continuing the lesson.

7 Press **Backspace** until the word "complete" and the space before it is erased.

Scrolling through the Letter

The word "immediate" is the next word that needs to be erased.

```
We are now planning to expand our business by opening several
retail outlets in major cities through the United States.  At the
same time, we would also like to include a line of Sundheim music
boxes.

We would like to order a selection of music boxes from the
following list for the conference:

Fairies
Pan's Pipes
Gondolier
Silver Harmonies
Return to the Danubue
Patterns
Autumn Memories
Paris at Night
Follow the Leader
Secrets
Symphony Strings
Black Forest Summer
Punting on the Thames
Winter's Wonder
Goatherd

In addition to the above music boxes, our marketing department
would also like to request one or more transparencies for as many
music boxes as possible for our catalog and other advertising
promotions.  For the immediate future, we would like to have
transparencies sent for the following:

Beautiful Dreamer
Always
```

However, the line with the correction is probably not on your screen right now. This is because most screens only let you see 24 lines at a time (25 if there is no status line).

```
1030 Harrington Blvd.
Newark, NJ 07112

Dear Ms. Wilson,

After recently visiting the Sundheim booth at the WURLD trade
exposition in Amsterdam, I was very impressed with both the
```

```
quality and variety of hand-crafted music boxes displayed.  After
speaking with the Sundheim marketing director, he indicated that
distribution of the music boxes in the United States is handled
directly through your company.

As you know, HALVA International has retailed an exclusive line
of jewelry from Europe for over 50 years.  Until recently, we
have handled the majority of our business through a mail order
service.

We are now planning to expand our business by opening several
retail outlets in major cities through the United States.  At the
same time, we would also like to include a line of Sundheim music
boxes.

We would like to order a selection of music boxes from the
following list for the conference:

Fairies
Pan's Pipes
Gondolier
Silver Harmonies
Return to the Danube
Patterns
C:\WP50\LEARN\MUSICBOX.WKB                     Doc 1 Pg 1 Ln 6.5" Pos 1.8
```

```
Paris at Night
Follow the Leader
Secrets
Symphony Strings
Black Forest Summer
Punting on the Thames
Winter's Wonder
```

In order to move the paragraph onto the screen, you need to use Down Arrow to scroll the top part of the letter off the screen.

8 Press **Down Arrow** (↓) several times until the paragraph following the list of music boxes is on your screen.

▲ PARAGRAPH AFTER MUSIC BOXES

```
We would like to order a selection of music boxes from the
following list for the conference:

Fairies
Pan's Pipes
Gondolier
Silver Harmonies
Return to the Danube
Patterns
Autumn Memories
Paris at Night
Follow the Leader
Secrets
Symphony Strings
Black Forest Summer
Punting on the Thames
Winter's Wonder
Goatherd

In addition to the above music boxes, our marketing department
would also like to request one or more transparencies for as many
music boxes as possible for our catalog and other advertising
promotions.  For the immediate future, we would like to have
transparencies sent for the following:
C:\WP50\LEARN\MUSICBOX.WKB                     Doc 1 Pg 1 Ln 9" Pos 1"
```

As you press Down Arrow, the lines at the top of the screen move off to make room for the lines below. The lines that are not on the screen, which include most of the music box letter, are available at any time by simply using the Home and/or arrow keys to scroll them back onto the screen.

You may want to take a few moments right now to try scrolling through the entire letter. If you do, make sure that you return to the same paragraph before continuing the lesson.

9 Use **Backspace** or **Delete** (Del) to erase the word "immediate" from the last sentence in the paragraph below the list.

Erasing a Word

As you learn more about WordPerfect, you will discover there are several ways to move the cursor and erase text. For example, the phrase "one or more" in the same paragraph needs to be erased.

```
retail outlets in major cities through the United States.  At the
same time, we would also like to include a line of Sundheim music
boxes.

We would like to order a selection of music boxes from the
following list for the conference:

Fairies
Pan's Pipes
Gondolier
Silver Harmonies
Return to the Danubue
Patterns
Autumn Memories
Paris at Night
Follow the Leader
Secrets
Symphony Strings
Black Forest Summer
Punting on the Thames
Winter's Wonder
Goatherd

In addition to the above music boxes, our marketing department
would also like to request one or more transparencies for as many
music boxes as possible for our catalog and other advertising
promotions.  For the future, we would like to have transparencies
sent for the following:

Beautiful Dreamer
Always
```

You could use Backspace to erase the phrase a character at a time. However, try erasing the phrase a word at a time with Delete Word.

10 Place the cursor on the word "one" in the first sentence of the paragraph.

11 Press **Delete Word** (Ctrl-Backspace) to erase the word.

Once the word "one" is erased, the text moves in from the right, and you can then use the Delete Word feature to erase the next word.

12 Press **Delete Word** (Ctrl-Backspace) to erase the word "or", and then press **Delete Word** again to erase the word "more."

Erasing a Line

For the next editing change, you can use Delete to End of Line to erase "Symphony Strings" from the list of music boxes.

```
retail outlets in major cities through the United States.  At the
same time, we would also like to include a line of Sundheim music
boxes.

We would like to order a selection of music boxes from the
following list for the conference:

Fairies
Pan's Pipes
Gondolier
Silver Harmonies
Return to the Danubue
Patterns
Autumn Memories
Paris at Night
Follow the Leader
Secrets
Symphony Strings
Black Forest Summer
Punting on the Thames
Winter's Wonder
Goatherd

In addition to the above music boxes, our marketing department
would also like to request transparencies for as many music boxes
as possible for our catalog and other advertising promotions.
For the future, we would like to have transparencies sent for the
following:

Beautiful Dreamer
Always
```

13 Place the cursor at the beginning of the "Symphony Strings" line in the list.

14 Press **Delete to End of Line** (Ctrl-End) to erase both words at the same time.

Notice that only the text in the line is erased. The Hard Return [HRt] is still keeping the line open for typing more text. You can erase the Hard Return by simply pressing Backspace.

15 Press **Backspace** to erase the empty line.

Starting a New Page

When you first start WordPerfect, all four margins (left, right, top, and bottom) are at one inch. For example, you may have noticed that the memo you printed in Lesson 5 had one-inch margins.

▲ ONE INCH MARGINS

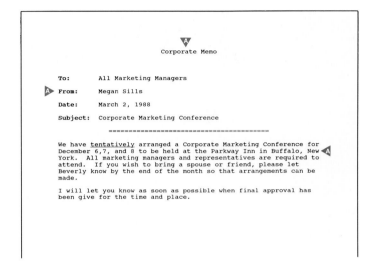

```
                            ▼A
                        Corporate Memo


        To:       All Marketing Managers
     ▷  From:     Megan Sills

        Date:     March 2, 1988

        Subject:  Corporate Marketing Conference

                  =========================================

        We have tentatively arranged a Corporate Marketing Conference for
        December 6,7, and 8 to be held at the Parkway Inn in Buffalo, New ◁A
        York.  All marketing managers and representatives are required to
        attend.  If you wish to bring a spouse or friend, please let
        Beverly know by the end of the month so that arrangements can be
        made.

        I will let you know as soon as possible when final approval has
        been give for the time and place.
```

WordPerfect is also set to print on a standard letter-sized page (8 1/2"x11"). Because WordPerfect already knows the width of the page (8 1/2") and that the left and right margins are one inch, it also knows that a line is full when it is 6 1/2" long. When a line is full, WordPerfect automatically wraps the cursor to the left margin to start a new line.

The same is true when a page fills up. WordPerfect automatically wraps the next line to the top of a new page. To help you see where the old page ends and the new page begins, WordPerfect places a page break (a line of dashes) across the screen.

For example, in the music box letter a page break falls in the middle of the second list of music boxes.

16 Press **Down Arrow** (↓) until you see the page break on your screen.

 PAGE BREAK

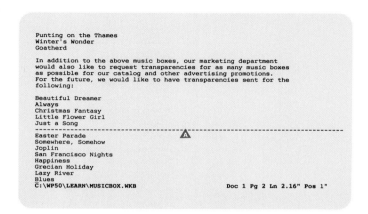

The editing remarks indicate that the beginning of the second list needs to start at the top of the second page.

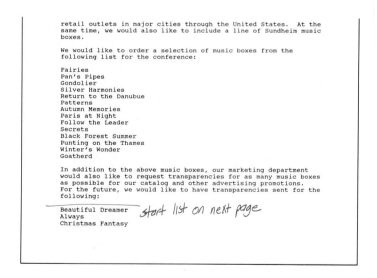

One way of solving the problem is to push the beginning of the list to the top of the second page by adding some extra lines.

17 Place the cursor at the beginning of the "Beautiful Dreamer" line.

18 Press **Enter** until "Beautiful Dreamer" is at the top of the second page.

▲ TOP OF SECOND PAGE

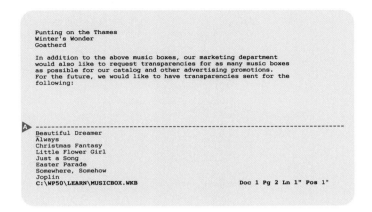

```
Punting on the Thames
Winter's Wonder
Goatherd

In addition to the above music boxes, our marketing department
would also like to request transparencies for as many music boxes
as possible for our catalog and other advertising promotions.
For the future, we would like to have transparencies sent for the
following:



-------------------------------------------------------------------------------
Beautiful Dreamer
Always
Christmas Fantasy
Little Flower Girl
Just a Song
Easter Parade
Somewhere, Somehow
Joplin
C:\WP50\LEARN\MUSICBOX.WKB                    Doc 1 Pg 2 Ln 1" Pos 1"
```

Notice that the page break stayed in the same place, while the lines moved past it. This is because the page break is a *soft* page break that stays in the same place, just like the *soft* return that stays at the end of a line in a paragraph, allowing the words to wrap through it.

However, just like pressing Enter to create a shorter line, you can also use Hard Page to create a shorter page. For example, instead of forcing the beginning of the list to the next page by adding empty lines, try using Hard Page.

19 Place the cursor at the beginning of the "Beautiful Dreamer" line (if it is not already there).

20 Press **Backspace** until the empty lines you added are erased.

21 Press **Hard Page** (Ctrl-Enter) to insert your own page break.

```
Punting on the Thames
Winter's Wonder
Goatherd

In addition to the above music boxes, our marketing department
would also like to request transparencies for as many music boxes
as possible for our catalog and other advertising promotions.
For the future, we would like to have transparencies sent for the
following:


==========================================================================
Beautiful Dreamer                              ⚠
Always
Christmas Fantasy
Little Flower Girl
Just a Song
Easter Parade
Somewhere, Somehow
Joplin
San Francisco Nights
Happiness
Grecian Holiday
Lazy River
C:\WP50\LEARN\MUSICBOX.WKB                     Doc 1 Pg 2 Ln 1" Pos 1"
```

If the page break is in the wrong place, simply press Backspace to erase it, then make sure your cursor is at the very beginning of the "Beautiful Dreamer" line before pressing Hard Page.

Notice that the page break you put in with Hard Page is displayed as a line of equal signs (=====) instead of a line of dashes (-----). This is done because the Hard Page Break stays with the text instead of remaining in the same place while the text moves past it.

22 Place the cursor at the end of the paragraph above the list.

23 Press **Enter** until a soft page break appears.

Notice that WordPerfect pushes the Hard Page Break down and will even add a page break of its own (if necessary) to keep the list at the top of the page. In fact, WordPerfect will do everything it can to make sure that the Hard Page Break stays in exactly the same place you inserted it.

24 Press **Backspace** until you erase the empty lines you inserted with Enter and the Soft Page Break is gone.

Numbering Pages

In most business correspondence styles, page numbering begins in a heading at the top of the second page. WordPerfect's Page Numbering feature can be used to print a page number at the top center of the second and third pages.

25 Press **Page Down** (PgDn) to move the cursor to the very beginning of the second page.

26 Press **Format** (Shift-F8), select Page (2) to display the Page Format menu, and then select Page Numbering (7) from the menu.

A menu is displayed from which you can select the position of the page number when it is printed or displayed in the preview screen.

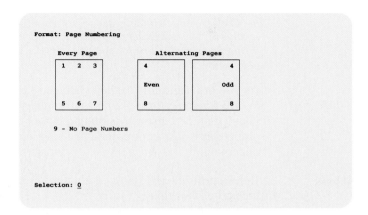

27 Type **2** to select the top center position for every page, and then press **Exit** (F7) to return to the letter.

After selecting a numbering position, WordPerfect places a page numbering code in the letter.

28 Press **Reveal Codes** (Alt-F3) to see the page numbering code.

▲ PAGE NUMBERING CODE

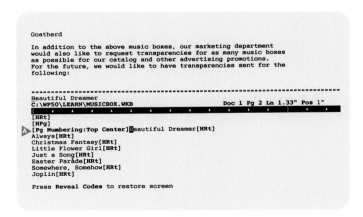

Notice you used Page Down to make sure that the cursor was at the very beginning of the second page before inserting the page numbering code. All formats on the Page Format menu should be placed at the beginning of the page before any other text or codes; otherwise, they will not begin working until the next page.

While the page number is not displayed in the document screen, it is displayed in the Preview screen and printed on the page. In fact, whenever you select page numbering, WordPerfect automatically subtracts two lines from each page—one for the number and one for spacing between the number and the text of the document.

As you are beginning to see, whenever you type text *or* select a WordPerfect feature (bold, page numbering, etc.), the text or code is inserted at the cursor. Making sure your cursor is in the right place before you begin is just as important as using WordPerfect to type or format a document.

Typing the Initials

Before printing and saving the letter, the typist's initials need to be added to the end of the letter.

29 Press **Reveal Codes** (Alt-F3) to return to the document screen.

30 Press **Home** twice and then press **Down Arrow** (↓) to move to the end of the third page.

Whenever you press Home twice (before pressing an arrow key), the cursor moves to the beginning or end of the line or the document. Pressing Home once simply moves the cursor to the edges of the screen.

31 Press **Enter** twice to move the cursor two lines below "HALVA International" and then type **cjg** for the initials.

▲ TYPIST'S INITIALS

```
Samuel A. Roberts
6120 Cottage Way, Suite #456
Sacramento, CA 95825
(916) 878-4550

Scott L. Ziegler
450 S. Flower St.
Los Angeles, CA 90014
(213) 937-3370

We look forward to establishing a working relationship with you,
and would be very interested in any other items you feel might
fit well with our current expansion plans.

Sincerely yours,


Bryan Metcalf
President
HALVA International
```
▲ cjg_
C:\WP50\LEARN\MUSICBOX.WKB   Doc 1 Pg 3 Ln 7.66" Pos 1.3"

Saving the Letter

Now that the editing is completed, you can use Save to save the letter before printing.

32 Press **Save** (F10) and enter **musicbox** to create a new file for the letter.

Instead of printing before saving a document (as you've done in the past few lessons), some individuals prefer to save the document first and then send it to the printer. This is especially true if the document is more than one page, and has not been saved while creating or editing.

Selecting a Printer

With the letter saved, you can use Print to print a second draft of the letter.

33 Press **Print** (Shift-F7) to display the Print menu.

Notice that the selected printer (in the lower half of the menu) is the Standard Printer. This is because the letter was created for the lesson with the Standard Printer selected. When you retrieved the letter at the beginning of the lesson, WordPerfect automatically switched to the Standard Printer for you.

However, to print the letter, you should select your own printer.

34 Type **s** (for Select Printer) to display a list of printer selections.

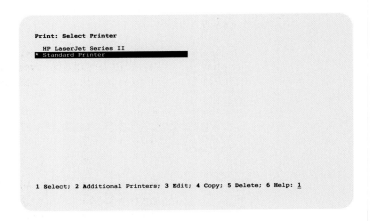

The list should include at least the Standard Printer and the printer you selected when installing WordPerfect.

35 Place the reverse video cursor on the name of your printer, and then press **Enter** to select the printer and return to the Print menu.

The name of the printer displayed in the Print menu should now be the one you selected from the list.

Also notice that the Text Quality is set to "High." You may want to change the quality to "Draft" before sending a draft of a letter to the printer. The Draft quality will usually print the letter using a faster (but lower quality) font.

Printing the Letter

36 Select Full Document (1) to send the letter to the printer.

All the documents that you retrieve from the Learn directory or Workbook diskette have been created using the Standard Printer so that the steps in the exercises work correctly. However, you need to select your own printer before printing the document.

37 Press **Exit** (F7) and type **n** twice to clear the screen without saving the letter.

Summary

During this lesson, you were introduced to the following tasks:

- Erasing a line of text.
- Erasing a word.
- Erasing characters.
- Moving the cursor a page at a time.
- Moving the cursor a screen at a time.
- Moving the cursor to the beginning or end of a document.
- Numbering pages.
- Restoring deleted text.
- Selecting a printer.
- Starting a new page.

For a complete listing of all tasks introduced in the lessons, turn to *Feature Summary* at the end of the workbook.

Lesson 9: Document Screens

One of WordPerfect's more powerful editing features is the ability to edit two documents at the same time, with each document in a separate screen. The first screen is called document 1 (Doc 1), and the second screen is called document 2 (Doc 2).

Opening the Second Document Screen

Until now, you have been using the document 1 screen to do word processing. In this lesson, you'll also use the document 2 screen. Right now, you are probably in the document 1 screen.

▲ DOCUMENT 1

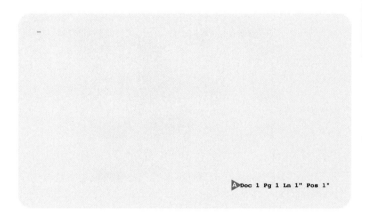

Opening the second document screen is as easy as pressing Switch.

1 Press **Switch** (Shift-F3) to open the second document screen.

You can always check the status line to find out which screen is currently active.

Switching Between Screens

When you want to return to the first document screen, simply press Switch again.

2 Press **Switch** (Shift-F3) to return to the first document screen.

As you continue using the two document screens throughout the lesson, you'll discover that all WordPerfect features are available in either screen. It's like running two copies of WordPerfect at the same time.

Filling In the Memo

Now that you have been introduced to both WordPerfect screens, try retrieving the memo form (created in Lesson 3) in the first screen and filling it out.

3 Press **Retrieve** (Shift-F10), and then enter **memo** for the filename.

Remember that the word "enter" means to type the bolded text and then press Enter.

Because you have already filled out the memo form once (Lesson 5), the information for filling out the memo is simply listed below. Remember to press End before typing the "To," "From," and "Subject."

4 Fill in the memo heading with the following information:

Megan Sills (to)
Bryan Metcalf (from)
New account with Swiss America, Inc. (subject)

5 Type the following paragraph in the message area below the double line:

Following our discussion at lunch the other day, I immediately wrote a letter to Swiss America, Inc. informing them of our decision to include their music boxes in our expanded line of merchandise.

6 Press **Enter** twice at the end of the paragraph to add extra spacing.

When you finish, the memo should look similar to the one illustrated below.

```
                        Corporate Memo


     To:       Megan Sills

     From:     Bryan Metcalf

     Date:     September 15, 1988

     Subject:  New account with Swiss America, Inc.


               ========================================

     Following our discussion at lunch the other day, I immediately
     wrote a letter to Swiss America, Inc. informing them of our
     decision to include their music boxes in our expanded line of
     merchandise.


       _


     C:\WP50\LEARN\MEMO                      Doc 1 Pg 1 Ln 4.16" Pos 1"
```

Moving a Paragraph from the Letter

Along with the text you have already typed, some information needs to be included from the letter to Swiss America, Inc..

While you could re-type the text from a printed copy of the letter, you can save time by using the second document screen and Move to quickly copy the text from the letter into the memo.

7 Press **Switch** (Shift-F3) to display the second document screen (check for "Doc 2" on the status line).

8 Press **Retrieve** (Shift-F10) and enter **musicbox.wkb** to retrieve the rough draft of the Swiss America letter.

Now you can use Move to copy and move the paragraph into the memo.

9 Press **Home** and then **Down Arrow** (↓) to move to the bottom of the screen.

10 Press **Home** and then **Down Arrow** (↓) again to scroll the first list of music boxes onto the screen.

11 Press **Up Arrow** (↑) until the cursor is in the "We would like to order. . ." paragraph above the list.

12 Press **Move** (Ctrl-F4), select Paragraph (2), and then select Copy (2).

The message displayed tells you to move the cursor to the place where you want the copied text inserted, and then to press Enter to retrieve the text. This message not only applies to the document currently on your screen, but also the document in screen 1.

13 Press **Switch** (Shift-F3) to return to the memo in the first document screen. Make sure the cursor is two lines below the text.

14 Press **Enter** to insert the paragraph into the memo.

While you've just completed quite a few keystrokes without much explanation, it is important to see just how quickly and smoothly you can move text between two documents in WordPerfect.

15 Press **Home** and then **Down Arrow** (↓) to place the cursor at the end of the memo.

Besides moving the text of the paragraph, notice that WordPerfect also moved the two Hard Returns after the paragraph. Although the paragraph is only one sentence long, by selecting "Paragraph" instead of "Sentence," WordPerfect will move any extra Hard Return's along with the text.

Moving a List from the Letter

Now, you need to return to the letter and move the list of music boxes.

16 Press **Switch** (Shift-F3) to return to the Swiss America letter, and then place the cursor on the first letter of "Fairies" at the beginning of the list.

The first three options on the Move menu give you the choice of moving a sentence, paragraph, or page. Once you select an option, the text to be moved is automatically highlighted for you.

But what about part of a sentence, paragraph, or page? Or what about text (like the list) that doesn't fit in any of the three categories?

In order to let you select exactly what you want to move, WordPerfect provides a Block feature that lets you do the highlighting yourself. Simply turn on Block, use Home and/or the arrow keys to highlight the text, and then select Move.

For example, try using Block to highlight the list. The cursor should already be at the beginning of the list.

17 Press **Block** (Alt-F4), and then move the cursor down to the beginning of the paragraph below the list.

Your screen should look similar to the one below, with the cursor under the "I" in the word "In," and the list completely highlighted.

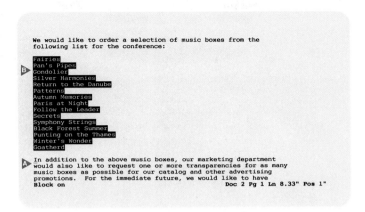

```
We would like to order a selection of music boxes from the
following list for the conference:
Fairies
Pan's Pipes
Gondolier
Silver Harmonies
Return to the Danube
Patterns
Autumn Memories
Paris at Night
Follow the Leader
Secrets
Symphony Strings
Black Forest Summer
Punting on the Thames
Winter's Wonder
Goatherd

In addition to the above music boxes, our marketing department
would also like to request one or more transparencies for as many
music boxes as possible for our catalog and other advertising
promotions.  For the immediate future, we would like to have
Block on                               Doc 2 Pg 1 Ln 8.33" Pos 1"
```

A "Block on" message at the bottom of the screen lets you know that Block is on.

18 Press **Move** (Ctrl-F4), select Block (1), and then select Copy (2).

After selecting Copy, WordPerfect automatically turns off Block for you. With the list saved, you are ready to move back into the memo.

19 Press **Switch** (Shift-F3) to display the memo in the first document screen.

20 Press **Enter** to insert the list into the memo.

Your screen should now look similar to the one below, with the cursor at the beginning of the list.

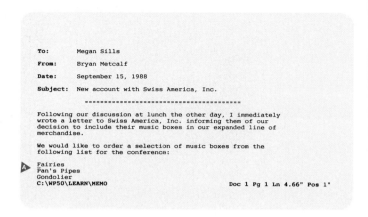

```
To:      Megan Sills

From:    Bryan Metcalf

Date:    September 15, 1988

Subject: New account with Swiss America, Inc.

         ========================================

Following our discussion at lunch the other day, I immediately
wrote a letter to Swiss America, Inc. informing them of our
decision to include their music boxes in our expanded line of
merchandise.

We would like to order a selection of music boxes from the
following list for the conference:
Fairies
Pan's Pipes
Gondolier
C:\WP50\LEARN\MEMO                          Doc 1 Pg 1 Ln 4.66" Pos 1"
```

Block is a wonderful editing tool that can be used with many other WordPerfect features (e.g., deleting a block of text). However, you may never need to use more than the Sentence, Paragraph, or Page option when moving text.

Deleting Several Words

Before finishing the memo, the text at the beginning of the paragraph that you moved needs to be changed.

```
                        Corporate Memo

          To:      Megan Sills

          From:    Bryan Metcalf

          Date:    March 2, 1988

          Subject: New account with Swiss America, Inc.
          ========================================
          Following our discussion at lunch the other day, I immediately
          wrote a letter to Swiss America, Inc. informing them of our
          decision to include their music boxes in our expanded line of
          merchandise.
                    I have already ordered
          We would like to order a selection of music boxes from the
          following list for the conference:

          Fairies
          Pan's Pipes
          Gondolier
          Silver Harmonies
          Return to the Danubue
          Patterns
          Autumn Memories
          Paris at Night
          Follow the Leader
          Secrets
          Symphony Strings
```

21 Place the cursor at the beginning of the "We would like. . ." paragraph.

22 Press **Escape** (Esc), type **5** for the repeat value, and then press **Delete Word** (Ctrl-Backspace) to delete the first five words of the sentence.

When you were first introduced to the repeat value (Lesson 3), you used it to automatically type a line of equal signs in the memo form. Notice that the repeat value can also be used with keys such as Delete Word to repeat the feature an exact number of times.

For a complete list of all the features that can be used with the repeat value, check your WordPerfect reference manual.

23 Type **I have already ordered** and then press the **Space Bar**.

Finishing the Memo

Now that the first few words of the paragraph have been edited, the memo can be finished.

24 Press **Home** twice and then **Down Arrow** (↓) to move to the end of the memo.

25 Type:

An account will be set up with Swiss America within the week. Order any other samples you feel we may need for the marketing conference and charge them to the account.

With the final paragraph typed, you are ready to print and save the memo.

26 Press **Print** (Shift-F7), and then select Full Document (1) to print the memo.

Exiting the Second Document Screen

Before saving the memo and clearing the screen, return to the letter and exit the second document screen.

27 Press **Switch** (Shift-F3) to display the letter.

28 Press **Exit** (F7) and type **n** to indicate that you do not want to save the letter.

When using one document screen, WordPerfect simply asks if you want to exit the program ("Exit WP?"). Now, because there are two active editing screens, WordPerfect asks if you want to exit document 2.

```
We would like to order a selection of music boxes from the
following list for the conference:

Fairies
Pan's Pipes
Gondolier
Silver Harmonies
Return to the Danube
Patterns
Autumn Memories
Paris at Night
Follow the Leader
Secrets
Symphony Strings
Black Forest Summer
Punting on the Thames
Winter's Wonder
Goatherd

In addition to the above music boxes, our marketing department
would also like to request one or more transparencies for as many
music boxes as possible for our catalog and other advertising
promotions.  For the immediate future, we would like to have
▲ Exit doc 2? (Y/N) No                          (Cancel to return to document)
```

29 Type **y** to exit the second document screen and return to the memo.

You could have also chosen to type "n" to clear the second document screen without exiting.

Saving the Memo

With the first document screen displayed, you are ready to save the memo.

30 Press **Exit** (F7), type **y** to save the memo, and then enter **musbmemo** to create a file for the memo.

31 Type **n** to clear the screen and stay in WordPerfect.

If you feel that you need more time to become acquainted with the features in the lessons, try repeating the steps one or more times.

For details on other methods of moving a block of text, turn to the Special Techniques lesson at the end of Fundamentals.

Summary

During this lesson, you were introduced to the following tasks:

- Blocking (highlighting) part of your text.
- Clearing and exiting the second document screen.
- Editing two documents.
- Moving a block of text.
- Moving a paragraph.
- Opening the second document screen.
- Repeating a WordPerfect feature.
- Switching between document screens.

For a complete listing of all tasks introduced in the lessons, turn to *Feature Summary* at the end of the workbook.

Lesson 10: Letter 2 – Final Draft

The second draft of the Swiss America letter has been returned with a note to alphabetize the two lists of music boxes and change the style of page numbering. The current date should also be added to the letter.

Inserting the Date

Let's begin by retrieving the letter and adding the date.

1 Press **List Files** (F5) and then press **Enter** to display the list of files on your disk.

2 Move the cursor to the "Musicbox" filename, and then select Retrieve (1) to retrieve the file.

3 Press **Date/Outline** (Shift-F5) and select Date Text (1) to insert the current date.

4 Press **Enter** twice to add extra spacing.

Changing the Page Numbering Style

The style of page numbering needs to be changed to a more standard form that includes the receiver's name and the current date with the page number.

While WordPerfect's automatic page numbering prints a page number, you need to create a header if you want to include text with page numbering.

Erasing a Code

Before creating the header, however, you should first erase the old page numbering code.

5 Press **Page Down** (PgDn) to move the cursor to the very beginning of the second page.

6 Press **Reveal Codes** (Alt-F3) to display the codes at the beginning of the second page.

△ PAGE NUMBERING CODE

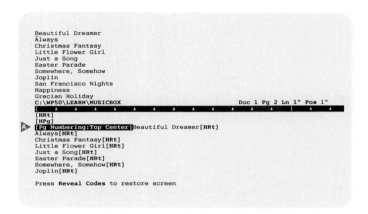

Because page formats need to be at the very beginning of the page (before any text) for the feature to work correctly, using Page Up and Page Down to move from page to page will always place the cursor is in the correct position for adding a page format.

Instead of deleting the page numbering code in the Reveal Codes screen, try erasing the code from the document screen.

7 Place the cursor on the page numbering code (if it is not already there).

8 Press **Reveal Codes** (Alt-F3) to display the full document screen.

9 Press **Delete** (Del) to erase the page numbering code.

You should now see a message at the bottom of your screen asking if you actually want to delete the code from the letter.

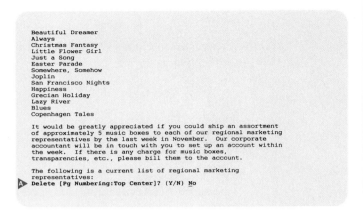

Because you cannot see codes in the document screen, WordPerfect makes sure that you know you are about to delete a formatting code whenever Backspace or Delete is being used to erase text.

10 Type **y** to have WordPerfect erase the page numbering code.

11 Press **Reveal Codes** (Alt-F3) to display the codes at the beginning of the second page.

The page numbering code should no longer appear at the beginning of the page.

▲ NO PAGE NUMBERING CODE

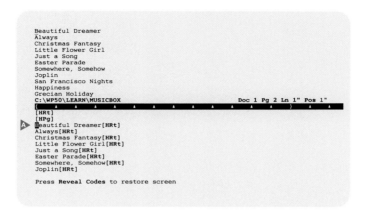

12 Press **Reveal Codes** (Alt-F3) to return to the full document screen.

Creating a Header

With the page numbering code deleted and the cursor at the very beginning of the second page, you are ready to create the header.

13 Press **Format** (Shift-F8), select Page (2), and then select Headers (3).

A menu on the status line indicates how many headers can be printed on one page (two).

▲ TWO HEADERS AVAILABLE

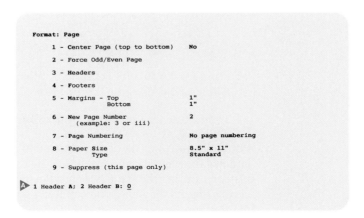

14 Select Header A (1), and then select Every Page (2) from the next menu that appears on the status line.

After selecting the type of header, WordPerfect places you in an editing screen very similar to the one you use for typing and editing documents.

⚠ EXIT MESSAGE

⚠ MISSING DOC AND PAGE INDICATORS

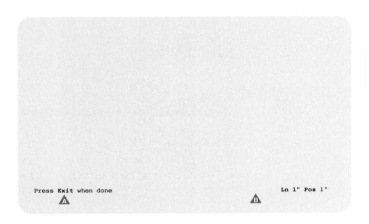

```
Press Exit when done                                    Ln 1" Pos 1"
            ⚠                              ⚠
```

In fact, the screens are so similar that some people have actually typed an entire document in the header/footer editing screen. If you do become confused, simply check the status line and notice the "Press Exit when done" message. Also notice that there are no document (Doc) or page (Pg) indicators on the status line, as you normally don't need a header that is larger than a page.

While there is a limitation (one page) on the size of the header, there are very few limits on the features that can be used while creating a header. We'll show you some creative ways that headers can be used in other lessons.

15 Type **Ms. Wilson** and press **Enter** to return to the left margin.

16 Press **Date/Outline** (Shift-F5), select Date Code (2), and then press **Enter** to return to the left margin.

17 Type **Page** and press the **Space Bar**.

For the actual page number, you need to put in a code that automatically updates the page number each time a new page is printed. However, instead of using the Page Number Position feature to place the page numbering on the page, you can use a special ^B code to print page numbers.

18 Hold down **Ctrl** and type **B** to place a ^B code next to the "Page" title.

The header you've created should now look like the one on the header/footer editing screen below.

```
Ms. Wilson
September 15, 1988
Page ^B_




Press Exit when done                              Ln 1.33" Pos 1.7"
```

You do not need to add extra spacing after the header because WordPerfect adds a double space between a header and the text. The lines for the header and spacing are automatically subtracted from the overall length of the page.

19 Press **Exit** (F7) to save the header, and then press **Exit** again to return to the letter.

Previewing the Header   The header can be seen by displaying the letter in the Preview screen.

20 Press **Print** (Shift-F7) and select View Document (6) to display the header.

21 Press **Page Up** (PgUp) or **Page Down** (PgDn) to scroll a page at a time through the letter.

Notice that you can see the page as it will be printed with the page number in the heading.

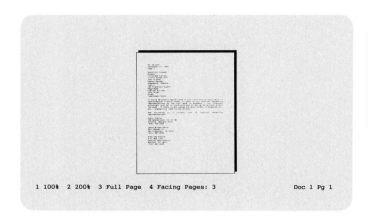

While in the graphics preview screen, you can press **Switch** (Shift-F3) to display the screen normally or in reverse video. The illustrated screens in the manual were created with reverse video off.

22 Press **Exit** (F7) to return to the document screen.

Sorting the Lists

The final editing change to the letter involves alphabetizing the two lists of music boxes. You could re-type the lists or use Move to re-shuffle the music box titles.

However, there is a feature in WordPerfect that can do all the sorting for you. All you need to do is highlight the list with Block, and then press two keys.

23 Place the cursor on the letter "B" in "Beautiful Dreamer" at the top of page 2 (if it is not already there).

24 Press **Block** (Alt-F4) and move the cursor to the end of the last music box title in the list ("Copenhagen Tales").

With all the titles in the list completely highlighted, you are ready to begin sorting.

25 Press **Merge/Sort** (Ctrl-F9) to display the Sort menu.

The title at the top of the menu should be "Sort by Line." If another title is displayed, simply select Type (7) and then select Line (2) before continuing.

26 Select Perform Action (1) from the menu that appears at the bottom of your screen.

After a moment, the menu disappears, and the letter is redisplayed with the sorted list.

▲ SORTED LIST

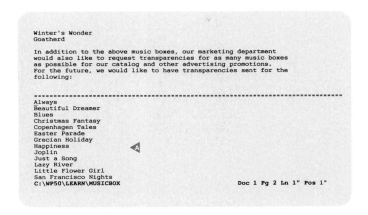

```
Winter's Wonder
Goatherd

In addition to the above music boxes, our marketing department
would also like to request transparencies for as many music boxes
as possible for our catalog and other advertising promotions.
For the future, we would like to have transparencies sent for the
following:


-----------------------------------------------------------------------
Always
Beautiful Dreamer
Blues
Christmas Fantasy
Copenhagen Tales
Easter Parade
Grecian Holiday
Happiness
Joplin
Just a Song
Lazy River
Little Flower Girl
San Francisco Nights
C:\WP50\LEARN\MUSICBOX                    Doc 1 Pg 2 Ln 1" Pos 1"
```

You probably noticed that the Sort menu took up half of the screen and offers several options. Although WordPerfect's sorter is a powerful feature, it is quite easy to use if all you want to do is alphabetize a list.

For other lessons that use Sort, check Sort in the index.

Now that you see how easy it is to sort a list of names, try sorting the list on the first page. However, instead of using Home and the arrow keys to move the cursor to the beginning of the list, you can use Search.

Searching for a Word

Search helps you move the cursor to an exact location in a document by letting you give WordPerfect a word to find. You already know that the first title in the list on page 1 is "Fairies," so,

27 Press ◆**Search** (Shift-F2) to search back through the letter.

28 Type **fairies** and press ◆**Search** (F2) to start the search.

The cursor should stop at the end of "Fairies" when the word is found.

```
have handled the majority of our business through a mail order
service.

We are now planning to expand our business by opening several
retail outlets in major cities through the United States.  At the
same time, we would also like to include a line of Sundheim music
boxes.

We would like to order a selection of music boxes from the
following list for the conference:

Fairies
Pan's Pipes
Gondolier
Silver Harmonies
Return to the Danube
Patterns
Autumn Memories
Paris at Night
Follow the Leader
Secrets
Black Forest Summer
Punting on the Thames
Winter's Wonder
C:\WP50\LEARN\MUSICBOX                         Doc 1 Pg 1 Ln 6" Pos 1.7"
```

If a " Not found *" message appears, you may have typed the title incorrectly. Try repeating steps 27 and 28.*

29 Press **Home** and then **Left Arrow** (←) to move to the beginning of the title.

With the cursor at the beginning of the first title in the list, you are ready to sort again.

30 Press **Block** (Alt-F4) and move the cursor to the end of the last title in the list ("Goatherd").

31 Press **Merge/Sort** (Ctrl-F9) and select Perform Action (1) from the sort menu.

Finishing the Editing

Now that both lists have been sorted, you can spell-check and preview the letter, save it on disk, and then send it to the printer. Because you have already done all three before, the steps are provided for these tasks without much explanation.

Just remember that during the spell-check, WordPerfect frequently stops at proper names it does not recognize. Simply select Skip (2) to continue spell-checking.

32 Press **Spell** (Ctrl-F2) and select Document (3) to check the spelling of the letter. Press any key when the spell-checking is completed to return to the letter.

33 Press **Save** (F10), press **Enter** to use the "Musicbox" filename, and then type **y** to replace the file.

34 Press **Print** (Shift-F7), type **s** to choose Select Printer, highlight the name of your printer, and then press **Enter** to select the printer.

35 Select Full Document (1) to print the letter.

36 Press **Exit** (F7) and type **n** twice to clear the screen.

You have been introduced to headers and sorting in this lesson—both of which are powerful features of WordPerfect.

As you are introduced to other WordPerfect features, keep in mind that most features do not demand a lot of time to learn if you are using them for simple tasks. However, the flexibility is always there if you want to use the features for more advanced applications.

Summary

During this lesson, you were introduced to the following tasks:

- Creating a header for every page.
- Erasing codes in the document screen.
- Numbering pages in a header.
- Searching for text or codes.
- Sorting a list of items (alphabetically).

For a complete listing of all the tasks introduced in the lessons, turn to *Feature Summary* at the end of the workbook.

Lesson 11: File Management

Most of the documents you create in WordPerfect will be saved in files. After several weeks, these files will begin to accumulate. Some will be worth saving; others can be erased from the disk. You may decide that some files need to be renamed, while others can be copied to a diskette for long-term storage.

WordPerfect includes a List Files feature from which you can perform most of your file management tasks quickly and efficiently.

This lesson is designed for individuals who are running WordPerfect from a hard disk. If you are running WordPerfect from two disk drives, then turn to the Two Disk Drives information in the Special Techniques lesson at the end of Fundamentals *before continuing.*

Backing up Files

Let's assume that it is the end of the day, and you are about to leave the office. Is there anything you should do with your files before exiting WordPerfect and turning off your computer?

The most important thing to remember is that your files are simply electronic information on a disk. If something happens to the disk, there is a good chance that you will not be able to recover the information. However, because the information is electronic, it can also be quickly copied to another diskette for safekeeping.

A diskette to which you copy files for safekeeping is called a backup diskette. Let's begin by copying the final draft of the reservation letter to a backup diskette.

For this exercise, you will need an extra formatted diskette. If you do not know how to format a diskette, turn to the Formatting a Disk information in the Special Techniques lesson at the end of Fundamentals.

1 Press **List Files** (F5) and then press **Enter** to display a list of filenames.

Searching for a Filename

If you have completed all the lessons to this point, you should have at least the following files in the list on your screen.

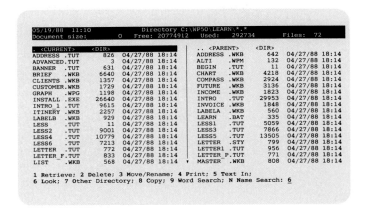

Other files may be listed with the ones above if you have created other files on your own. If the Learning files are not listed at all, then you are probably in the wrong directory. Select Other Directory (7) and enter the name of the directory where the files are kept.

2 Select Name Search (n), type **park**, and then press **Enter** to end the search.

3 Place a formatted diskette in drive A.

Copying a Single File

4 Select Copy (8) from the menu at the bottom of the screen.

5 When you see the "Copy this file to:" message, type **a:** and press **Enter**.

The file is copied to the formatted diskette, which has now become your backup diskette for keeping an extra copy of important files. Let's check and make sure that a copy of the file is actually on the diskette in drive A.

Checking the Backup Diskette

6 Move the cursor to the "<CURRENT>" directory at the top of the list.

7 Press **Enter**, type **a:** and then press **Enter** to display all the files on drive A.

Unless you have other files on the diskette in drive A, your list files screen should look like the one illustrated below.

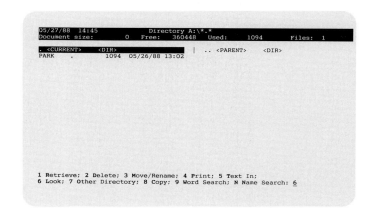

You can return to the directory where your files are stored by using the "<CURRENT>" directory again.

8 Make sure that the cursor is on the "<CURRENT>" directory.

9 Press **Enter**, type **c:\wp50\learn**, and then press **Enter** to return to the directory where the original files are stored.

If you are keeping your WordPerfect files in a directory other than "C:\WP50\LEARN," you need to type the name of that directory for step 9.

Copying Several Files

While you're copying files to a backup diskette, you may as well copy any other important files. For example, you should make sure that the two memos, the memo form, and the music box letter are also copied to the backup diskette.

However, instead of copying them one at a time, you can use WordPerfect's file marking feature to mark each file, and then copy them all at once.

10 Move the cursor to the "Parkmemo" filename by using the arrow keys or Name Search (n).

11 Type an asterisk (*) to mark the file.

An asterisk should appear next to the file size, indicating that the file has been marked. Now that you know how to mark one file, go ahead and mark the rest of the files you need to copy.

12 Mark the following files:

Memo
Musbmemo
Musicbox

Once you have marked the files, the rest is as easy as copying a single file to the backup diskette.

13 Select Copy (8) and type **y** (for yes) when you see the "Copy marked files?" question at the bottom of the screen.

14 When the "Copy all marked files to:" message is displayed, enter **a:** to copy the files to the diskette in drive A.

The files are copied one at a time while a "* Please Wait *" message is displayed at the bottom of the screen.

When the copying is completed, the files are still marked. Often when you copy files to a backup diskette, you may no longer want them on your hard disk. This is especially true if the files have been stored for several weeks and are no longer useful.

Deleting Several Files

Let's assume that the memos and letters do not need to be kept on the hard disk. However, you will probably still want to keep the "Memo" file for creating other memos.

15 Place the cursor on the "Memo" file, and then type an asterisk (*) to unmark the file.

With the memo form unmarked, Delete can be used to erase the rest of the files from the list.

16 Place the cursor on the "Park" file, and then type an asterisk (*) to mark the file.

Before using Delete, check your screen to make sure that only the following files are marked.

 MARKED FILES

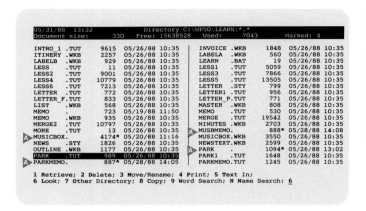

```
05/31/88  13:32              Directory C:\WP50\LEARN\*.*
Document size:       330  Free: 15638528   Used:    7043       Marked: 4

  INTRO_1 .TUT    9615 05/26/88 10:35 | INVOICE .WKB    1848 05/26/88 10:35
  ITINERY .WKB    2257 05/26/88 10:35 | LABELA  .WKB     560 05/26/88 10:35
  LABELB  .WKB     929 05/26/88 10:35 | LEARN   .BAT      19 05/26/88 10:35
  LESS    .TUT      11 05/26/88 10:35 | LESS1   .TUT    5059 05/26/88 10:35
  LESS2   .TUT    9001 05/26/88 10:35 | LESS3   .TUT    7866 05/26/88 10:35
  LESS4   .TUT   10779 05/26/88 10:35 | LESS5   .TUT   13505 05/26/88 10:35
  LESS6   .TUT    7213 05/26/88 10:35 | LETTER  .STY     799 05/26/88 10:35
  LETTER  .TUT     772 05/26/88 10:35 | LETTER1 .TUT     956 05/26/88 10:35
  LETTER_F.TUT     833 05/26/88 10:35 | LETTER_P.TUT     771 05/26/88 10:35
  LIST    .WKB     568 05/26/88 10:35 | MASTER  .WKB     808 05/26/88 10:35
  MEMO    .        723 05/19/88 11:50 | MEMO    .TUT     530 05/26/88 10:35
  MEMO    .WKB     935 05/26/88 10:35 | MERGE   .TUT   19542 05/26/88 10:35
  MERGE2  .TUT   10797 05/26/88 10:35 | MINUTES .WKB    2703 05/26/88 10:35
  MORE    .TUT      13 05/26/88 10:35 | MUSBMEMO.        888* 05/28/88 14:08
▶ MUSICBOX.       4174* 05/20/88 11:16 | MUSICBOX.WKB    3550 05/26/88 10:35
  NEWS    .STY    1826 05/26/88 10:35 | NEWSTEXT.WKB    2599 05/26/88 10:35
  OUTLINE .WKB    1177 05/26/88 10:35 |▶PARK    .        1094* 05/28/88 13:02
  PARK    .TUT     989 05/26/88 10:35 | PARK1   .TUT    1648 05/26/88 10:35
▶ PARKMEMO.        887* 05/28/88 14:05 | PARKMEMO.TUT    1245 05/26/88 10:35

1 Retrieve; 2 Delete; 3 Move/Rename; 4 Print; 5 Text In;
6 Look; 7 Other Directory; 8 Copy; 9 Word Search; N Name Search: 6
```

It is important to understand that once a file is erased, you cannot get it back without using special recovery programs. Even then, the file may not ever be put back together exactly the way it was first created. So, always check twice to make sure that you are deleting the file(s) you no longer want on your disk.

17 Select Delete (2) and type **y** when you see the "Delete marked files?" message.

A second message appears, letting you know that the marked files will be deleted if you continue. Because the marked files have already been copied to a backup diskette, it is safe to go ahead and delete them from the hard disk. They can always be copied back on to the hard disk when they are needed.

18 Type **y** to delete the marked files.

WordPerfect erases the files from the directory, and then re-displays the list with the remaining files in alphabetical order.

While keeping the files in your directory well-organized is easier if you backup and delete every day, some people wait until their hard disk "crashes" and then realize that there are no backup copies of their files and no way of getting them from the hard disk.

If you do nothing else, always take a moment to make a copy of the files you create or edit before exiting WordPerfect or turning off your computer. It's the best protection plan available for your files, and can be done quickly and easily from the List Files screen.

Deleting a Single File

The first ten lessons in *Fundamentals* provide an overview of some basic word processing skills. In order to set up your directory for repeating these lessons, you should also delete the "Memo" file.

19 Move the cursor to the "Memo" file, select Delete (2), and then type **y** to delete the file.

Printing a List of Files

As a convenience in helping you keep a record of your files, you can use Print to send a copy of the file list on your screen to the printer. All files in the directory or on the diskette are included—even those not currently on the screen.

20 Press **Print** (Shift-F7) to send the list of files on your screen to the printer.

The printed list includes the heading information you see on your screen with the current date, time, and directory. Other items include the size of the document currently on your screen, the amount of free space on the disk, the amount used by the directory, and the number of files in the directory.

All this information can be valuable in helping you to keep your diskettes or hard disk organized. You may want to keep a printed list of each directory and backup diskette for quick and easy reference.

Exiting WordPerfect

Assuming that you have finished your file management for the day, it's time to exit WordPerfect and turn off the computer before leaving the office.

21 Press **Exit** (F7) to return to the document screen.

22 Press **Exit** (F7) again, type **n** to indicate that you do not want to save anything from your screen, and then type **y** to exit WordPerfect.

WordPerfect creates several files of its own whenever you first start the program. By using Exit to leave the program, WordPerfect has a chance to erase these program files.

If you simply turn off the computer without exiting properly, WordPerfect is not able to erase the files, and the next time you start WordPerfect you will probably see a message asking if there is another copy of WordPerfect running. Type **n** (for no), and WordPerfect will delete the old program files and replace them with new ones.

Once you leave WordPerfect, you are returned to the place where you started the program. If you started from DOS, then you should see the DOS prompt at the top of the screen.

▲ DOS PROMPT

If you started WordPerfect from a menu, such as the one in the WordPerfect Library, then you are returned to that menu.

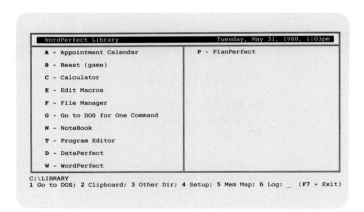

The topic of file management includes a lot of information about the way your computer stores and organizes files. In this lesson you have been introduced to copying and deleting files as important tasks of word processing. You have also been introduced to some terms, such as "directory," that may be unfamiliar to you.

If you feel you need more information about maintaining files, turn to the WordPerfect reference manual for detailed instructions.

An exercise on document summaries in the Special Techniques lesson in Formatting Documents *gives you additional information on how to find files from the List Files screen.*

Summary

During this lesson, you were introduced to the following tasks:

- Copying a file to a backup diskette.
- Copying a group of files to a backup diskette.
- Deleting a file.
- Deleting a group of files.
- Displaying another directory from the List Files screen.
- Exiting WordPerfect.
- Marking and unmarking files in the List Files screen.
- Printing a list of files.
- Searching for a filename in the List Files screen.

For a complete listing of all tasks introduced in the lessons, turn to *Feature Summary* at the end of the workbook.

Lesson 12: Special Techniques

Now that you have completed Fundamentals, we'd like to share with you some insights and special techniques that many people have found to be valuable when first learning WordPerfect.

Like the Getting Help lesson, the following information can be referred to as you need it. While special methods discussed below are not included in *Feature Summary* at the end of the workbook, you can find them listed in the index.

Filenames

While retrieving the music box letter, you probably noticed that a period (.) and a "wkb" follow the word "musicbox" in the filename. Characters that follow a period in a filename are called an *extension* of the filename. You can have up to 3 characters in an extension, and up to 8 characters before typing a period to begin the extension.

Extensions help you to organize your files into groups that can be easily managed. They can also provide additional information about a file (month, date, year). For example, all of the files provided with the workbook have an extension of .WKB.

Formatting a Diskette

Formatting a diskette is the process of laying down a "map" on your diskette so that the computer can store and then find and retrieve files. You cannot create files on a diskette that is not formatted.

The following steps guide you through formatting a diskette for storing files. If you are formatting a diskette that already has files on it, be aware that the files will be erased during the formatting.

1 Press **Shell** (Ctrl-F1) and select Go to DOS (1). Select Go to Shell (1) and then Go to DOS (1) if you are running WordPerfect from the WordPerfect Library.

If you are running WordPerfect from two disk drives, you need to remove both the WordPerfect diskette and the Learning diskette before continuing.

2 Place your DOS diskette in drive A and the diskette to be formatted in drive B.

You should have received a DOS diskette when you purchased your computer. It is usually labeled with the letters "DOS."

3 Type **a:format b:** and press **Enter**.

4 Type **y** to begin formatting (you may also need to press **Enter** on some versions of DOS).

When formatting has been completed, you will see a message asking if you want to format another diskette.

5 Type **n** to indicate you have finished (you may also need to press **Enter** on some versions of DOS).

If you are running WordPerfect from two disk drives, you need to insert the WordPerfect diskette in drive A and the Learning diskette in drive B before continuing.

6 Type **exit** and press **Enter** to return to WordPerfect.

Now that the diskette in drive B has been formatted, you can remove the DOS diskette from drive A, place the formatted diskette in drive A, and then return to Lesson 11 (if you have not completed the lesson).

Initial Settings

As you are beginning to notice, many of the formatting features (justification, tabs, margins, etc.) are already set for you. For example, tab stops are set for every half-inch on the tab ruler.

These settings are called the *initial settings*, and they let you begin typing immediately when you first start WordPerfect. If you want to change a setting for a document you are typing, simply use Format (as you did in Lesson 5) to insert a formatting code in the document. The new setting will change the text from the code *forward* through the document. Initial settings still apply for text to the left and above the codes.

Whenever you want to change an initial setting, press Setup (Shift-F1) select Initial Settings (5), and then select Initial Codes (4). After you select the option, a Reveal Codes screen is displayed that lets you enter the new setting by simply inserting a WordPerfect code with Format (Shift-F8).

After you change an initial setting, each document you create in WordPerfect will have the new initial setting saved with the document. If you find that you are changing an initial setting frequently, then it would be wise to leave the initial setting alone, and use Format to insert a code into the document.

Check the index at the end of the workbook for other lessons that mention Setup. You may also want to turn to the WordPerfect reference manual for complete details on using Setup to customize your copy of WordPerfect.

Justification

WordPerfect is set to keep each line exactly the same length when a document is printed (a justified right margin), however, the spacing between words on a page may not be equal.

Because many business offices no longer use justification for their correspondence, most of the illustrations of printed pages in the workbook show an unjustified (ragged) right margin.

If you want your printed documents to have a ragged right margin, use Setup to turn off justification.

1 Press **Setup** (Shift-F1), select Initial Settings (5), and then select Initial Codes (4).

2 Press **Format** (Shift-F8), and then select Line (1).

3 Select Justification (3), type **n** (for no), and then press **Exit** (F7).

A [Just Off] code should be displayed on your screen.

4 Press **Exit** (F7) to save the change, and then press **Exit** again to return to the document screen.

Each document you send to the printer will have justification off. If you want to turn justification back on for a single document, then place your cursor at the beginning of the document, and follow steps 2 and 3 above before printing (type **y** to turn on justification).

Moving Text

The Move menus let you move or copy text that is highlighted. When using Copy, a copy of the text is saved, while the original text *remains* in your document. When using Move, a copy of the text is saved, while the original text is *removed* (erased) from your document.

The text is saved until you exit the WordPerfect program.

Although Move is specifically designed for moving text from one location to another, there are two other methods of copying and cutting text that some people prefer to use while editing in WordPerfect. Both methods are particularly useful if you are blocking text that needs to be moved.

Copying a block of text

To copy a block of text without using Move,

1 Highlight the text with **Block** (Alt-F4).

2 Press **Save** (F10), and then press **Enter** to save the highlighted text.

3 Place the cursor at the location where you want the text inserted.

4 Press **Retrieve** (Shift-F10), and then press **Enter** to insert the text into your document.

Moving a block of text
To delete and move a block of text without using Move,

1 Highlight the text with **Block** (Alt-F4).

2 Press **Backspace**, and then type **y** to erase the text from your document.

3 Place the cursor at the location where you want the text inserted.

4 Press **Cancel** (F1) and then select Restore (1) to insert the text into your document.

You can delete up to three blocks of text before moving them by repeating steps 1 and 2 for each block of text. When you want to insert the text at the new location, simply select Show Previous Deletion (2) after pressing Cancel until the text you want to insert is displayed, and then select Restore (1) to insert the text.

For details on what WordPerfect considers a deletion, turn to Undelete in the WordPerfect reference manual.

Two Disk Drives

If you are running WordPerfect from two disk drives, you will need to keep your WordPerfect diskette in drive A during the lesson. You should be saving and retrieving files from the Learning diskette in drive B.

When you are asked to press List Files and then Enter during Lesson 11, check the bottom of the screen before pressing Enter for a "Dir B:*.*" message. If the message reads "Dir A:*.*," then you need to change the directory before continuing. Type an equal sign (=), type **b:** for the drive letter, and then press **Enter** twice to display the files on your Learning diskette.

When copying files from your Learning diskette to a backup diskette during the lesson, you will need to remove the WordPerfect diskette from drive A and replace it with the backup diskette *before* selecting Copy (8) from the List files screen. After the copying is completed, replace the backup diskette with the WordPerfect diskette before continuing the lesson.

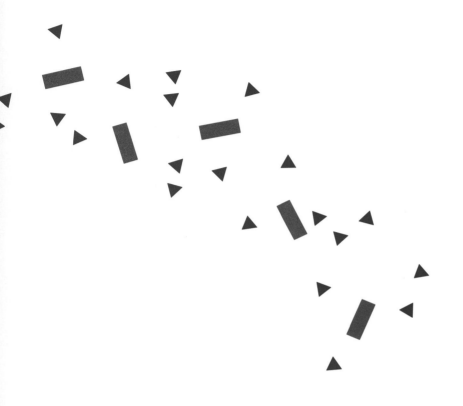

Lesson 13: Business Letters

One of the most popular ways of communicating in the business world continues to be the letter. Because a letter is often the first impression someone has of a company, styles have been developed to make letters look as professional as possible.

Although each company eventually develops its own style, there are some standard styles frequently used as models. In this lesson, you retrieve and format a letter in several of these styles.

1 Press **Retrieve** (Shift-F10) and enter **retaila.wkb** to retrieve a letter to Robin Pierce.

Printing the Block Style

Notice that each part of the letter on your screen (except for the list) is lined up at the left margin. This style is called a Block Letter.

2 Press **Print** (Shift-F7) and type **s** to display the list of printers.

3 Highlight the name of your printer, then press **Enter** to select the printer and return to the Print menu.

4 Select Full Document (1) to print the letter.

The length of the lines in the letter may now be longer (or shorter) after selecting your own printer. WordPerfect automatically adjusts the format of the letter on your screen so you know exactly how many words and lines will be printed on a page.

Your printed copy of the letter should contain the following information.

```
November 6, 1989

Robin Pierce
InterChange, Inc.
544 Westminster Circle NW
Atlanta, Georgia 30327

Dear Robin,

We are proud to announce the grand opening of several HALVA
International retail stores throughout the country.  Stores are
scheduled to open in the following cities during the first
quarter of the year:

        Manhattan, New York        January 18
        Boston, Massachusetts      January 26
        San Francisco, California  February 10
        Los Angeles, California    February 24
        Atlanta, Georgia           March 9
        Chicago, Illinois          March 17

As a preferred customer, you will be receiving a special
invitation, and I personally look forward to meeting you at the
opening.

Sincerely yours,


Bryan Metcalf
President
HALVA International

coc
Enclosures (2)
```

Because you have selected a printer other than the Standard Printer, the illustrations in the lesson may not exactly match your own screen and printed pages. However, the steps will work correctly with any printer selected.

You may want to take a moment and label your printed copy with "Block Letter Style" to keep for future reference. In fact, as you print other styles throughout the lesson, you may also want to label and keep them as samples of letter styles.

Aligning Text at the Right Margin

While the Block Letter style is quite common, many people choose to modify the style by moving the date line, closing, and signature block flush against the right margin. By using the Flush Right feature you can do this automatically.

5 Place the cursor at the beginning of the date line (if it is not already there), then press **Delete to End of Line** (Ctrl-End) to erase the date.

6 Press **Flush Right** (Alt-F6) and type **November 6, 1989** for the date.

As you type the date, it is lined up against the right margin. You can end the flush right and return to the left margin by pressing Enter or Down Arrow. If there is already text below the flush right, and you don't want to add an extra line of spacing, simply press Down Arrow.

7 Press **Down Arrow** (↓) to end the flush right and return to the left margin.

Another way of using Flush Right is to line up an *existing* line of text at the right margin.

8 Place the cursor at the beginning of the complimentary close (Sincerely yours).

9 Press **Flush Right** (Alt-F6) to begin the right margin alignment, and then press **Down Arrow** (↓) to end the alignment.

If you are typing text, you need to use Flush Right at the beginning of each new line. However, you can use Block with Flush Right to align several lines of existing text at one time.

10 Place the cursor at the beginning of the first line in the signature block (Bryan Metcalf).

11 Press **Block** (Alt-F4), and then press **Down Arrow** (↓) until the signature block is highlighted.

12 Press **Flush Right** (Alt-F6), and then type **y** to align the entire signature block at the right margin.

Block can also be used with Center (Shift-F6) to center several lines of text at the same time.

Printing the Modified Block Style

Now that you've created a modified block letter using Flush Right, try printing the letter to see how the modified style compares to the simple block style.

13 Press **Print** (Shift-F7) and select Full Document (1) to print the letter.

Your letter should look similar to the one illustrated below.

The Block Letter and Modified Block Letter styles both keep the paragraphs in the message flush against the left margin. The only exception is text (such as the list) that needs to be set apart from the body of the message.

Indenting the First Line of a Paragraph

If you want to "soften" the look of the text in a block style, you can use Tab to indent the first line of each paragraph. This is sometimes called the Semi-Block Letter style.

14 Place the cursor at the beginning of the first paragraph (We are proud to announce. . .), and then press **Tab** to indent the first line.

15 Place the cursor at the beginning of the last paragraph (As a preferred customer,. . .), and then press **Tab** to indent the first line.

Printing the Semi-Block Style

16 Press **Print** (Shift-F7) and select Full Document (1) to print the letter.

Your letter should look similar to the illustration below.

You may want to label your copy of the printed letter "Modified Semi-Block Letter Style" to indicate that you are combining two styles to create a third.

Creating a Hanging Indent

The final style is called the Hanging-Indented Letter style because the first line of each paragraph "hangs" at the left margin, while the rest of the lines are indented one tab stop.

17 Erase the tab in the first line of both paragraphs by using Backspace or Delete.

18 Place the cursor at the beginning of the first line in the first paragraph.

19 Press ♦**Indent** (F4) to indent all the lines in the paragraph one tab stop over.

20 Press ♦**Margin Release** (Shift-Tab) to release the first line back to the left margin.

21 Press **Screen** (Ctrl-F3) and select Rewrite (0) to rewrite the text on your screen.

You can use Rewrite any time you want the text on your screen formatted, or if the text has not been displayed correctly by the computer. If your copy of WordPerfect is set to automatically format and rewrite as you type (Setup), then you may never need to use Rewrite.

Your first paragraph should now look like the one illustrated in the screen below.

▲ HANGING INDENT

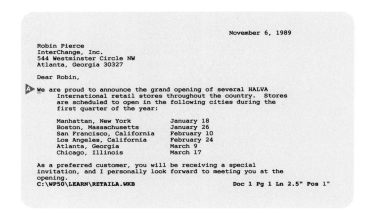

```
                                                November 6, 1989

Robin Pierce
InterChange, Inc.
544 Westminster Circle NW
Atlanta, Georgia 30327

Dear Robin,

We are proud to announce the grand opening of several HALVA
     International retail stores throughout the country.  Stores
     are scheduled to open in the following cities during the
     first quarter of the year:

        Manhattan, New York       January 18
        Boston, Massachusetts     January 26
        San Francisco, California February 10
        Los Angeles, California   February 24
        Atlanta, Georgia          March 9
        Chicago, Illinois         March 17

As a preferred customer, you will be receiving a special
invitation, and I personally look forward to meeting you at the
opening.
C:\WP50\LEARN\RETAILA.WKB             Doc 1 Pg 1 Ln 2.5" Pos 1"
```

Indenting Single Lines

Now that the first paragraph is indented, the list of places and dates should be indented one more tab stop by using Tab.

22 Place the cursor at the beginning of each line in the list and press **Tab** to indent the line another tab stop.

Notice that you used Tab instead of ♦Indent to indent the list. Tab is used to indent a single line of text that ends with a Hard Return (Enter), or to indent the first line of a paragraph.

However, ♦Indent is designed to indent all the lines of a paragraph without having to change the left margin setting. Because paragraphs normally end with a Hard Return, the ♦Indent feature also ends at the first Hard Return. For each new paragraph, you need to press ♦Indent again.

Let's finish formatting the letter by creating a hanging indent for the last paragraph, and then send the letter to the printer.

23 Place the cursor at the beginning of the last paragraph.

24 Press ♦**Indent** (F4), and then press ◄**Margin Release** (Shift-Tab) to format the paragraph (use Rewrite if needed).

Printing the Hanging-Indented Style

25 Press **Print** (Shift-F7) and select Full Document (1) to print a copy of the Hanging-Indented Letter style.

Label the printed copy "Hanging-Indented Style" and keep it with the other style examples.

Adjusting for Letterhead

Besides developing a style for the body of the letter, most companies use a printed letterhead for the first page of a letter. Three lines of spacing are normally recommended between the letterhead and the date line.

For an example of designing letter and memo headings with WordPerfect, turn to the Headings lesson in Formatting Documents.

You could use Enter to add extra spacing for the letterhead and the three lines. However, because the letterhead is not displayed on your screen, it might be difficult to estimate the exact number of lines you need to add to the top of the letter.

Advancing Text from the Top of the Page

A more precise way of printing the date line exactly where you need it is to use Advance.

26 Press **Home** three times and then **Up Arrow** (↑) to place the cursor at the very beginning of the letter.

27 Press **Format** (Shift-F8), select Other (4), and then select Advance (1).

Advance lets you select from several options to place text on the page exactly where you want it printed.

▲ ADVANCE OPTIONS

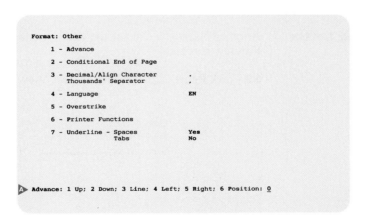

```
Format: Other

     1 - Advance

     2 - Conditional End of Page

     3 - Decimal/Align Character          .
         Thousands' Separator             ,

     4 - Language                        EN

     5 - Overstrike

     6 - Printer Functions

     7 - Underline - Spaces             Yes
                     Tabs               No




A▶ Advance: 1 Up; 2 Down; 3 Line; 4 Left; 5 Right; 6 Position: 0
```

If the letterhead for HALVA International requires 1.5" from the top edge of the page, and three lines of spacing takes up about another .5", the date line needs to be printed 2" from the top edge of the page.

You could use Down to advance the text, but Down advances the text from the *current cursor position*. To advance an exact distance from the *top edge of the page*, you need to use Line.

28 Select Line (3), enter **2** for two inches, and then press **Exit** (F7) to return to the letter.

You will not be able to see the extra spacing on your document screen. However, you can check the Line (Ln) number on the status line to see the advance.

29 Press **Reveal Codes** (Alt-F3) to display the codes in the letter, and then place the cursor on the [AdvToLn:2"] code.

Notice that the Line number indicates that the cursor is on Line 1.

30 Press **Right Arrow** (→) to move the cursor past the [AdvToLn:2"] code.

Now check the status line and notice that the Line number has increased to two inches.

If you would rather have the status line display another measurement for the Line and Position numbers, then turn to the Units of Measure heading in the Special Techniques lesson at the end of Formatting Documents.

31 Press **Reveal Codes** (Alt-F3) to display the full document screen.

Previewing the Letter

Another place you can see the extra spacing for the letterhead is in the Preview screen.

32 Press **Print** (Shift-F7) and select View Document (6).

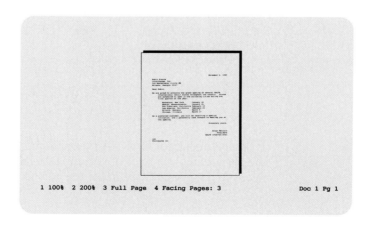

The above Preview screen is displayed if you have a graphics card (select Full Page to see the entire page at once). If you do not have a graphics card, you can still see the extra spacing at the top of the page. Remember that you can press Switch (Shift-F3) to turn reverse video on and off.

Printing the Hanging-Indented Style

Now that you've seen the results of the extra spacing, you can send the letter to the printer.

33 Press **Cancel** (F1) to return to the Print menu, and then select Full Document (1) to print the letter.

34 Press **Exit** (F7) and type **n** twice to clear the screen.

After the letter is printed, you may want to label it "Letterhead" and keep it with the other examples of business letter styles.

WordPerfect includes a Style feature for organizing and editing styles, and a Document Summary feature for organizing your letters. If you are interested in learning about Style, turn to the Styles lesson in *Formatting Documents.*

Summary

During this lesson, you were introduced to the following tasks:

- Advancing text from the top edge of the page.
- Aligning text at the right margin (one line).
- Aligning text at the right margin (several lines).
- Indenting a paragraph with a hanging indent.
- Indenting all the lines of a paragraph.
- Indenting single lines of text.
- Indenting the first line of a paragraph.
- Rewriting (formatting) the text on your screen.
- Selecting a printer.

For a complete listing of all tasks introduced in the lessons, turn to *Feature Summary* at the end of the workbook.

Lesson 14: Minutes

Of the many types of business documents that have become standardized, minutes offer some unique formatting challenges.

Printing the Minutes

Let's begin by reviewing the first page of minutes taken at a directors' meeting of HALVA International.

1 Press **Retrieve** (Shift-F10) and enter **minutes.wkb** to retrieve the minutes of the meeting.

2 Press **Print** (Shift-F7), type **s** to display the list of printers, and highlight the name of your printer.

3 Press **Enter** to select your printer, and then select Full Document (1), to print to the minutes.

Now, compare your printed copy of the minutes with the page below.

Notice that there is a break in the underlining, and that the page and minutes numbering needs to be changed in the header.

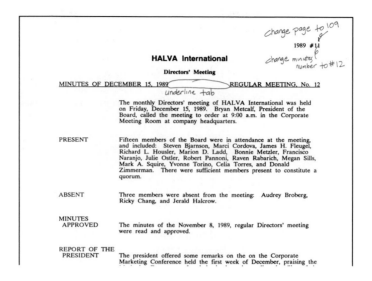

Also notice that text for the last two subtitles needs to be moved up one line.

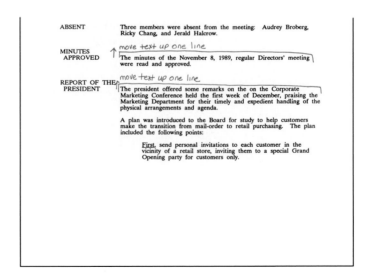

Underlining Spaces and Tabs

The break in the underlining is simply the way WordPerfect is initially set to underline text. Spaces are underlined, while tabs, indents, and other text alignment features are not.

4 Press **Reveal Codes** (Alt-F3) to see the codes in the minutes.

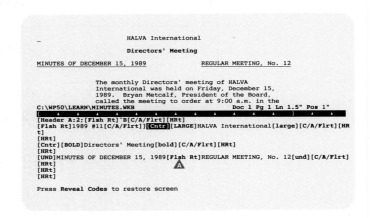
Notice that a Flush Right code separates the text. Because flush right is a text alignment feature, WordPerfect is not underlining the space in the middle of the line. However, this can be changed by inserting a new format setting.

5 Press **Format** (Shift-F8) and select Other (4).

The Other formatting options include a variety of features available to help with special formatting needs.

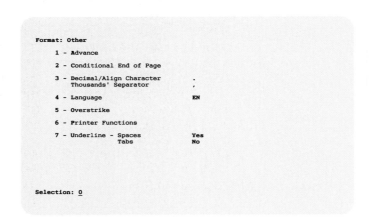

Underline can be used to set underlining for spaces *and* tabs.

6 Select Underline (7), type **y** twice to underline tabs and spaces, and then press **Exit** (F7) to return to the document screen.

The code placed at the beginning of the minutes tells WordPerfect to underline both spaces and tabs (including all text alignment features).

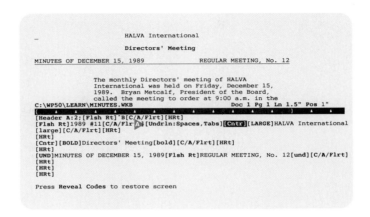

7 Press **Reveal Codes** (Alt-F3) to display the full document screen.

Editing the Header

A standard way of filing minutes is to assign a number to the set of minutes and then to number the pages. Both numbers are kept continuous throughout the year.

Assuming that the last set of minutes is #11, and that the last page number of the set is 108, the set of minutes on your screen should be #12 with the page numbering starting at 109.

8 Press **Format** (Shift-F8), select Page (2), and then select Headers (3).

9 Select Header A (1), and then select Edit (5) from the menu on the status line.

The header should now appear in a screen very similar to the document screen.

 HEADER

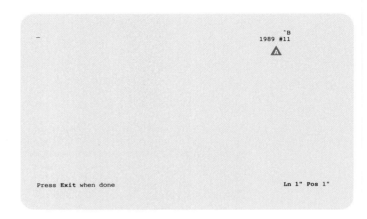

This same type of editing screen is used for several features in WordPerfect, and works just like the document screen. This means that you can create or edit a header just like you would edit a document.

10 Move the cursor to the "#11" and change it to read "#12".

11 Press **Exit** (F7) twice to save the edited header and return to the document screen.

Setting a New Page Number

While editing the header, you may have noticed that page numbering is accomplished with a ^B. The number WordPerfect prints at the ^B depends on the current page number displayed on the status line.

You can change the current page number from 1 to 109 by placing the cursor at the beginning of the page and using New Page Number on the Format menu.

12 Press **Home** three times and then **Up Arrow** (↑) to move the cursor to the beginning of the minutes (before any codes).

13 Press **Format** (Shift-F8), select Page (2), and then select New Page Number (6).

14 Enter **109** for the new page number, and then press **Exit** (F7) to return to the document screen.

The Page (Pg) number on the status line should now read "109." Like all features on the Page Format menu, the cursor needs to be at the beginning of the page, or the feature may not work correctly.

Advancing Text Up the Page

Whenever a subtitle is one line in length (e.g., PRESENT), the subtitle is typed, and then ♦Indent is pressed to align the paragraph at the next tab stop.

However, with subtitles two lines in length (e.g., MINUTES APPROVED), indenting needs to be done after the *second* line of the subtitle.

15 Press **Page Down** (PgDn) to scroll to the end of the minutes.

A FIRST LINE
B SECOND LINE

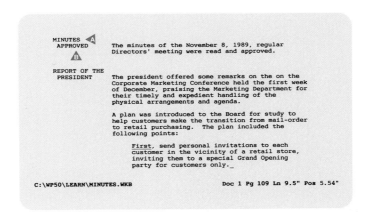

If you try indenting the text after the first *and* second lines of the subtitle, you will have problems with the paragraph formatting correctly.

The solution is to keep the paragraph indented after the second line of the subtitle, and then move the entire paragraph back up the page one line using Advance.

16 Press **Up Arrow** (↑) to move to the "MINUTES APPROVED" subtitle.

17 Place the cursor on the word "MINUTES," and then write down the Line (Ln) number on the status line at the bottom of the screen.

18 Place the cursor on the "T" at the beginning of the "The minutes of the November 8,. . ." paragraph.

19 Press **Format** (Shift-F8), select Other (4), and then select Advance (1) to display the menu of Advance options.

While all of the options let you place text anywhere on the printed page, Line lets you indicate a specific line (without calculating distances) on which to print the text.

20 Select Line (3) and type the number you wrote down.

21 Press **Enter** to save the setting, and then press **Exit** (F7) to return to the document screen.

You will not be able to see the text line up with the subtitle in the document screen. However, you can see the results at the printer *and* in the preview screen.

22 Press **Print** (Shift-F7) and select View Document (6).

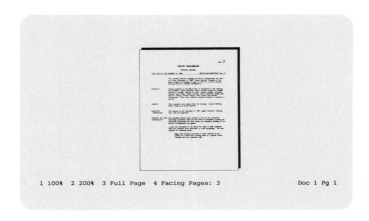

1 100%   2 200%   3 Full Page   4 Facing Pages: 3   Doc 1 Pg 1

23 Press **Exit** (F7) to return to the document screen.

Now that you have aligned the "MINUTES APPROVED" text with the subtitle, try using Advance to align the "REPORT OF THE PRESIDENT" text with the subtitle.

24 Use Line (3) on the Advance menu to align the last subtitle on the page with the corresponding text.

Printing the Edited Minutes

With the formatting changes made, you can print the minutes to see the results. You may want to use the preview screen to see the changes before printing.

25 Press **Print** (Shift-F7) and select Full Document (1) to print the page of minutes.

Now, compare your printed copy with the one illustrated below.

26 Press **Exit** (F7) and type **n** twice to clear the screen.

Summary

During this lesson, you were introduced to the following tasks:

- Advancing text up the page.
- Editing a header.
- Setting a new page number.
- Underlining spaces and tabs.

For a complete listing of all tasks introduced in the lessons, turn to *Feature Summary* at the end of the workbook.

Lesson 15: Itineraries

While minutes provide some interesting problems in aligning text, itineraries offer the unique challenge of typing text in columns.

1 Press **Retrieve** (Shift-F10) and enter **itinery.wkb** to retrieve an itinerary for a marketing conference in Buffalo, NY.

A FIRST COLUMN

B SECOND COLUMN

C THIRD COLUMN

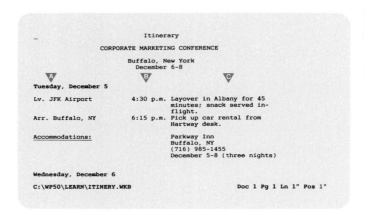

Tabs and Indents

There are three columns of information in the itinerary. The first column is at the left margin and is being used for flight destinations and titles. The second column contains times of flights and events, and the third column contains comments about both.

The second and third columns are lined up at two tab stops that have already been set for you.

2 Press **Escape** (Esc) and then press **Down Arrow** (↓) to place the cursor on the "Tuesday, December 5" heading.

3 Press **Reveal Codes** (Alt-F3) to see the codes in the flight information.

The flight times are lined up at the second column with a Tab. However, the comments are lined up at the third column with an ◆Indent.

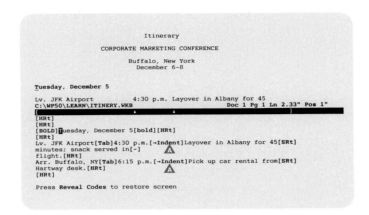

Because using ◆Indent is like setting a temporary left margin, all the lines of each comment are aligned at the third column.

Typing the Flight Information

Let's try filling out the flight arrival information for the last day of the conference using Tab and ◆Indent to line up the text in columns.

4 Press **Reveal Codes** (Alt-F3) to display the full document screen again.

5 Press **Home** twice and then **Down Arrow** (↓) to place the cursor at the end of the itinerary.

6 Type **Arr. JFK Airport** and press **Tab** to move to the second column.

7 Type **11:05 a.m.** for the arrival time.

Instead of using ◆Indent to move to the third column, try using Tab to line up the text of the comment.

8 Press **Tab** to move to the third column, and then type the following comment:

Meet Suzanne at airport; conference at noon.

Notice that the comment wrapped all the way back to the left margin as you typed:

▲ WRAPPED TO LEFT MARGIN

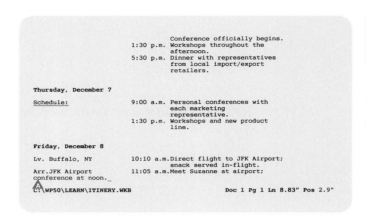

```
                                      Conference officially begins.
                             1:30 p.m. Workshops throughout the
                                      afternoon.
                             5:30 p.m. Dinner with representatives
                                      from local import/export
                                      retailers.


Thursday, December 7

Schedule:                    9:00 a.m. Personal conferences with
                                      each marketing
                                      representative.
                             1:30 p.m. Workshops and new product
                                      line.


Friday, December 8

Lv. Buffalo, NY              10:10 a.m.Direct flight to JFK Airport;
                                      snack served in-flight.
Arr.JFK Airport             11:05 a.m.Meet Suzanne at airport;
conference at noon._
▲
C:\WP50\LEARN\ITINERY.WKB                        Doc 1 Pg 1 Ln 8.83" Pos 2.9"
```

Now, substitute an indent for the last tab and see what happens to the note.

9 Place the cursor on the "M" of the word "Meet" at the beginning of the comment.

10 Press **Backspace** to delete the tab, and then press **♦Indent** (F4) to insert an indent.

11 Press **Home** and then **Down Arrow** (↓) to rewrite the screen (if necessary).

The text of the note should be lined up at the last tab stop (column) on the page.

Adding an Event

Now that the flight information is completed, an event needs to be added to Thursday's schedule.

12 Move the cursor to the "Friday, December 8" title.

13 Press **Up Arrow** (↑) twice to place the cursor at the left margin below the 1:30 p.m. workshop entry.

14 Press **Tab** to move to the second column and type **7:00 p.m.** for the time of the event.

15 Press ➧**Indent** (F4) to move to the third column and type the following comment:

Dinner theater at Andre's Place in downtown Buffalo. Reservations made for invited guests and regional marketing representatives.

Your schedule for Thursday should look like the one illustrated below.

```
                              Conference officially begins.
                      1:30 p.m. Workshops throughout the
                              afternoon.
                      5:30 p.m. Dinner with representatives
                              from local import/export
                              retailers.


Thursday, December 7

Schedule:             9:00 a.m. Personal conferences with
                              each marketing
                              representative.
                      1:30 p.m. Workshops and new product
                              line.
                      7:00 p.m. Dinner theater at Andre's
                              Place in downtown Buffalo.
                              Reservations made for invited
                              guests and regional marketing
                              representatives._


Friday, December 8
Lv. Buffalo, NY       10:10 a.m.Direct flight to JFK Airport;
C:\WP50\LEARN\ITINERY.WKB              Doc 1 Pg 1 Ln 8.33" Pos 6.05"
```

The Parallel Columns heading in the Special Techniques lesson introduces you to Text Columns, which is designed to handle any length of text in any column. However, for simple documents such as an itinerary, it may be just as effective to use tabbed columns.

Adjusting the Columns

Sometimes you may need to adjust the columns to allow more (or less) room for information in a column. Tabbed columns can be quickly adjusted by simply changing the tab stop settings.

For example, the time and comments columns could be moved to the left to make more room for the notes in the last column.

16 Press **Home** three times and then **Up Arrow** (↑) to move the cursor to the beginning of the itinerary.

17 Press **Format** (Shift-F8), select Line (1), and then select Tab Set (8).

18 Press **Home** and **Left Arrow** (←), and then press **Delete to End of Line** (Ctrl-End) to erase all the tab stop settings.

19 Press **Right Arrow** (→) until the cursor is at 3" on the tab ruler, then type **L** to set a tab stop for the scheduled times.

20 Press **Right Arrow** (→) to move to the 4" mark, then type **L** to set a tab stop for the comments.

21 Press **Exit** (F7) twice to save the tab stop settings and return to the itinerary.

Deleting Old Codes

Although you've set new tabs stops, they are not being used because the original tab setting code is still in the itinerary.

22 Press **Reveal Codes** (Alt-F3) to see the two tab setting codes (original and new).

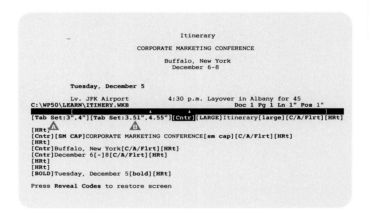

The first code contains the new tab settings, while the second code contains the original tab settings. Because the original code comes *after* the new code, WordPerfect continues to use the original tab settings. To correct the problem, the original code needs to be deleted.

23 Make sure that the cursor is on the second (original) tab setting code, then press **Reveal Codes** (Alt-F3) to display the full document screen.

24 Press **Delete** (Del) and type **y** to delete the original code.

25 Press **Screen** (Ctrl-F3) and select Rewrite (0) to reformat the itinerary (if necessary).

The times and descriptions should jump to the new tab settings, leaving more room in the last column for each comment.

Printing the Itinerary

Because the itinerary was created with the Standard Printer selected, you will need to select your own printer before printing the edited version.

26 Press **Print** (Shift-F7) and type **s** to display the list of printers.

27 Highlight the name of your printer and press **Enter** to select the printer.

28 Select Full Document (1) to print the edited itinerary.

29 Press **Exit** (F7) and type **n** twice to clear the screen.

Summary

During this lesson, you were introduced to the following tasks:

- Defining tabbed columns.
- Setting a tab stop.
- Typing text in tabbed columns.

For a complete listing of all tasks introduced in the lessons, turn to *Feature Summary* at the end of the workbook.

Lesson 16: Printed Forms

Using forms is one of the most reliable and economical ways of exchanging information. Most forms are professionally printed, and then filled in by hand or with a typewriter.

However, if you fill in the same form frequently, you may want to consider using Advance to help you print the information on the form.

For example, the following is an invoice for HALVA International that was filled in with WordPerfect.

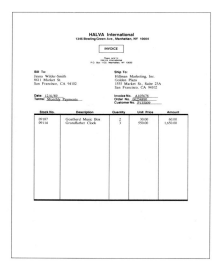

The information in the invoice was printed using Advance to place the text in the correct position on the page.

1 Press **Retrieve** (Shift-F10) and enter **invoice.wkb** to retrieve the document with the Advance codes.

Comments and Advance Codes

Notice that the document you retrieved does not look like the invoice form. Instead, there are comments on the page (in boxes) that indicate the information you need to type to fill in the invoice.

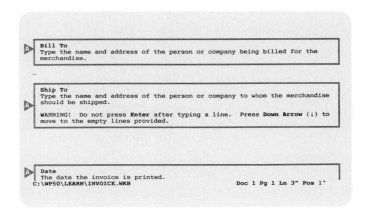

▲ COMMENTS

Below each comment is an empty line (or lines) where the information is typed. Advance codes at the beginning of each line tell WordPerfect exactly where to print the information on the form.

For example, the empty line for the "Bill To" information includes Advance codes to print the information 3" from the top edge of the form and 1" from the left edge of the form.

2 Press **Reveal Codes** (Alt-F3) to see the Advance codes in the document.

▲ ADVANCE CODES

Besides the Advance codes, notice that each comment displayed in the document screen is a single WordPerfect code. The comment appears on the screen, but is not printed.

3 Press **Reveal Codes** (Alt-F3) to display the full document screen.

Creating a Comment

Let's add a comment and Advance codes for the Customer No. on the invoice form.

4 Press **Page Down** (PgDn) to move to the end of the invoice information document, and then press **Up Arrow** (↑) to place the cursor on the empty line below the "Order No." comment.

5 Press **Enter** to insert an extra line.

6 Press **Text In/Out** (Ctrl-F5), select Comment (5), and then select Create (1).

An empty box appears on your screen in which you can type the comment.

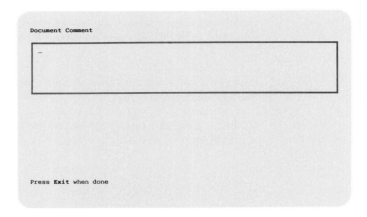

```
Document Comment

 ┌─────────────────────────────────────────────────────┐
 │ _                                                     │
 │                                                       │
 │                                                       │
 │                                                       │
 └─────────────────────────────────────────────────────┘




Press Exit when done
```

Besides typing and editing text in the box, you can also use Bold and Underline to highlight text.

7 Press **Bold** (F6), type **Customer No.** for the comment, and then press **Exit** (F7) to return to the information document.

Your comment should look like the one illustrated on the screen below.

⚠ CUSTOMER COMMENT

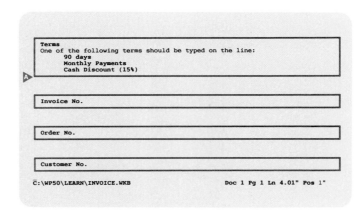

Adding Advance Codes

Now that the comment has been created, the Advance codes need to be placed in the line to print the customer number in the blank line provided on the invoice form. The blank line is 4.15" down from the top of the form, and 5.3" in from the left edge of the form.

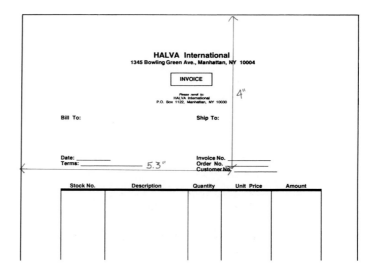

When measuring from the top edge of the form, the measurement *should not* include the line of text that will be printed.

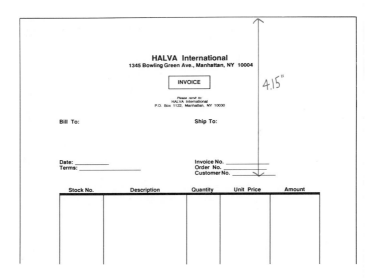

For example, the blank Customer No. line on the form is 4.15" from the top of the form. However, because a line of printed text is approximately .15" (for an 11 point font), the .15" should be subtracted from the 4.15" to get the correct measurement.

8 Press **Format** (Shift-F8), select Other (4), and then select Advance (1).

9 Select Line (3) and enter **4** for the vertical measurement.

10 Select Advance (1), select Column (6), and enter **5.3** for the horizontal measurement.

11 Press **Exit** (F7) to return to the information document.

If you want another measurement for the Line (Ln) and Position (Pos) numbers on the status line to compare the Advance code settings to the cursor position, turn to the Units of Measure heading in the Special Techniques lesson at the end of Formatting Documents.

Saving the Invoice Document

Now that the invoice information document is complete, you can save and then retrieve it any time an invoice needs to be printed. However, because the information document is currently using the Standard Printer selection, you need to select your own printer before saving the document.

12 Press **Print** (Shift-F7), type **s** to for the Select Printer option, select your printer, and then press **Exit** (F7) to return to the information document.

13 Press **Save** (F10) and enter **invoice** to create a new file for the edited information document.

When a document is saved with one selected, WordPerfect automatically selects the same printer when you retrieve the document.

Filling In the Invoice

The invoice information document can now be filled in and sent to the printer.

14 Press **Home** twice and then **Up Arrow** (↑) to place the cursor on the empty line below the "Bill To" comment.

15 Type the following name and address for the "Bill To" information, pressing **Enter** after each line:

Robin Pierce
InterChange, Inc.
544 Westminster Circle NW
Atlanta, GA 30327

16 Press **Down Arrow** (↓) to place the cursor on the empty line below the "Ship To" comment.

Notice the warning in the comment box about Enter.

 WARNING

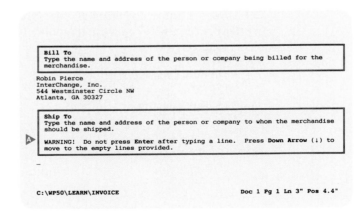

Because the "Bill To" address is printed at the left margin, only one set of Advance codes is needed to print the address in the correct place. However, because the "Ship To" address is in the middle of the page, *each* line of the "Ship To" address needs to start with a set of Advance codes to print correctly.

The empty lines below the "Ship To" comment have Advance codes already inserted. If you press Enter when typing the "Ship To" address, the Advance codes are pushed below the text, and the address will not be printed properly on the invoice form.

17 Type the following address in the empty lines below the "Ship To" comment, using **Down Arrow** (↓) to move from line to line:

InterChange, Inc.
Old Dominion Drive
Atlanta, GA 30338

If you press Enter while typing, simply press Backspace, and then press Down Arrow to move to the next empty line.

18 Press **Down Arrow** (↓) twice to place the cursor on the empty line below the "Date" comment, and then type **09/25/1989** for the date.

19 Press **Down Arrow** (↓) to place the cursor on the empty line below the "Terms" comment, and then type **90 days** for the payment terms.

20 Press **Down Arrow** (↓) to place the cursor on the empty line below the "Invoice No." comment.

21 Type the following invoice, order, and customer numbers, pressing **Down Arrow** (↓) after each number to place the cursor below the correct comment:

A105678 (invoice number)
00254890 (order number)
P135009 (customer number)

Typing in Tabbed Columns

The final information to be filled out is the merchandise ordered. Notice the special directions in the comment for filling in the information.

⚠ SPECIAL DIRECTIONS

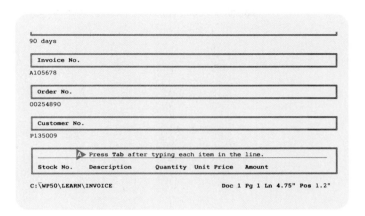

Tabs have been set to place each item of information (stock no., description, etc.) at the correct position when the invoice is printed. All you need to do is type an item and press Tab to move to the next position.

As you type, notice that the Quantity column tab is set to align the number to the right, while the Unit Price and Amount column tabs align the prices at the decimal point.

22 Type the following information for an order of music boxes. Remember to press **Tab** between each item:

09187 (stock no.)
Spring Rain Music Box (description)
10 (quantity)
15.00 (unit price)
150.00 (amount)

Printing the Information

With the invoice information completed, you are ready to print the information.

23 Press **Print** (Shift-F7) and select Full Document (1) to print the information.

Check the position of the customer number on the printed page.

24 Measure 4" down from the top of the printed page, and 5.3" in from the left edge of the page.

Your measurements should mark the top and beginning of the "P" in the customer number.

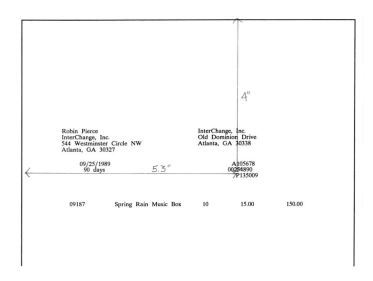

Even if you use a larger or smaller font to print the information, the measurements in the Advance codes are *absolute* and should always place the text in exactly the same place on the page.

25 Press **Exit** (F7) and type **n** twice to clear the screen.

Adding Math Columns

The last column in the merchandise information is the total amount for the item ordered.

△ TOTAL AMOUNT

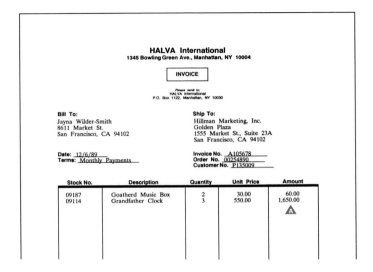

While you could calculate the amount by multiplying the quantity by the unit price for each item, you can also use Math to have WordPerfect do the calculating for you.

26 Press **Retrieve** (Shift-F10) and enter **invoice** to retrieve the edited information document.

27 Press **Page Down** (PgDn) to place the cursor at the very end of the document.

28 Press **Math/Columns** (Alt-F7) and select Math Define (2).

You should see the following Math Definition menu on your screen.

```
Math Definition          Use arrow keys to position cursor

Columns                  A B C D E F G H I J K L M N O P Q R S T U V W X

Type                     2 2 2 2 2 2 2 2.2 2 2 2 2 2 2 2 2 2 2 2 2 2 2 2

Negative Numbers         ( ( ( ( ( ( ( ( ( ( ( ( ( ( ( ( ( ( ( ( ( ( ( (

Number of Digits to      2 2 2 2 2 2 2 2 2 2 2 2 2 2 2 2 2 2 2 2 2 2 2 2
  the Right (0-4)

Calculation      1
  Formulas       2
                 3
                 4

Type of Column:
      0 = Calculation    1 = Text      2 = Numeric    3 = Total

Negative Numbers
      ( = Parentheses (50.00)          - = Minus Sign  -50.00


Press Exit when done
```

Math lets you define columns (A-X) for typing text, entering numbers, calculating totals, or creating your own formula for calculating. The columns are the tabbed columns that you set up using Format.

For example, the first column (A) is the description and is used for typing text.

29 Type **1** to define the first tab stop (column A) as a text column.

The next two columns (B and C) are the quantity and unit price, and are used for typing numbers. Because WordPerfect has preset all columns as numeric columns, you do not need to change the settings.

30 Press **Right Arrow** (→) twice to leave the second and third tab stops (columns B and C) defined as numeric columns.

The final column (D) is the amount that needs to be calculated by multiplying the quantity by the unit price.

31 Type **0** to define the last tab stop (column D) for calculating.

The cursor jumps to the middle of the menu, where you can enter the formula for the column.

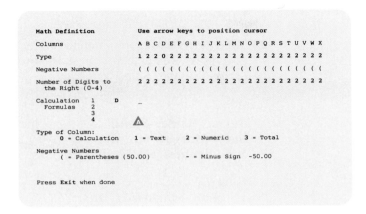

```
Math Definition            Use arrow keys to position cursor

Columns                    A B C D E F G H I J K L M N O P Q R S T U V W X

Type                       1 2 2 0 2 2 2 2 2 2 2 2 2 2 2 2 2 2 2 2 2 2 2 2

Negative Numbers           ( ( ( ( ( ( ( ( ( ( ( ( ( ( ( ( ( ( ( ( ( ( ( (

Number of Digits to        2 2 2 2 2 2 2 2 2 2 2 2 2 2 2 2 2 2 2 2 2 2 2 2
   the Right (0-4)

Calculation    1    D      _
  Formulas     2
               3
               4         ▲

Type of Column:
   0 = Calculation    1 = Text    2 = Numeric    3 = Total

Negative Numbers
   ( = Parentheses (50.00)        - = Minus Sign  -50.00


Press Exit when done
```

If you are familiar with calculators, then you know that the asterisk (*) is the symbol used for multiplying. Because you want to multiply column B (the quantity) by column C (the unit price) for the total amount, you can enter the formula "B*C" to have WordPerfect do the calculating for you.

32 Type **b*c** for the formula, press **Enter**, and then press **Exit** (F7) to leave the Math Define menu.

33 Select Math On (1) to turn on Math for the columns.

Now that you have added Math to the information document, it is ready to save, complete, and then calculate.

34 Press **Exit** (F7), type **y**, and press **Enter** to use the "Invoice" filename.

35 Type **y** to replace the file, and then type **n** to clear the screen.

The lesson on financial statements in Special Applications *provides additional exercises in using Math.*

Filling In the Invoice

Because you have already filled in the invoice once, the steps below simply provide information you can use to fill in the invoice again.

36 Press **Retrieve** (Shift-F10) and enter **invoice** to retrieve the information document.

37 Type the following information for the "Bill To" and "Ship To" addresses. Remember to press **Down Arrow** (and not Enter) after each line in the "Ship To" address:

(bill to)
Jayna Wilder-Smith
8611 Market St.
San Francisco, CA 94102

(ship to)
Hillman Marketing, Inc.
Golden Plaza
1555 Market St., Suite 23A
San Francisco, CA 94102

38 Type the following information for the date, terms, and numbers, pressing **Down Arrow** (↓) after each item to move the cursor below the next comment:

12/6/89 (date)
Monthly Payments (terms)
A105678 (invoice number)
00254890 (order number)
P135009 (customer number)

After typing the customer number and pressing Down Arrow, the cursor should be below the final comment, with a "Math" message displayed on the status line.

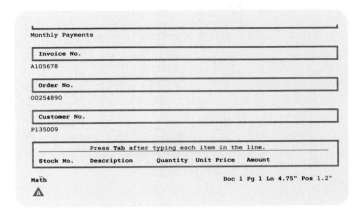

The message lets you know that you can begin typing in the Math columns you defined.

If the "Math" message does not appear, try pressing Page Down (PgDn).

39 Type the following information for the stock number, description, quantity, and unit price. Remember to press **Tab** after typing an item of information:

09187 (stock no.)
Goatherd Music Box (description)
2 (quantity)
30.00 (unit price)

After typing the unit price and pressing Tab, an exclamation point (!) should appear in the Amount column.

EXCLAMATION POINT

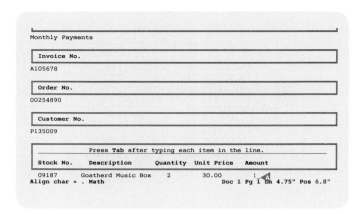

The exclamation point indicates that WordPerfect will calculate the amount for you when you select Calculate from the Math/Columns menu.

40 Press **Enter** to start a new line.

41 Type the following information for the second item of merchandise ordered. Remember to press **Tab** after typing the unit price to have WordPerfect display the "!" in the last column:

09114 (stock no.)
Grandfather Clock (description)
3 (quantity)
550.00 (unit price)

Calculating the Amounts

Now that the information document is completed, you can calculate the amounts.

42 Press **Math/Columns** (Alt-F7) and select Calculate (2).

The following amounts should appear in the last column of the merchandise information.

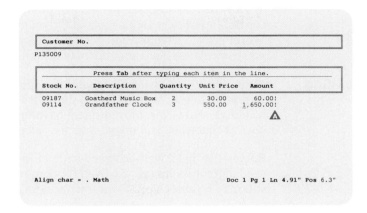

While the exclamation points are still displayed on your screen, they (and the comments) will not be printed.

43 Press **Print** (Shift-F7) and select Full Document (1) to send the information document to the printer.

44 Press **Exit** (F7) and type **n** twice to clear the screen.

For information on using Merge and Macros to automate the process of filling in and printing invoices, turn to the Printed Forms lesson in *Merging Documents*.

Summary

During this lesson you were introduced to the following tasks:

• Advancing text from the left edge of the page.
• Advancing text from the top of the page.
• Calculating Math columns.
• Creating a Math formula.
• Creating and editing comments.
• Defining Math columns.

For a complete listing of all tasks introduced in the lessons, turn to *Feature Summary* at the end of the workbook.

Lesson 17: Headings

WordPerfect is designed to take maximum advantage of your printer's capabilities. Every font available for your printer can be used from WordPerfect. If your printer can print graphics images and characters, then you can create a document that will print those images.

Designing a Heading

Because of these powerful capabilities, a number of businesses are beginning to use WordPerfect to print their own letterhead and memo headings. However, most of them have invested in a printer that produces quality characters and images (such as a laser printer).

Remember that a well-designed letter or memo heading does not always need a graphics image. So even if your printer cannot handle graphics, you still may be able to print your own heading for business documents.

Before continuing, check the Print menu (Shift-F7) to see if your printer is selected. If not, use Select Printer to select your printer so that your fonts are available.

Creating a Letterhead Format

For example, you can use Headers and Footers to create a format for a sheet of letterhead paper for HALVA International.

1 Press **Format** (Shift-F8), select Page (2), and then select Headers (3).

2 Select Header A (1) and then select Every Page (2).

The font attributes on the Font menu can be used to quickly select different styles and sizes of fonts. Let's center and type HALVA on the first line of the header using the Large attribute, and then center and type International on the second line using the Bold attribute.

3 Press **Center** (Shift-F6), press **Font** (Ctrl-F8), select Size (1), and then select Large (5).

4 Type **HALVA** for the title, press **End** to move past the [large] code, and then press **Enter** to start a new line.

While text can be bolded by using Bold (F6), bolding is also a font attribute available on the Appearance menu.

5 Press **Center** (Shift-F6), press **Font** (Ctrl-F8), select Appearance (2), and then select Bold (1).

6 Type **International** for the second line of the title.

Your header should now look similar to the one illustrated on the screen below.

▲ HEADING

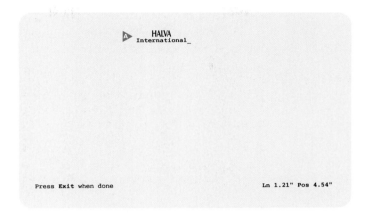

7 Press **Exit** (F7) to return to the Page Format menu.

Creating a Footer

The footer for the letterhead includes the name, address, and phone number of the company.

8 Select Footers (4), select Footer A (1), and then select Every Page (2).

9 Press **Center** (Shift-F6), press **Font** (Ctrl-F8), select Size (1), and then select Small (4).

10 Type the following information in one continuous line without pressing Enter:

HALVA International, 1345 Bowling Green Ave., Manhattan, NY 10004

Your footer should look similar to the one illustrated below.

11 Press **Exit** (F7) to return to Page Format menu.

Setting a Bottom Margin

Because the bottom margin is set to 1 inch, the footer will be too far up the page to leave enough space for the text of the letter. You can correct the problem by resetting the bottom margin to .3" to place the footer closer to the bottom of the page.

12 Select Margins (5), press **Enter** to keep the 1 inch top margin, enter **.3** for the bottom margin, and then press **Exit** to return to the document screen.

Previewing and Printing the Letterhead

With the bottom margin set, you can preview the letterhead format before sending it to the printer.

13 Press **Print** (Shift-F7) and select View Document (6) to display the letterhead in the preview screen.

Whether or not you have a graphics card, you should be able to see the text in the header and footer on your screen. If you have a graphics card, then the page should look similar to the following screen.

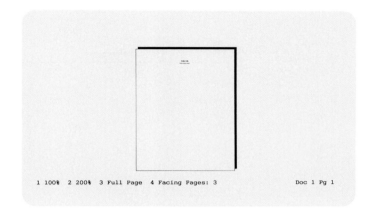

1 100%   2 200%   3 Full Page   4 Facing Pages: 3   Doc 1 Pg 1

14 Press **Cancel** (F1) to leave the preview screen, select Full Document (1) to print the letterhead.

If the text printed on the page is all the same size and style, you may not have any fonts assigned to your attributes. You can try using other attributes, or simply use Base Font on the Font menu to select from a complete list of fonts. The base font code should be inserted at the beginning of the line before pressing Center.

You can save the letterhead as a file that can be retrieved and used whenever you want to print a letter. If you will be typing more than one page, you will need to use Discontinue on the Headers and Footers menus at the top of the second page to insert codes to discontinue the header and footer. You may also want to reset the bottom margin to 1 inch.

15 Press **Exit** (F7) and type **n** twice to clear the screen.

The Styles feature is an excellent way of organizing formats by simply selecting a format style from a menu. For an example of using a style list, see the Styles lesson in Formatting Documents.

Creating a Memo Heading

If you have a printer that can print graphics images (such as a laser printer), you may want to try this exercise to discover how Graphics in WordPerfect can be used to create a memo heading similar to the following.

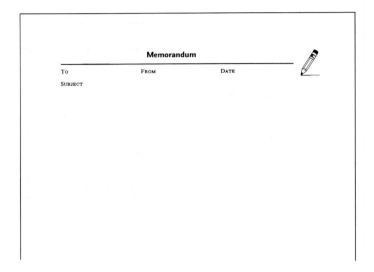

The first step is to change the left and right margins to increase the space in the lines. At the same time, you can set tabs for the titles below the line.

16 Press **Format** (Shift-F8), select Line (1), and then select Margins Left/Right (7).

17 Enter **.75** for the left margin, and then enter **.75** for the right margin.

18 Select Tab Set (8) and then press **Delete to End of Line** (Ctrl-End) to erase the current settings.

19 Enter **2.7** for the first tab stop, enter **4.85** for the second tab stop, and then press **Exit** (F7) twice to return to the document screen.

With the margins and tabs set, you can begin creating the heading.

20 Press **Center** (Shift-F6), press **Font** (Ctrl-F8), select Size (1), and then select Extra Large (7).

21 Type **Memorandum**, press **Font** (Ctrl-F8), select Normal (3), and then press **Enter** to insert a new line.

Creating the
Horizontal Line

The horizontal line can be added below the title by using Line on the Graphics menu.

22 Press **Graphics** (Alt-F9), select Line (5), and then select Horizontal Line (1).

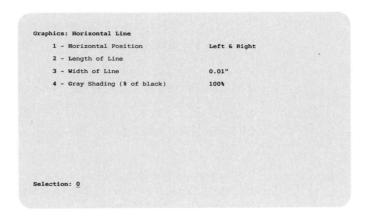

```
Graphics: Horizontal Line
      1 - Horizontal Position          Left & Right
      2 - Length of Line
      3 - Width of Line                0.01"
      4 - Gray Shading (% of black)    100%




Selection: 0
```

As you can see, the line is set to extend from the left to the right margins, is .01" in width, and will be printed in 100% shading (black).

23 Select Width of Line (3), enter **.02** to increase the thickness of the line, and then press **Exit** (F7) to return to the memo heading.

24 Press **Print** (Shift-F7) and select View Document (6) to preview the heading.

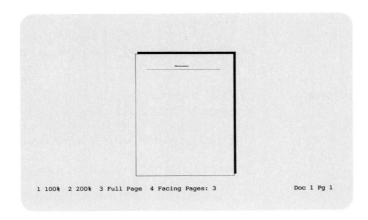

```
1 100%   2 200%   3 Full Page   4 Facing Pages: 3              Doc 1 Pg 1
```

If you have a graphics card, you may want to use View Document after each step that follows to check the memo heading design.

25 Press **Exit** (F7) to return to the document screen.

Creating the Information Titles

After creating the main title, the information titles need to be placed below the horizontal line.

26 Press **Page Down** (PgDn) to move the cursor to the end of the document.

27 Press **Enter** twice to double space, type **To**, press **Tab**, type **From**, press **Tab**, and then type **Date**.

28 Press **Enter** twice to double space, and then type **Subject** for the last title.

Besides using the font attributes as you type, you can also block existing text and select an attribute. The Small Caps attribute is convenient for titles, as WordPerfect prints all the letters in uppercase, with the initial letter of each word in a larger size.

If a font is not assigned to the Small Caps attribute in your printer resource file (.Prs), then Small Caps will not work.

29 Place the cursor at the beginning of the "to" title, press **Block** (Alt-F4), and then press **Page Down** (PgDn) to highlight all four titles.

30 Press **Font** (Ctrl-F8), select Appearance (2), and then select Small Caps (7).

Adding a Graphics Figure

For the final step, a graphics figure can be added to the upper right corner of the heading.

31 Press **Page Up** (PgUp) to move to the very beginning of the memo heading.

Setting the Options

While WordPerfect is set to print a box around a graphics figure, the box is not needed for the memo heading.

32 Press **Graphics** (Alt-F9), select Figure (1), and then select Options (4).

33 Select Border Style (1), and then type **1** four times to eliminate the box.

You may also want to decrease the outside border space on the left to allow more room for the date.

34 Select Outside Border Space (2), enter **0** (zero) for the left border, and then press **Enter** three times to leave the rest of the spacing at ".16."

35 Press **Exit** (F7) to return to the memo heading

Retrieving the Image

Now that the options have been set for the box, you are ready to retrieve an image and create a WordPerfect graphics figure to add to the heading.

36 Press **Graphics** (Alt-F9), select Figure (1), and then select Create (1).

The Create menu contains all the options for retrieving and adjusting the graphics image.

37 Select Filename (1) and enter **pencil.wpg** to retrieve a pencil drawing a line.

38 Select Size (6), select Height (2), and then enter **.7** for the height of the pencil (the width is calculated automatically).

39 Press **Exit** (F7) to return to the memo heading.

40 Press **Print** (Shift-F7), and then select View Document (6) to display the heading one last time in the preview screen before sending it to the printer.

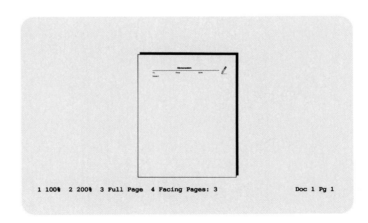

41 Press **Cancel** (F1) and select Full Document (1) to print the heading.

After the memo heading prints, you may want to try using another attribute for the titles, adjust the horizontal line, adjust the tabs, or place the pencil in a different position on the page. All of this (and more) can be done with features available in WordPerfect.

42 Press **Exit** (F7) and type **n** twice to clear the screen.

If you decide to use the memo heading, you will need to place each title in its own set of attribute codes, or the text you type will be in the same font (small caps) as the titles.

Summary

During this lesson you were introduced to the following tasks:

- Creating a graphics figure.
- Creating a horizontal line.
- Creating a footer for every page.
- Selecting a font attribute.
- Setting options for a graphics figure.
- Setting top and bottom margins.

For a complete listing of all tasks introduced in the lessons, turn to *Feature Summary* at the end of the workbook.

Lesson 18: Styles

WordPerfect helps you automate the process of formatting a document by providing a Style feature that lets you store and retrieve a group of formats at the same time. Each group of formats is called a *style*, and is displayed in a list where styles can be created, edited, deleted, etc.

Let's retrieve the letter to Swiss America, and then try creating a hanging-indented style for the paragraphs.

1 Press **Retrieve** (Shift-F10) and enter **musicbox.wkb** to retrieve the letter.

2 Press **Style** (Alt-F8) to display the style list.

Creating a Style

Notice that the style list is empty when you start a new document.

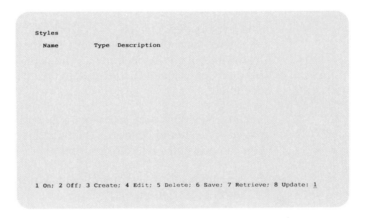

```
Styles
  Name          Type  Description




1 On; 2 Off; 3 Create; 4 Edit; 5 Delete; 6 Save; 7 Retrieve; 8 Update: 1
```

If you have chosen a style library with Setup, then a list of styles will appear. However, you can continue following the steps in the exercise.

3 Select Create (3) to add a style to the list.

The menu for the style information is displayed on the screen.

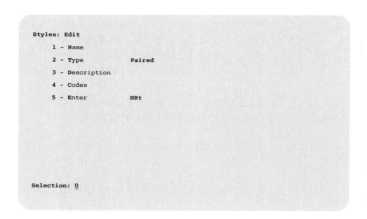

```
Styles: Edit
       1 - Name
       2 - Type          Paired
       3 - Description
       4 - Codes
       5 - Enter          HRt




Selection: 0
```

4 Select Name (1) and enter **Hanging** for the name of the style.

The Type option lets you select from an open or paired style. The open style (like the settings) is inserted once, and affects all text from the style forward through the document. The paired style uses on and off codes (like Bold or Center), and can be used to create a style for part of the text in your document.

Because you only want the paragraphs formatted with a hanging indent, the paired style should be used. The paired style is already selected for you, so you can continue on to the description.

5 Select Description (3) and enter **Hanging-indented paragraph style** for the description.

6 Select Codes (4) to create the codes for the style.

Notice that the Reveal Codes screen for a paired style includes a comment.

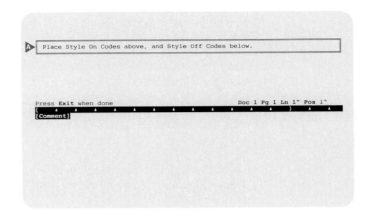

Any codes before (above) the comment are placed in the on style code, while any codes after (below) the comment are placed in the off style code.

7 Press ♦**Indent** (F4) and then press ♦**Margin Release** (Shift-Tab) to insert these two codes before the comment.

Because a hanging indent is created with two formatting codes at the beginning of the paragraph, there is no need to place any codes in the ending style code at this point. You are ready to exit and try using the hanging-indented style.

8 Press **Exit** (F7) three times to return to the letter.

Formating with a Paired Style

If you have already typed the text of a document, you can block the text you want included in the style, and then select the style from the list.

9 Place the cursor at the beginning of the first paragraph, press **Block** (Alt-F4), and then move the cursor to the end of the paragraph.

10 Press **Style** (Alt-F8) and then select On (1).

You are returned to the letter where the first paragraph is now displayed in a hanging-indented style.

11 Press **Reveal Codes** (Alt-F3) to see the on and off codes around the paragraph.

12 Place the cursor on the [Style On:Hanging] code at the beginning of the paragraph.

The code immediately expands to let you see the indent and margin release that you placed before the comment.

13 Place the cursor on the [Style Off:Hanging] code at the end of the paragraph.

Because there were no formats placed after the comment, there are no formats for WordPerfect to display.

At this point you may want to try repeating steps 9 and 10 to assign the hanging-indented style to two or more paragraphs before continuing with the exercise.

Editing a Style

One of the more important features of using styles is the ability to change a style once from the list, and then let WordPerfect change the style for the entire document.

For example, if you want all the hanging-indented paragraphs double-spaced, all you need to do is add the code to the style, and then let WordPerfect do all the formatting for you.

14 Press **Style** (Alt-F8), place the cursor on the Hanging style, and then type **4** twice to edit the codes in the style.

15 Press **Format** (Shift-F8), select Line (1), and then select Line Spacing (6).

16 Enter **2** for the spacing number, and then press **Exit** (F7) to return to the codes in the style.

17 Press Exit (F7) four times to return to the letter on your screen.

18 Place the cursor on a [Style On: Hanging] code.

The paragraph(s) with the Hanging style are double-spaced because a Line Spacing code has been added to each [Style On: Hanging] code.

19 Place the cursor on a [Style Off: hanging] code.

Notice that the Style Off code now contains a line spacing code that changes the line spacing back to single spacing.

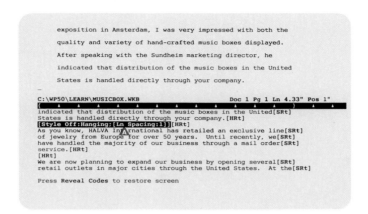

By using a paired set of style codes, WordPerfect automatically adds whatever format codes are needed to change the format back to the initial settings of the document. You can add other fromats to the style off code by placing them to the right of the Comment in the style editing screen.

20 Press **Reveal Codes** (Alt-F3) to display the full document screen again.

While the styled paragraphs are double-spaced, the rest of the letter is still single-spaced because you used a paired style.

Retrieving a Style List

Once you create the styles you need, you can use Save at the bottom of the Style menu to save them as a file that can be retrieved whenever you start a new document.

For example, a style list has already been saved for formatting letters.

21 Press **Style** (Alt-F8) to display the style list.

22 Select Retrieve (7) and enter **letter.sty** for the name of the style list.

Four styles are retrieved from the file and added to the hanging-indented style already in the list.

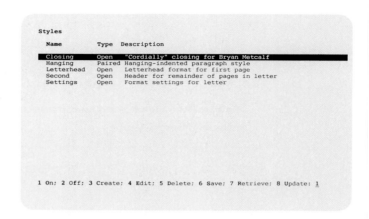

```
Styles

  Name          Type   Description

  Closing       Open   "Cordially" closing for Bryan Metcalf
  Hanging       Paired Hanging-indented paragraph style
  Letterhead    Open   Letterhead format for first page
  Second        Open   Header for remainder of pages in letter
  Settings      Open   Format settings for letter









  1 On; 2 Off; 3 Create; 4 Edit; 5 Delete; 6 Save; 7 Retrieve; 8 Update: 1
```

The styles include a standard closing, a letterhead format, a format for the second page of a letter, and format settings to be inserted at the beginning of a letter.

Displaying the Contents of a Style

Let's take a look at the contents of a couple of styles to see what they contain.

23 Highlight the Settings style, and then select Edit (4).

24 Select Codes (4) to display the group of codes for the Settings style.

As you can see, there is one code for justification, and one for widow/orphan protection.

25 Press **Exit** (F7) twice to return to the list of styles.

26 Place the cursor on the Closing style, and then type **4** twice to see the formats in the style.

Inserting a Text Style

Notice that the Closing style is simply text with no format codes included. You can include both formats *and* text in a style. Creating a text style can be valuable if you use the same phrase, title, or block of text continually in a document.

27 Press Exit (F7) three times to return to the letter.

28 Press **Home** twice and then **Down Arrow** (↓) to move the cursor to the end of the letter.

29 Place the cursor on the "S" of the word "Sincerely," press **Delete to End of Page** (Ctrl-PgDn) and then type **y** to erase the closing to the letter.

30 Select **Style** (Alt-F8), highlight the Closing style, and then select On (1).

A closing for the letter is automatically inserted for you. While this is a convenient feature, remember that the text being displayed is inside a style code, and can only be edited from the style list.

For example, notice that the cursor is at the end of the closing at the moment.

31 Press **Reveal Codes** (Alt-F3), and then place the cursor on the [Open Style:Closing] code.

The style code expands to show the closing in the Reveal Codes screen, but the cursor in the document screen has jumped to the beginning of the closing.

32 Press **Reveal Codes** (Alt-F3) to return to display the full document screen.

Style is a very powerful feature of WordPerfect, and includes many other options that can help you in organizing and designing styles for your documents.

33 Press **Exit** (F7) and type **n** twice to clear the screen.

The lesson on newsletters in Special Applications *contains an additional exercise using styles. For complete details on Style, turn to the WordPerfect reference manual.*

Summary

During this lesson you were introduced to the following tasks:

- Creating a style.
- Editing a style.
- Formatting with styles.
- Retrieving a style list.
- Setting line spacing.

For a complete listing of all tasks introduced in the lessons, turn to *Feature Summary* at the end of the workbook.

Lesson 19: Special Techniques

Now that you have completed *Formatting Documents*, we'd like to take a moment to give you some insights and special techniques that many people have found to be valuable when formatting and managing documents.

While not all the special methods discussed below are included in *Feature Summary* at the end of the workbook, you can find them listed in the index.

Document Summaries

Many companies like to organize their letters, memorandums, and other business documents by adding a document summary to each file created.

Creating a Letter Summary

For example, let's add a document summary to the letter of introduction (Lesson 8).

1 Press **Retrieve** (Shift-F10) and enter **musicbox.wkb** for the filename of the letter.

2 Press **Format** (Shift-F8), select Document (3), and then select Summary (5).

A document summary appears on your screen for the letter you have retrieved.

A FILENAME
B CURRENT DATE

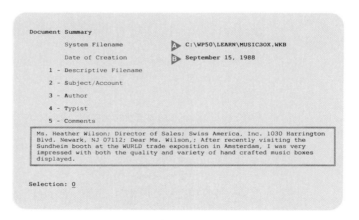

```
Document Summary

        System Filename           A   C:\WP50\LEARN\MUSICBOX.WKB

        Date of Creation          B   September 15, 1988

    1 - Descriptive Filename

    2 - Subject/Account

    3 - Author

    4 - Typist

    5 - Comments
   ┌──────────────────────────────────────────────────────────────────┐
   │ Ms. Heather Wilson; Director of Sales; Swiss America, Inc. 1030 Harrington │
   │ Blvd. Newark, NJ 07112; Dear Ms. Wilson,; After recently visiting the      │
   │ Sundheim booth at the WURLD trade exposition in Amsterdam, I was very       │
   │ impressed with both the quality and variety of hand crafted music boxes     │
   │ displayed.                                                                  │
   └──────────────────────────────────────────────────────────────────┘

Selection: 0
```

Notice that the filename (system filename) and current date (date of creation) are already inserted. The filename is added to the document summary whenever you name the document. When typing a letter, you may want to create a document summary before saving the letter so that the date inserted is the date of creation.

The first few lines of the letter are automatically inserted into the comments as a reminder of the letter's contents. The rest of the information can be filled in as needed.

For example, HALVA International requires that the account, author, and typist be entered for every letter.

3 Select Subject/Account (2) and enter **Swiss America, Inc.** for the account name.

4 Select Author (3) and enter **Bryan Metcalf** for the author.

5 Select Typist (4) and enter **cjg** for the typist's initials.

Your document summary should look similar to the one illustrated in the screen below.

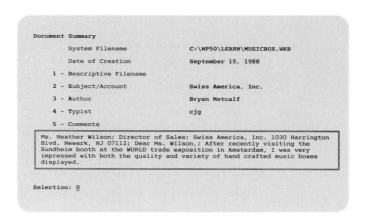

6 Press **Exit** (F7) to save the document summary and return to the letter.

7 Press **Exit** (F7), type **y**, enter **musicbox.1** to save the letter, and then type **n** to clear the screen.

Setting the Subject Title for a Memo Summary
When creating a document summary for memorandums, the subject line of the memo is automatically inserted into the document summary. However, you need to make sure that WordPerfect knows the title you are using for the subject line.

8 Press **Retrieve** (Shift-F10) and enter **memo.wkb** to retrieve a memo form.

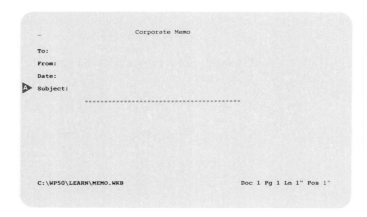

Notice that the title "Subject:" is being used for the subject line title in the memo form.

9 Press **Setup** (Shift-F1), select Initial Settings (5), and then select Document Summary (3).

10 Select Subject Search Text (2), press **Delete to End of Line** (Ctrl-End) and then enter **Subject:** for the name of the title.

Now, when WordPerfect finds a "Subject:" title in a document, the text following the title will be inserted into the document summary.

If your company is using "RE:" or another title, you should return to the Document Summary menu after the exercise to change the title.

The Create on Save/Exit option on the Document Summary menu lets you set WordPerfect to automatically display a document summary for you to fill in (if one does not already exist) whenever you save a document.

Creating a Memo Summary
Let's return to the memo form and fill in the subject line.

11 Press **Exit** (F7) to return to the memo form.

12 Place the cursor on the Subject title, press **End**, and then type **New Account with Swiss America, Inc.** for the subject.

13 Press **Format** (Shift-F8), select Document (3), and then select Summary (5).

Notice that the subject has been automatically entered for you by WordPerfect:

 SUBJECT

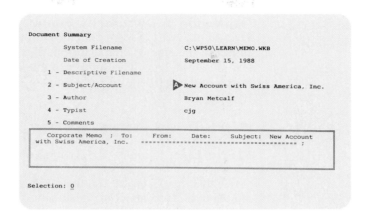

```
Document Summary

        System Filename            C:\WP50\LEARN\MEMO.WKB

        Date of Creation           September 15, 1988

    1 - Descriptive Filename

    2 - Subject/Account          ▶ New Account with Swiss America, Inc.

    3 - Author                     Bryan Metcalf

    4 - Typist                     cjg

    5 - Comments

    Corporate Memo  ; To:    From:    Date:    Subject: New Account
with Swiss America, Inc.  ==================================== ;



Selection: 0
```

The author and typist are also included from the first document summary in the case they are the same for the memo.

14 Press **Exit** (F7) to save the document summary and return to the memo form.

15 Press **Exit** (F7), type **y**, enter **memo.1** for the name of the memo, and then type **n** to clear the screen.

Searching Through the Document Summaries

Once a document summary is added to a letter or memo, the document can be quickly found on the List Files screen.

16 Press **List Files** (F5), and then press **Enter** to display the files you have been saving.

After a few weeks or months, finding a file can be difficult. However, you can use Word Search to look through the document summaries, first pages, or the entire text of each file in a directory (or on a disk) to find the document you need.

For example, let's try using Word Search to find the letter and memo you just saved.

17 Select Word Search (9), and then select Document Summary (1).

18 Type **swiss** for the word pattern, and then press **Enter** to start the search.

WordPerfect looks through the document summary of every file for the word "Swiss," and then redisplays the list of files with those files marked that have a word that matches "swiss."

Displaying a Document Summary

Because the word "Swiss" is in the comments of the letter summary and the subject of the memo summary, both files are marked with an asterisk (*) next to the file size. The number of marked files (two) is also displayed at the top of the list. The cursor is conveniently on the first marked file (memo.1).

19 Press **Tab** to move the cursor to the next marked file (Musicbox.1).

20 Press **Enter** to look at the contents of the letter.

Notice that the document summary information is displayed first, giving you the basic facts about the document.

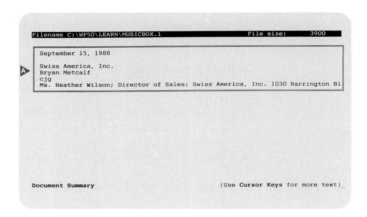

▲ DOCUMENT SUMMARY INFORMATION

```
Filename C:\WP50\LEARN\MUSICBOX.1                    File size:      3900

     September 15, 1988

     Swiss America, Inc.
     Bryan Metcalf
     cjg
     Ms. Heather Wilson; Director of Sales; Swiss America, Inc. 1030 Harrington Bl




   Document Summary                    (Use Cursor Keys for more text)
```

21 Press **Down Arrow** (↓) to display the contents of the letter.

22 Press **Exit** (F7) to return to the list of files.

Once you have found several files that match the word pattern, you can always use Word Search again to search through only the marked files. In addition, the Conditions menu lets you set more detailed specifications for the search.

23 Select Word Search (9) and then select Conditions (4).

```
Word Search

   1 - Perform Search on          2 Marked File(s)

   2 - Undo Last Search

   3 - Reset Search Conditions

   4 - File Date                    No
         From (MM/DD/YY):           (All)
         To   (MM/DD/YY):           (All)

                  Word Pattern(s)

   5 - First Page
   6 - Entire Doc
   7 - Document Summary             swiss
         Creation Date (e.g. Nov)
         Descriptive Name
         Subject/Account
         Author
         Typist
         Comments

Selection: 1
```

The options on the Conditions menu provide a large variety of limitations you can set for the search. All of these are explained in the WordPerfect reference manual under *Word Search*.

24 Press **Exit** (F7) twice to return to the document screen.

Parallel Columns

Whenever you are typing text in columns across the page, you can set a tab stop for each column and then press Tab to move from column to column.

▲ TAB STOP

```
We are proud to announce the grand opening of several HALVA
International retail stores throughout the country.  Stores are
scheduled to open in the following cities during the first
quarter of the year:

      Manhattan      New York        January 18    full size
      Boston         Massachusetts   January 26    full size
      San Francisco  California      February 10   modified
      Los Angeles    California      February 24   superstore
      Atlanta        Georgia         March 9       co-occupancy
      Chicago        Illinois        March 17      full size

As a preferred customer, you will be receiving a special
invitation, and I personally look forward to meeting you at the
opening.

Sincerely,


Bryan Metcalf
President
HALVA International

C:\WP50\LEARN\RETAIL.WKB                     Doc 1 Pg 1 Ln 1" Pos 1"
```

If one of the columns has text with more than one line, you can keep the text lined up at the tab stop by pressing ◆Indent instead of Tab. However, ◆Indent can only be used for the last column.

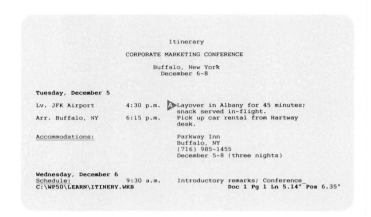

If you want to set up your columns so that any number of lines can be typed in any column, then you need to use the Parallel Columns feature of WordPerfect.

What Parallel Columns lets you do is set a left and right margin for each column. When the text reaches the right column of a margin, it automatically wraps to the left margin of the same column. You can also press Enter to end a short line and return to the left margin of the column.

If you want each column to be the same width, with the same spacing between columns, then WordPerfect automatically calculates the left and right margins of each column for you.

Creating Parallel Columns
For example, to create a phone list with the name at the left margin, the address in the middle, and the phone number in the last column, you need to set up parallel columns to keep the 2 or more lines of each address together in the middle column.

1 Press **Exit** (F7) and type **n** twice to clear the screen.

2 Press **Math/Columns** (Alt-F7) and select Column Define (4) to display the Column Definition menu.

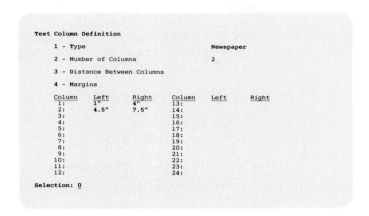

```
Text Column Definition

    1 - Type                                Newspaper

    2 - Number of Columns                   2

    3 - Distance Between Columns

    4 - Margins

    Column   Left    Right      Column   Left     Right
      1:     1"      4"           13:
      2:     4.5"    7.5"         14:
      3:                          15:
      4:                          16:
      5:                          17:
      6:                          18:
      7:                          19:
      8:                          20:
      9:                          21:
     10:                          22:
     11:                          23:
     12:                          24:

    Selection: 0
```

There are several options available for setting up columns, and you can have up to 24 columns across the page with columns of uneven widths. However, all you need to do for the phone list is simply set up 3 columns of equal width and let WordPerfect calculate the margins for you.

3 Select Type (1) and then select Parallel with Block Protect (3).

Block protection means that if a name, address, and phone number for an individual do not fit at the bottom of a page, then all three items of information are kept together (protected) by moving them to the top of the next page.

4 Select Number of Columns (2), enter **3** for the number of columns (the margins are calculated and displayed), and then press **Exit** (F7) to return to the Math/Columns menu.

5 Select Columns On/Off (3) to turn on Parallel Columns.

Typing in Parallel Columns

After returning to the document screen, you'll notice that a Col number has been added to the status line to let you know in which column you are typing text.

6 Type **Paul Magleby** for the name, and then press **Hard Page** (Ctrl-Enter) to move the cursor to the left margin of the next column.

Notice that you pressed Hard Page to move to the next column. Each column is handled by WordPerfect like a page. If you want to end one "column page" and move to the beginning of the next "column page," then Hard Page needs to be pressed.

Now that you have pressed Hard Page, the cursor is at the top of the next column, and the status line displays "Col 2" for the column number. You are ready to type the address.

7 Type the following address:

**1820 Harbor Ave.
Chicago, IL 60617**

8 Press **Hard Page** (Ctrl-Enter) after typing the Zip code, and then type **(312) 377-3980** for the phone number in the third column.

9 Press **Hard Page** (Ctrl-Enter) to return to the left margin of the first column.

The name, address, and phone number are all aligned at the left margin of each column.

△ LEFT MARGIN OF COLUMN

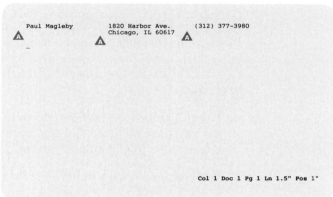

At this point, you may want to try typing more information in the columns, or simply clear the screen.

10 Press **Exit** (F7) and type **n** twice to clear the screen.

For details on Parallel Columns, turn to Columns, Text heading in the WordPerfect reference manual.

Passwords

Whenever you want to provide extra security for a file, you can add a password to the file. The file becomes locked so that the contents cannot be displayed from List Files, retrieved, or printed until the password is entered.

1 Press **Retrieve** (Shift-F10) and enter **musicbox.wkb** to retrieve the letter of introduction.

2 Press **Text In/Out** (Ctrl-F5), select Password (2), and then select Add (1).

To make sure that no one can see the password while you are typing it, the password is not shown on the screen. For this reason, WordPerfect has you enter the password twice when assigning to a document.

3 Enter **music** once, and then enter **music** again when requested by WordPerfect.

4 Press **Exit** (F7), type **y**, and then enter **musicbox.2** to save the locked letter in a new file.

5 Type **n** to clear the screen.

You can also save the locked document in the same file by simply pressing Enter to use the same filename when saving the document.

Now, let's try retrieving the locked letter file to see if WordPerfect requests a password.

6 Press **Retrieve** (Shift-F10) and enter **musicbox.2** to retrieve the locked document.

7 Enter **music** for the requested password.

Once a file is locked only a person knowing the password can retrieve, print, or look at the contents of the file. However, after the file is retrieved, it can be unlocked again by using Password.

8 Press **Text In/Out** (Ctrl-F5), select Password (2), and then select Remove (2).

9 Press **Exit** (F7) , type **y**, press **Enter**, and type **y** to replace the file.

10 Type **n** to clear the screen.

Now the letter can be retrieved and printed without the password protection.

Remember that once you assign a password to a document, the only way to find out the contents of the file is to know the password. If you forget the password, the file will be off limits to everyone (including you!).

Units of Measure

Whenever you need to use a different measurement for the document on your screen, you can use Units of Measure to change the measurements shown on the menus and the status line.

For example, if you would rather use centimeters for measuring,

1   Press **Setup** (Shift-F1) and select Units of Measure (8).

2   Select display and Entry of Numbers (1) and type **c** for centimeters.

3   Select Status Line Display (2) and type **c** for centimeters.

4   Press **Exit** (F7) to return to the document screen.

Notice that the status line is now displaying measurements in centimeters.

▲ CENTIMETERS

Doc 1 Pg 1 Ln 2.54c Pos 2.54c

One advantage of using centimeters (vs. inches) is that you do not need to convert a fraction such as "3/8" to a decimal equivalent when entering the measurement. For some applications (such as desktop publishing), WordPerfect even provides a points measurement for detailed work. Measurements provide a more accurate way of relating the formats you set with the way they affect the document on your screen.

Summary

During this lesson you were introduced to the following tasks:

- Creating a document summary.
- Defining parallel columns.
- Displaying a document summary.
- Searching for a word in a file.
- Setting the units of measure.

For a complete listing of all tasks introduced in the lessons, turn to *Feature Summary* at the end of the workbook.

Lesson 20: Merge Fundamentals

As the word suggests, merging is the process of combining at least two items to make a third. For example, an artist produces the color green by combining blue and yellow pigments. While the green contains both blue and yellow, it is an entirely different color.

In word processing, merging refers to the process of combining information from at least two sources to produce an entirely new document.

Merging with Retrieve

A simple merge can be done by using Retrieve to combine a file on disk with the document on your screen.

1 Press **Retrieve** (Shift-F10) and enter **retail.wkb** to retrieve a letter.

The letter on your screen is complete except for the inside address and salutation. Instead of typing the information, you can retrieve it from another file on disk.

2 Make sure that the cursor is at the beginning of the letter.

3 Press **Retrieve** (Shift-F10) and enter **address.wkb** to insert an address and salutation into the letter.

By using Retrieve, you have merged the document on the screen with a file on disk to create a letter to Robin.

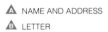
A NAME AND ADDRESS
B LETTER

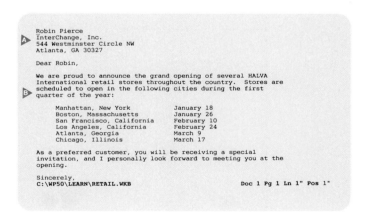

```
    Robin Pierce
    InterChange, Inc.
    544 Westminster Circle NW
    Atlanta, GA 30327

    Dear Robin,

    We are proud to announce the grand opening of several HALVA
    International retail stores throughout the country.  Stores are
    scheduled to open in the following cities during the first
    quarter of the year:

         Manhattan, New York          January 18
         Boston, Massachusetts        January 26
         San Francisco, California    February 10
         Los Angeles, California      February 24
         Atlanta, Georgia             March 9
         Chicago, Illinois            March 17

    As a preferred customer, you will be receiving a special
    invitation, and I personally look forward to meeting you at the
    opening.

    Sincerely,
    C:\WP50\LEARN\RETAIL.WKB                    Doc 1 Pg 1 Ln 1" Pos 1"
```

4 Press **Exit** (F7) and type **n** twice to clear the screen.

Primary and Secondary Files

Saving the inside address and salutation in a file and then retrieving it into a letter is one way of merging. However, if you wanted to send the same letter to several people, you would need an address file for each individual.

It would be much easier if all the names and addresses could be kept in a single file, and you could indicate the places in the letter where you want the information inserted.

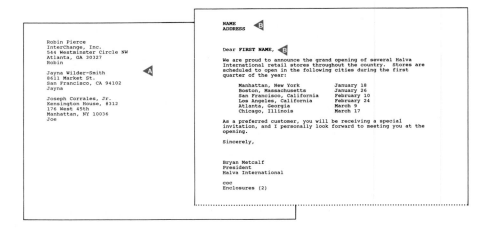

By merging the same letter with each individual in the list, a personalized letter could then be created for each person.

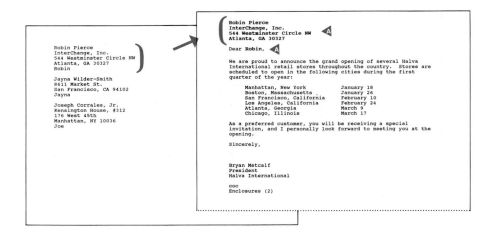

The Merge feature in WordPerfect is designed to work the same way. The letter for the merge is called the *primary file*, while the list of names and addresses is called the *secondary file*.

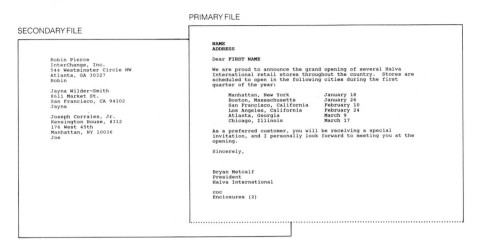

After the merging is completed, the merged document contains a letter for each individual in the secondary file. A page break between each letter makes it convenient to send the merged document to the printer and have each letter printed on a separate piece of paper.

Merging with Merge

For example,

5 Press **Merge/Sort** (Ctrl-F9) and select Merge (1).

6 Enter **stores.wkb** for the name of the primary file, and then enter **customer.wkb** for the name of the secondary file.

WordPerfect begins merging the two files, and, when the merging is completed, your cursor is at the end of all the merged letters.

7 Press **Home** twice and then **Up Arrow** (↑) to move to the beginning of the merged letters.

▲ FIRST MERGED LETTER

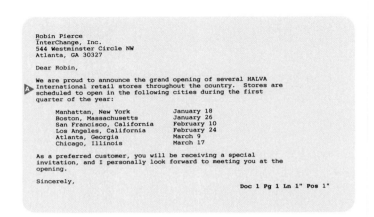

```
Robin Pierce
InterChange, Inc.
544 Westminster Circle NW
Atlanta, GA 30327

Dear Robin,

     We are proud to announce the grand opening of several HALVA
▲ International retail stores throughout the country.  Stores are
     scheduled to open in the following cities during the first
     quarter of the year:

         Manhattan, New York        January 18
         Boston, Massachusetts      January 26
         San Francisco, California  February 10
         Los Angeles, California    February 24
         Atlanta, Georgia           March 9
         Chicago, Illinois          March 17

As a preferred customer, you will be receiving a special
invitation, and I personally look forward to meeting you at the
opening.

Sincerely,

                                    Doc 1 Pg 1 Ln 1" Pos 1"
```

There should be several letters (one for each customer) in the merged document.

8 Press **Page Down** (PgDn) to scroll through the letters created during the merge.

9 Press **Exit** (F7) and type **n** twice to clear the screen.

Merge Codes

Indicating which information you want from the secondary file (the list), and where you want it placed in the primary file (the letter) is done by using special merge codes.

10 Press **Retrieve** (Shift-F10) and enter **customer.wkb** to retrieve the list of names and addresses.

Notice that two different merge codes are used in the secondary file.

```
     Robin Pierce^R  ◄A
     InterChange, Inc.
     544 Westminster Circle NW
     Atlanta, GA 30327^R
     Robin^R
     (404) 359-2828^R
   B►E
     ================================================================
     Jayna Wilder-Smith^R
     8611 Market St.
     San Francisco, CA 94102^R
     Jayna^R
     (415) 987-4598^R
     ^E
     ================================================================
     Anna Lee Pierce^R
     P.O. Box 1392
     Central Park Station
     Buffalo, NY 14215^R
     Anna^R
     (716) 453-5678^R
     ^E
     ================================================================
     Joseph Corrales, Jr.^R
     C:\WP50\LEARN\CUSTOMER.WKB              Doc 1 Pg 1 Ln 1" Pos 1"
```

The group of information about each customer is called a *record*. As you can see, each record ends with a ^E merge code and is separated from the other records with a Hard Page break. As already noted, WordPerfect creates a new letter for each record in the secondary file.

Each record is divided into smaller units of information called *fields*. As you can see, each field ends with a ^R merge code, and is separated from the other fields by a Hard Return.

For Merge to work properly, each record should have the same number of fields with the information arranged in the same order.

```
   A► Robin Pierce^R
      InterChange, Inc.
   B► 544 Westminster Circle NW
      Atlanta, GA 30327^R
   C► Robin^R
      (404) 359-2828^R  ◄D
      ^E
      ================================================================
      Jayna Wilder-Smith^R
      8611 Market St.
      San Francisco, CA 94102^R
      Jayna^R
      (415) 987-4598^R
      ^E
      ================================================================
      Anna Lee Pierce^R
      P.O. Box 1392
      Central Park Station
      Buffalo, NY 14215^R
      Anna^R
      (716) 453-5678^R
      ^E
      ================================================================
      Joseph Corrales, Jr.^R
      C:\WP50\LEARN\CUSTOMER.WKB              Doc 1 Pg 1 Ln 1" Pos 1"
```

Records and fields let you organize the information in the list, but how do you indicate where and what information to include in the letter from the secondary file?

11 Press **Switch** (Shift-F3) to display the second document screen.

12 Press **Retrieve** (Shift-F10) and enter **stores.wkb** to retrieve the primary file.

Opening a Window

Let's compare the primary file with the secondary file by using Window to split the screen.

13 Press **Screen** (Ctrl-F3), select Window (1), and then enter **12** to split the screen evenly between the two windows.

The secondary file in the document 1 screen is displayed in the top half, while the primary file in the document 2 screen is displayed in the bottom half.

▲ PRIMARY FILE
Ⓑ SECONDARY FILE

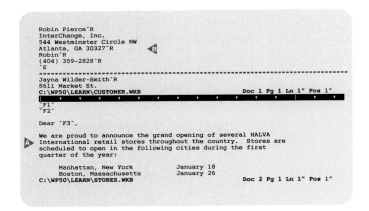

```
Robin Pierce^R
InterChange, Inc.
544 Westminster Circle NW
Atlanta, GA 30327^R                    ◄Ⓑ
Robin^R
(404) 359-2828^R
^E
-----------------------------------------------------------------
Jayna Wilder-Smith^R
8611 Market St.
C:\WP50\LEARN\CUSTOMER.WKB                    Doc 1 Pg 1 Ln 1" Pos 1"
[    ▼    ▼    ▼    ▼    ▼    ▼    ▼    ▼    ▼    ▼    )    ▼    ▼
^F1^
^F2^

Dear ^F3^,

      We are proud to announce the grand opening of several HALVA
 ▲   International retail stores throughout the country.  Stores are
      scheduled to open in the following cities during the first
      quarter of the year:

          Manhattan, New York        January 18
          Boston, Massachusetts      January 26
C:\WP50\LEARN\STORES.WKB                    Doc 2 Pg 1 Ln 1" Pos 1"
```

Both windows are independent of each other and can be used for editing as you normally would by pressing Switch to move back and forth between the document screens.

Fields and Records

Notice that wherever information is needed from the secondary file, a ^F merge code is placed in the primary file.

 ^F MERGE CODES

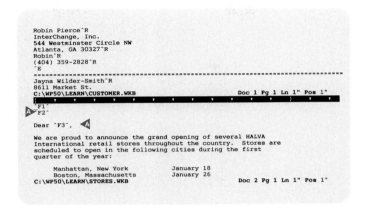

```
Robin Pierce^R
InterChange, Inc.
544 Westminster Circle NW
Atlanta, GA 30327^R
Robin^R
(404) 359-2828^R
^E
----------------------------------------------------------------
Jayna Wilder-Smith^R
8611 Market St.
C:\WP50\LEARN\CUSTOMER.WKB                    Doc 1 Pg 1 Ln 1" Pos 1"
[    ▼    ▼    ▼    ▼    ▼    ▼    ▼    ▼    ▼    ▼    ▼    }    ▼    ▼
 ^F1^
 ^F2^

Dear ^F3^,

We are proud to announce the grand opening of several HALVA
International retail stores throughout the country.  Stores are
scheduled to open in the following cities during the first
quarter of the year:

        Manhattan, New York          January 18
        Boston, Massachusetts        January 26
C:\WP50\LEARN\STORES.WKB                       Doc 2 Pg 1 Ln 1" Pos 1"
```

The ^F merge codes all include a number that indicates the field which should be inserted into the letter. The position of the ^F indicates the place where the information should be inserted into the letter.

For example, the ^F1^ code tells WordPerfect to insert the first field at the beginning of the letter.

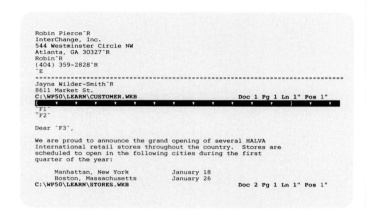

The first field in each record contains the full name of the customer. During the merge, the customer's full name is inserted at the position of the ^F1^.

The ^F2^ in the letter inserts the information from the second field of the record (the address), while the ^F3^ inserts the information from the third field (the first name).

Because the word "Dear" is used in every letter, you do not need to include it as part of the information in the third field. Only the information that changes from letter to letter (name, address, etc.) should be included in the secondary file.

The fourth field contains the customer's phone number, but a ^F4^ is not placed in the primary file because the phone number does not need to be inserted into the letter. However, the phone number may be important to include in other documents that you create with Merge.

For an example of using a phone number in a primary file, turn to the Lists lesson in **Merging Documents.**

Dividing the secondary file into records and fields is a common way of organizing information for many software programs. You may want to think of each record as an address card in a desktop card file.

The information to be filled in (name, address, phone number, etc.) is always in the same place on each card, even though the information may be longer or shorter. Even if there is no information for an item (e.g, a phone number), a place is still kept open for the information to be filled in later.

What is true for address cards is also true for the secondary file. The name, address, and first name are always in the same place in the record. And while some addresses are longer than others, there is always a field for an address, even if the field is empty.

14 Press **Switch** (Shift-F3) to place the cursor in the document 1 editing screen (top half).

15 Press **Page Down** (PgDn) until you reach the record for Ted Mortinthal.

Updating a Field

Notice that Ted Mortinthal's address is missing. However, a ^R holds the field open until an address can be entered.

16 Place the cursor at the beginning of the empty address field (to the left of the ^R).

17 Type the following address:

    1380 Georgia Ave.
    Silver Spring, MD 20910

The record for Ted Mortinthal should now include his address as well as his full name, first name, and phone number.

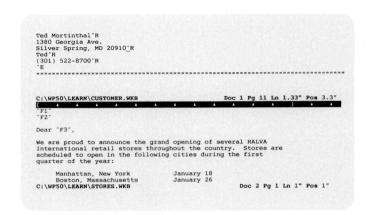

You can place as many lines of information as you want in a field. However, the last line should always end with a ^R.

18 Press **Exit** (F7), type **y**, and enter **customer** to save the list in a new file.

19 Type **n** to clear the document 1 screen.

Because the two windows are completely independent of each other, the messages for the document 1 editing screen are displayed at the bottom of the top window, instead of at the bottom of the screen.

20 Press **Switch** (Shift-F3) to place the cursor in the bottom window.

21 Press **Exit** (F7), and then type **n** twice to clear the document 2 screen.

Closing a Window
When you want to close the window, use Window on the Screen menu again.

22 Press **Switch** (Shift-F3) to place the cursor in the document 1 screen.

23 Press **Screen** (Ctrl-F3), select Window (1), and then enter **0** for the number of lines.

WordPerfect closes the bottom window (document 2) and returns the document 1 screen to its normal size.

Reviewing the Fundamentals

Let's review the basic concepts of merging documents in WordPerfect.

Ⓐ END OF FIELD
Ⓑ END OF RECORD
Ⓒ INSERT FIELDS

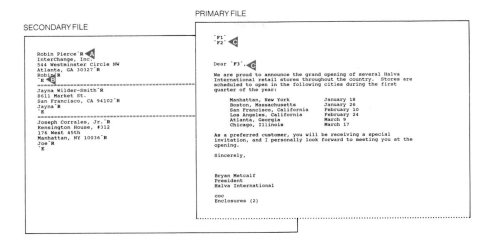

The idea of merging can be as simple as retrieving one document into another with Retrieve. However, most merging in WordPerfect is done by using a primary file (such as a letter) and a secondary file (such as an address list) with Merge.

The secondary file contains a record of information by ^E codes for each individual. The record is divided into fields by ^R codes so that parts of the information can be inserted at various locations in the primary file. The inserting is done by using ^F codes to indicate which fields you want from the record.

It is important to make sure that each record contains the same number of fields with the same type of information in each field. If not, you may get a name where you need an address, or a phone number where you need a name.

Summary

During this lesson, you were introduced to the following tasks:

- Merging a primary and secondary file.
- Opening (and closing) a window.

For a complete listing of all tasks introduced in the lessons, turn to *Feature Summary* at the end of the workbook.

Lesson 21: Business Letters

Now that you have been introduced to the idea of merging in WordPerfect, let's merge the store announcement letter with the customer list you edited in Lesson 20.

1 Press **Merge/Sort** (Ctrl-F9) and select Merge (1).

2 Enter **stores.wkb** for the name of the primary file, and then enter **customer** for the name of the secondary file.

As soon as you enter the name of the secondary file, the merge begins, and a "* Merging *" message appears at the bottom of the screen. The length of time it takes WordPerfect to perform the merge depends on the number of ^F codes in the primary file, the size of the primary file, and the number of records in the secondary file.

Computers process information at different rates of speed. The faster the processing chip you have in your computer, the faster the merging is in WordPerfect.

Moving to the Top of a Page

Because there are only eleven records in the customer list, the merge should go quickly. When merging is completed, the last letter in the merged document should be on your screen.

▲ LAST LETTER

```
International retail stores throughout the country.  Stores are
scheduled to open in the following cities during the first
quarter of the year:

     Manhattan, New York          January 18
     Boston, Massachusetts        January 26
     San Francisco, California    February 10
     Los Angeles, California      February 24
     Atlanta, Georgia             March 9
 A   Chicago, Illinois            March 17

As a preferred customer, you will be receiving a special
invitation, and I personally look forward to meeting you at the
opening.

Sincerely,


Bryan Metcalf
President
HALVA International_

                                        Doc 1 Pg 11 Ln 5.66" Pos 2.9"
```

3 Press **Go To** (Ctrl-Home) and then **Up Arrow** (↑) to scroll to the top of the last letter.

The address you typed in the customer list (Lesson 20) is included in the heading of the letter.

Once the merging is completed, the letters are ready to send to the printer. However, most people never save the merged letters because they can always be created again by simply merging the primary and secondary files.

4 Press **Exit** (F7), and then type **n** twice to clear the screen without saving the letters.

Adding a Record

As the number of HALVA International customers increases, a new record for each customer is added to the secondary file.

5 Press **Retrieve** (Shift-F10) and enter **customer** to retrieve the secondary file.

6 Press **Home** twice and then **Down Arrow** (↓) to move the cursor to the end of the list to add a new customer.

The first field contains the full name of the customer. The ^R merge code is used to end the field and can by inserted by using Merge R.

7 Type **Samantha Dance** and then press **Merge R** (F9) to create the first field.

Notice that a ^R merge code *and* a Hard Return are inserted for you when you press Merge R.

8 Type the following address and press **Merge R** (F9) to end the field:

1487 Lockwood Dr.
New Bedford, MS 02743

9 Type **Samantha** and press **Merge R** (F9) to end the field.

10 Type **(617) 687-5321** and press **Merge R** (F9) to end the field.

Now that the record information has been typed, you are ready to insert a ^E to end the record.

11 Press **Merge Codes** (Shift-F9) and then type **e** to select ^E.

Notice that a ^E *and* a page break are inserted for you when you use Merge Codes to end a record.

The record you have created for Samantha Dance should look exactly like the one on the screen below.

```
=======================================================================
Scott L. Ziegler^R
Merchants Exchange
450 S. Flower St.
Los Angeles, CA 90014^R
Scott^R
(213) 937-3370^R
^E
=======================================================================
Ted Mortinthal^R
1380 Georgia Ave.
Silver Spring, MD 20910^R
Ted^R
(301) 522-8700^R
^E
=======================================================================
Samantha Dance^R
1487 Lockwood Dr.
New Bedford, MS 02743^R
Samantha^R
(617) 687-5321^R
^E
=======================================================================
C:\WP50\LEARN\CUSTOMER                          Doc 1 Pg 13 Ln 1" Pos 1"
```

Remember that a ^R merge code is not needed at the end of each line, only at the end of a field. For example, a ^R should appear after the ZIP code in Samantha's record, but *not after* the street address. If you have placed ^R after the street address, simply erase it by using Backspace or Delete.

Inserting Merge Codes

When you pressed Merge Codes, you probably noticed an entire line of different merge codes. Each code begins with a caret (^) and includes a letter of the alphabet. However, you cannot create a merge code by simply *typing* the caret and then an uppercase letter.

For example, try deleting the ^E at the end of Samantha's record.

12 Place the cursor to the right of the ^E and press **Backspace** to erase the merge code.

You only needed to press Backspace *once* to erase both the caret and the E. Now, try creating a ^E using Shift.

13 Hold down **Shift**, type ^ at the top of your keyboard, type **e**, and then release **Shift**.

Now, try erasing the ^E you have just created with Shift.

14 Press **Backspace** until the ^E is erased.

You needed to press Backspace *twice* to erase the ^E. The ^E merge code (as with all merge codes) is a special character that is inserted by using Merge Codes. However, you can also insert a merge code by using Control.

15 Hold down **Control** (Ctrl) and type **e** to insert the ^E merge code at the end of the record.

The merge codes are often referred to as control characters because they can be inserted using Control. However, the advantage to using Merge R and Merge Codes for creating a secondary file is that they also insert the Hard Return and Hard Page break for you.

Merge codes can also be distinguished from other characters in the Reveal Codes screen because they are bolded like all other WordPerfect codes, and the Reveal Codes cursor highlights both the caret and the letter when the cursor is on the merge code.

Merging the Letters

With the new record added, you can save the edited list and start another merge.

16 Press **Exit** (F7), type **y**, press **Enter**, and then type **y** again to replace the original customer list with the edited list on the screen.

17 Type **n** to clear the screen for the merge.

18 Press **Merge/Sort** (Ctrl-F9) and select Merge (1).

19 Enter **stores.wkb** for the name of the primary file, and then enter **customer** for the name of the secondary file.

When the merge finishes, you should have a new letter for Samantha added to the end of all the merged letters.

20 Press **Go To** (Ctrl-Home) and then **Up Arrow** (↑) to move to top of the letter to Samantha.

A LETTER TO SAMANTHA DANCE

```
HALVA International
========================================================================
Samantha Dance
1487 Lockwood Dr.
New Bedford, MS 02743

Dear Samantha,

We are proud to announce the grand opening of several HALVA
International retail stores throughout the country.  Stores are
scheduled to open in the following cities during the first
quarter of the year:

     Manhattan, New York         January 18
     Boston, Massachusetts       January 26
     San Francisco, California   February 10
     Los Angeles, California     February 24
     Atlanta, Georgia            March 9
     Chicago, Illinois           March 17

As a preferred customer, you will be receiving a special
invitation, and I personally look forward to meeting you at the
opening.

                            Doc 1 Pg 12 Ln 1" Pos 1"
```

Adding a Field to the Primary File

Now that the secondary file has been edited, let's try editing the primary file to add a more personal tone to the letter.

21 Press **Exit** (F7) and type **n** twice to clear the screen.

22 Press **Retrieve** (Shift-F10) and enter **stores.wkb** to retrieve the primary file.

23 Move the cursor to the last paragraph, and place the cursor on the "y" of the word "you" after the phrase "As a preferred customer,. . .".

The customer's first name can be inserted at this point in the letter by using the ^F merge code.

24 Press **Merge Codes** (Shift-F9), type **f** to select ^F, and then enter **3** to insert field three (the first name) into the letter during a merge.

25 Type a comma, press the **Space Bar**, and then press **Down Arrow** (↓).

Your primary file should now look like the one illustrated below.

▲ NEW ^F3^ MERGE CODE

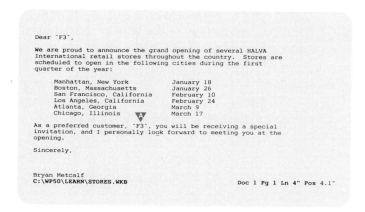

```
Dear ^F3^,

We are proud to announce the grand opening of several HALVA
International retail stores throughout the country.  Stores are
scheduled to open in the following cities during the first
quarter of the year:

     Manhattan, New York          January 18
     Boston, Massachusetts        January 26
     San Francisco, California    February 10
     Los Angeles, California      February 24
     Atlanta, Georgia             March 9
     Chicago, Illinois     ▼      March 17

As a preferred customer, ^F3^, you will be receiving a special
invitation, and I personally look forward to meeting you at the
opening.

Sincerely,


Bryan Metcalf
C:\WP50\LEARN\STORES.WKB                Doc 1 Pg 1 Ln 4" Pos 4.1"
```

The ^F is a very flexible merge code, and can be used to insert the same field as many times and wherever you want in a primary file.

Adding a Date to the Primary File

Before saving the edited primary file and starting the final merge of the lesson, let's insert one more merge code into the letter.

26 Press **Home** twice and then **Up Arrow** (↑) to move the cursor to the beginning of the letter.

27 Press **Merge Codes** (Shift-F9), and then type **d** to insert a ^D merge code.

28 Press **Enter** four times to add extra spacing.

The ^D merge code performs the same task as WordPerfect's Date Text feature. Whenever you merge the primary file, WordPerfect automatically inserts the current date at the position of the ^D.

29 Press **Exit** (F7), type **y** to save the edited letter, and then enter **stores** to create a new primary file.

30 Type **n** to clear the screen and stay in WordPerfect.

Merging the Letters

With the ^D added to the primary file, you are ready to begin the last merge of the lesson.

31 Press **Merge/Sort** (Ctrl-F9) and select Merge (1).

32 Enter **stores** for the primary file, and then enter **customer** for the secondary file.

After the merge is completed, check for the current date at the beginning of each letter and the first name in the last paragraph of each letter.

A FIRST NAME
B CURRENT DATE

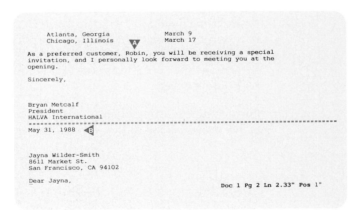

```
     Atlanta, Georgia          March 9
     Chicago, Illinois    ▼A   March 17
As a preferred customer, Robin, you will be receiving a special
invitation, and I personally look forward to meeting you at the
opening.

Sincerely,


Bryan Metcalf
President
HALVA International
=================================================================
May 31, 1988   ◄B


Jayna Wilder-Smith
8611 Market St.
San Francisco, CA 94102

Dear Jayna,                      Doc 1 Pg 2 Ln 2.33" Pos 1"
```

By using the ^D and another ^F3^, you saved the time of typing the current date, and the letter is more personal.

Printing the Letters

The letters are ready to send to the printer. However, because the primary file was created using the Standard Printer selection, the merged letters are also assigned to the Standard Printer.

33 Press **Print** (Shift-F7), and type **s** to display the list of printers.

34 Highlight the name of your printer, and then press **Enter** to select the printer.

Notice that the Print menu also includes an option for printing a page from the document.

35 Select Page (2) to print the letter on which the cursor is positioned.

36 Press **Exit** (F7) and type **n** twice to clear the screen and stay in WordPerfect.

When merging hundreds (or thousands) of documents, many companies choose to have each letter automatically sent to the printer *as soon as it is merged*. For details on merging to the printer, turn to the Merging to the Printer heading in the Special Techniques lesson at the end of *Merging Documents*.

Summary

During this lesson, you were introduced to the following tasks:

- Adding a record to a secondary file (^R and ^E).
- Inserting a field in a primary file (^F).
- Inserting merge codes into a document.
- Inserting the current date into a primary file (^D).
- Moving the cursor to the top or bottom of a page.
- Printing a page.

For a complete listing of all tasks introduced in the lessons, turn to *Feature Summary* at the end of the workbook.

Lesson 22: Envelopes and Labels

Once the letters are merged and printed (Lesson 21), envelopes need to be addressed for mailing. By using Merge with WordPerfect's formatting features, you can automate the process of printing addresses directly on envelopes or labels.

Setting the Envelope Size

If you want an address printed directly on an envelope, WordPerfect needs to know the size of the envelope and the place to print the address.

The size of the envelope can be indicated by using the Paper Size and Type option on the Page Format menu.

1   Press **Format** (Shift-F8), select Page (2), and then select Paper Size/Type (8).

A list of standard paper sizes is displayed on your screen.

```
Format: Paper Size
     1 - Standard              (8.5" x 11")
     2 - Standard Landscape    (11" x 8.5")
     3 - Legal                 (8.5" x 14")
     4 - Legal Landscape       (14" x 8.5")
     5 - Envelope              (9.5" x 4")
     6 - Half Sheet            (5.5" x 8.5")
     7 - US Government         (8" x 11")
     8 - A4                    (210mm x 297mm)
     9 - A4 Landscape          (297mm x 210mm)
     0 - Other

Selection: 1
```

Because most business correspondence is sent in a 9.5" x 4" envelope, an option is already set for that size. If your envelope is a different size, all you need to do is select Other and enter the correct width and height.

2   Select Envelope (5) to set the size for a standard business correspondence envelope.

A list of paper types appears, letting you indicate the type of paper on which you will be printing.

```
Format: Paper Type
        1 - Standard
        2 - Bond
        3 - Letterhead
        4 - Labels
        5 - Envelope
        6 - Transparency
        7 - Cardstock
        8 - Other




Selection: 1
```

Selecting a paper type makes sure that any special instructions for printing the form (e.g., bin number, landscape font) are sent to the printer.

3 Select Envelope (5) for the paper type.

When you return to the Page Format menu, a message similar to the following may indicate that the envelope form is not available.

⚠ NOT AVAILABLE MESSAGE

```
Format: Page
        1 - Center Page (top to bottom)    No
        2 - Force Odd/Even Page
        3 - Headers
        4 - Footers
        5 - Margins - Top                  1"
                      Bottom               1"
        6 - New Page Number                1
              (example: 3 or iii)
        7 - Page Numbering                 No page numbering
        8 - Paper Size                     *8.5" x 4"
              Type                         Envelope
                                          ⚠(*requested form is unavailable)
        9 - Suppress (this page only)

Selection: 0
```

WordPerfect will still print the address on the envelope, but there are no special instructions for printing an envelope.

For details on setting up an envelope type, turn to Form Types in the Special Techniques section of Merging Documents.

4 Press **Exit** (F7) to return to the document screen.

5 Press **Enter** until a page break appears on your screen.

Notice that only a few lines can be placed on a page before WordPerfect inserts a page break.

 PAGE BREAK

Doc 1 Pg 2 Ln 1" Pos 1"

After selecting the new paper size, WordPerfect subtracts the top and bottom margins (one inch per margin), and only allows you two inches of space for typing text.

6 Press **Home** twice and then **Up Arrow** (↑) to move the cursor to the beginning of the empty lines.

7 Press **Block** (Alt-F4), press **Page Down** (PgDn) twice to move to the end of the empty lines, and then press **Backspace** and type **y** to erase the lines.

Positioning the Address

A standard position for typing the address block on a 9.5" x 4" envelope is 4.5" in from the left edge of the envelope, and 2.5" down from the top edge of the envelope.

Advance could be used to print the address 4.5" in from the left margin, but an Advance code would need to be placed at the beginning of each address line. A simpler way is to set a new left margin.

8 Press **Format** (Shift-F8), select Line (1), and then select Margins (7).

9 Enter **4.5** for the left margin.

It would also be a good idea to set the right margin to "0" so that there will be plenty of room for the address lines.

10 Enter **0** for the right margin, and then press **Enter** to return to the main Format menu.

Besides setting the left and right margins, the top and bottom margins should be set to "0" to avoid any problems with advancing the envelope in some printers (top margin), and to make sure there are enough lines available for longer addresses (bottom margin).

11 Select Page (2) and then select Margins Top/Bottom (5).

12 Enter **0** for the top margin, and then enter **0** for the bottom margin.

13 Press **Enter** to return to the main Format menu.

With the margins set, you can use Advance to place the address down the page at exactly 2.5" from the top of the envelope.

14 Select Other (4), and then select Advance (1).

15 Select Down (2) and enter **2.5** to have WordPerfect advance 2.5" down the envelope.

16 Press **Exit** (F7) to return to the document screen.

17 Press **Reveal Codes** (Alt-F3) to see the formats you have set for the envelope.

Checking the Formats

Your screen should display the same codes as those illustrated below.

▲ ENVELOPE FORMATS

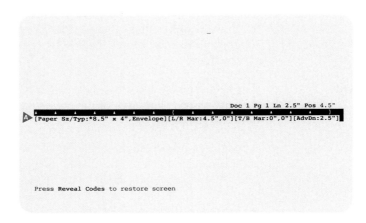

18 Press **Reveal Codes** (Alt-F3) to display the full document screen.

19 Press **Exit** (F7), type **y**, and enter **envelope** to save the settings in a file.

20 Type **n** to clear the screen.

Printing the Address

The envelope file can now be retrieved, filled in, and printed any time you want to print the forwarding address on an envelope.

21 Press **Retrieve** (Shift-F10) and enter **envelope** to retrieve the envelope formats.

22 Type the following address:

Robin Pierce
InterChange, Inc.
544 Westminster Circle NW
Atlanta, GA 30327

23 Press **Print** (Shift-F7) and select Full Document (1) to send the address to the printer.

WordPerfect may "beep" or the printer may display a message, waiting for you to insert an envelope into the printer. If you want to actually print on an envelope, insert it in the printer the same way you would normally insert a sheet of paper.

24 If WordPerfect "beeps," press **Print** (Shift-F7), select Control Printer (4), and then select Go (4) to start printing.

25 Press **Exit** (F7) to return to the document screen.

After the address is printed, you may want to measure the position of the address to see if it printed in the correct place.

Creating a Primary File

Once the formats for the envelope file are set, you can create a primary file for merging and printing several envelopes at the same time.

26 Press **Home** twice and then **Up Arrow** (↑) to place the cursor at the beginning of the address.

27 Press **Delete to End of Page** (Ctrl-PgDn), and then type **y** to erase the address and leave the formatting codes.

The full name and address of each customer in the "Customer.wkb" secondary file (Lesson 21) are in the first and second fields of each record.

28 Press **Merge Codes** (Shift-F9), type **f**, and then enter **1** to insert a ^F1^ for the first field.

29 Press **Enter** to start a new line.

30 Press **Merge Codes** (Shift-F9), type **f**, and then enter **2** to insert a ^F2^ for the second field.

31 Press **Exit** (F7), type **y**, press **Enter** to use the "Envelope" filename, and then type **y** to replace the file.

32 Type **n** to clear the screen.

Merging the Addresses

With "Envelope" saved as a primary file, you can merge with a secondary file to create addresses for printing on envelopes.

33 Press **Merge/Sort** (Ctrl-F9) and select Merge (1).

34 Enter **envelope** for the primary file, and then enter **customer.wkb** for the secondary file.

35 When the merging is completed, press **Home** twice and then press **Up Arrow** (↑) to move to the first address.

An address for each envelope is ready to be sent to the printer.

 ENVELOPE ADDRESS

```
         Robin Pierce
         InterChange, Inc.
         544 Westminster Circle NW
         Atlanta, GA 30327
-------------------------------------------------------
         Jayna Wilder-Smith
         8611 Market St.
         San Francisco, CA 94102
-------------------------------------------------------
         Anna Lee Pierce
         P.O. Box 1392
         Central Park Station
         Buffalo, NY 14215
-------------------------------------------------------
         Joseph Corrales, Jr.
         Kensington House, #312
         176 West 45th
         Manhattan, NY 10036
-------------------------------------------------------
         Kathleen O'Hara
         678 Forestvale Road
         Boston, MA 02136
-------------------------------------------------------
         Mary Anna Pickford
                      Doc 1 Pg 1 Ln 2.75" Pos 4.5"
```

If you want to try printing an envelope, use Page on the Print menu to print the first address. Otherwise,

36 Press **Exit** (F7) and type **n** twice to clear the screen.

Formatting for Continuous Forms Labels

Now that you have set up a file that merges addresses for printing on envelopes, the same basic steps can be followed for setting up a primary file that merges addresses for printing on labels.

For example, labels are available with holes (perforations) on both sides for feeding continuously through many printers. One of the standard sizes for these labels is 4" x 1 7/16".

Let's set formatting codes for margins and advance, and then set the paper size and type.

37 Press **Format** (Shift-F8), and then enter the following format settings for the labels:

0" (top and bottom margins)
.5" (left margin)
0" (right margin)
.25" (advance down)

Because the height of the label (1 7/16") is less than the total of the preset top and bottom margins (2"), the top and bottom margins should be reset before setting the form size.

Now that the margins and advance code have been set, you are ready to select the paper size and type.

38 Press **Format** (Shift-F8), select Page (2), and then select Paper Size/Type (8).

39 Select Other (O) from the Page Size menu (there is no preset label size), enter **4** for the width, and then enter **1.44** for the height.

40 Select Labels (4) for the page.

41 Press **Exit** (F7) to return to the document screen.

If a label type is not available, then an asterisk in the Page Format menu indicates that there are no special instructions to send to the printer for printing labels.

42 Press **Reveal Codes** (Alt-F3) to display all the formatting codes for the label.

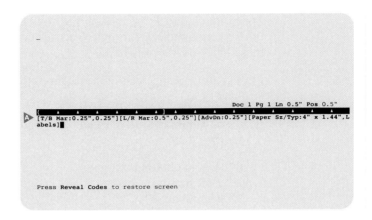

Doc 1 Pg 1 Ln 0.5" Pos 0.5"

[T/B Mar:0.25",0.25"][L/R Mar:0.5",0.25"][AdvDn:0.25"][Paper Sz/Typ:4" x 1.44",Labels]█

Press **Reveal Codes** to restore screen

Creating a Primary File

You are now ready to insert the ^F codes for creating a primary file.

43 Press **Page Down** (PgDn) to place the cursor at the end of the format codes.

44 Press **Merge Codes** (Shift-F9), type **f**, and enter **1** to insert a ^F1^ merge code.

45 Press **Enter** to insert a new line.

46 Press **Merge Codes** (Shift-F9), type **f**, and enter **2** to insert a ^F2^ merge code.

Your primary file should look like the one illustrated below.

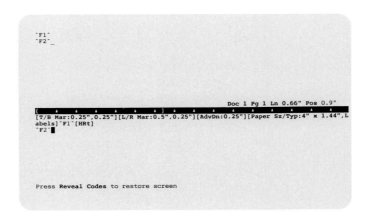

47 Press **Exit** (F7), type **y**, and enter **labels** for the name of the primary file.

48 Type **n** to clear the screen, and then press **Reveal Codes** (Alt-F3) to display the full document screen.

Merging the Labels

You can now merge the "Labels" primary file with a secondary file to create the labels you need for addressing envelopes, packages, etc.

49 Press **Merge/Sort** (Ctrl-F9) and select Merge (1).

50 Enter **labels** for the primary file, and then enter **customer.wkb** for the secondary file.

51 When merging is finished, press **Home** twice and then **Up Arrow** (↑) to move to the beginning of the addresses.

Printing the Labels

Before sending all the merged addresses to the printer, you may want to send only a few to experiment with positioning the first label in the rollers. Normally, the top edge of the first label should be aligned with the horizontal marks on the guide. However, the alignment will vary from printer to printer.

For details on setting up a file to print addresses on multiple-column labels (individual sheets or continuous forms), turn to the Multiple-Column Labels heading in the Special Techniques lesson at the end of Merging Documents.

Once you print the labels,

52 Press **Exit** (F7) and type **n** twice to clear the screen.

Summary

During this lesson, you were introduced to the following tasks:

- Advancing text down the page.
- Erasing a block of text.
- Selecting a paper size and type.
- Sending a "Go" to the printer.
- Setting left and right margins.
- Setting top and bottom margins.

For a complete listing of all tasks introduced in the lessons, turn to *Feature Summary* at the end of the workbook.

Lesson 23: Memorandums

The memorandum is a standard way of communicating important news, reminders, and other brief information to all or part of the people in a company or organization.

For an example of designing letter and memo headings with WordPerfect, turn to Document Headings in the Special Techniques lesson at the end of Formatting Documents.

In *Fundamentals* you were introduced to the idea of creating a memo form you could retrieve and fill in whenever you needed to create a memo. In this lesson, you'll learn how to automate the process of filling in the memo and sending it to the printer.

Retrieving the Memo Form

Let's retrieve a memo form like the one you created in *Fundamentals*.

1 Press **Retrieve** (Shift-F10) and enter **memo.wkb** to retrieve the memo form to your screen.

Inserting a Pause

At this point, you could begin filling in the memo by moving the cursor to the "To:" title and then typing. However, you can automate the memo form to have WordPerfect move the cursor from place to place as you fill in the memo.

2 Place the cursor at the beginning of the "To:" line, and then press **End** to move the cursor to the end of the line.

Because a tab is already in the memo, your cursor should be a few spaces to the right of the title.

3 Press **Merge Codes** (Shift-F9) and type **c** to insert a ^C at the cursor.

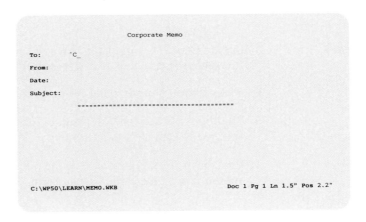

```
                          Corporate Memo

         To:        ^C_
         From:
         Date:
         Subject:
                    ==========================================



         C:\WP50\LEARN\MEMO.WKB          Doc 1 Pg 1 Ln 1.5" Pos 2.2"
```

The ^C merge code pauses WordPerfect during a merge to let you enter information from the keyboard.

4 Move the cursor to the end of the "From:" line, press **Merge Codes** (Shift-F9) and type **c** to insert a ^C.

Inserting the Date

Besides using the ^C to have WordPerfect stop in a merge, you can also use the ^D code to have WordPerfect automatically insert the current date during a merge.

5 Move the cursor to the end of the "Date:" line, press **Merge Codes** (Shift-F9) and type **d** to insert a ^D for the current date.

6 Move the cursor to the end of the "Subject:" line, press **Merge Codes** (Shift-F9) and type **c** to insert a ^C.

7 Press **Home** and then **Down Arrow** (↓) to move to the end of the memo, press **Merge Codes** (Shift-F9) and type **c** to insert a ^C.

Your memo form should now look similar to the one illustrated below.

Saving the Memo Form

With the ^D and ^C's in place, you can save the memo form (with your printer selected), and then use Merge to fill in the form.

8 Press **Print** (Shift-F7) and type **s** to display the list of printers.

9 Highlight the name of your printer, press **Enter** to select the printer, and then press **Exit** (F7) to return to the document screen.

10 Press **Exit** (F7), type **y** to save the memo form, and then enter **memo.2** to create a file for the form.

11 Type **n** to clear the screen.

Starting the Merge

Until now, you have been using a primary and secondary file to merge documents. The primary file contains the merge codes that control the merge, while the secondary file is a list of records from which you can retrieve information into the primary file.

You always need a primary file to start a merge. However, the secondary file is optional. In this case, the memo form contains ^C codes that control the merge. A secondary file is not needed because the information will all be typed from the keyboard.

12 Press **Merge/Sort** (Ctrl-F9) and select Merge (1).

13 Enter **memo.2** for the name of the primary file, and then press **Enter** for the name of the secondary file to start the merge.

Typing Text from the Keyboard

WordPerfect immediately stops the cursor at the position of the first ^C.

 MERGE PAUSE

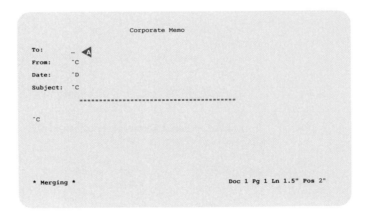

```
                           Corporate Memo


        To:          _  ◄
        From:       ^C
        Date:       ^D
        Subject:    ^C

                    ========================================


        ^C





        * Merging *                              Doc 1 Pg 1 Ln 1.5" Pos 2"
```

14 Type **All Marketing Managers** and press **Merge R** (F9) to continue on to the next ^C.

When you press Merge R during the memo merge, the cursor jumps to the next ^C. If you forget and move the cursor yourself, then press **Up Arrow** (↑) until the cursor is above the ^C and press Merge R again.

If you press Enter by mistake (instead of Merge R), press Backspace to delete the extra line and press Merge R to continue the merge.

15 Type **Megan Sills** and press **Merge R** (F9) to continue.

As the cursor passes the ^D, the current date is automatically inserted.

16 Type **Corporate Marketing Conference** and press **Merge R** to fill in the message.

17 Type the following message:

The reservations for the December marketing conference have now been confirmed. See you there!

Inserting a Center Code

Often the author's initials are used to close the memo, and are placed to the right of "dead center." You can position text to the right of center by using Center.

18 Press **Reveal Codes** (Alt-F3) to see what happens with the Center codes.

19 Press **Enter** twice to add extra spacing.

20 Press **Center** (Shift-F6), and then press **Enter** to end centering.

Notice that a pair of empty Center codes are inserted in the line.

▲ EMPTY CENTER CODES

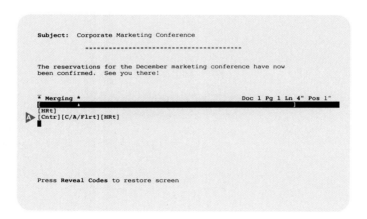

21 Press **Left Arrow** (←) to return to the line with the Center code, and then type **M. S.** for the author's initials.

When you press Left Arrow (←), the cursor moves back to the right of the empty Center codes. Any text typed after the codes is forced to the right of the center position.

22 Press **Reveal Codes** (Alt-F3) to return to the full document screen.

23 Press **Merge R** (F9) to end the merge.

Printing the Memo

Your filled-in memo should look like the one illustrated below.

As you discovered while filling in the memo, both text *and* WordPerfect codes can be typed when you are stopped at a ^C during a merge. You can even use the Reveal Codes screen for editing. And when you finish typing the message, simply press Merge R to end the merge.

If you want to stop the merge at any time, you can press Merge Codes and type "e" to end merging.

24 Press **Exit** (F7) and type **n** twice to clear the screen.

Creating a Macro to Start the Merge

While starting a merge to fill in a memo form requires very few keystrokes, some people completely automate the process by using one macro to start the merge and another macro to send the memo to the printer.

A macro is a special feature of WordPerfect that lets you record keystrokes in a file that can be used over and over again. The file can even be assigned to a key on the keyboard.

For complete details on macros, turn to the WordPerfect reference manual. You can also find other examples of macros in the workbook by turning to the Macros heading in the index.

For example, you can create a macro that starts the memo form merge, and assign it to the Alt-M keystroke.

25 Press **Macro Define** (Ctrl-F10), and then hold down **Alt** and type **m** to assign the macro file Alt-M.

26 Press **Enter** when you see the "Description:" message to bypass entering a description.

A description is only helpful if you want to edit the macro file later on. For simple macros, such as the one you are creating, editing is not usually necessary.

A "Macro Def" message appears at the bottom of the screen, letting you know that WordPerfect is ready to record every key you press.

27 Press **Merge/Sort** (Ctrl-F9) and select Merge (1).

28 Enter **memo.2** for the primary file, and then press **Enter** for the name of the secondary file to start the merge.

As soon as a merge starts, WordPerfect ends the macro definition process and the keystrokes up to that point are then saved in the macro file on disk.

Testing the Macro

Although the memo form is ready for you to fill in the information, let's end the merge and then test the macro you've created.

29 Press **Merge Codes** (Shift-F9) and type **e** to end the merge.

30 Press **Exit** (F7) and type **n** twice to clear the screen.

Because your macro is assigned to Alt-M on the keyboard, all you need to do is press those keys to start the memo form merge.

31 Hold down **Alt** and type **m** to start the merge.

The memo form should be on your screen, ready to fill in.

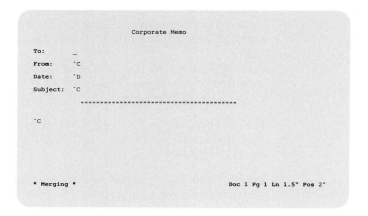

```
                          Corporate Memo


         To:        _
         From:     ˆC
         Date:     ˆD
         Subject:  ˆC

                  ==========================================



         ˆC






         * Merging *                          Doc 1 Pg 1 Ln 1.5" Pos 2"
```

By using Merge and Macro, you have created a memo form that is only a keystroke away.

32 Press **Merge Codes** (Shift-F9) and type **e** to end the merge.

33 Press **Merge Codes** (Shift-F9) and type **c** to insert another ^C.

Creating a Macro to Print the Memo

Once the memo is filled in, it would be wonderful if WordPerfect could send it to the printer, and then clear the screen for you. However, because the Alt-M macro ends when the merge starts, you'll need to create another macro to send the memo to the printer after the merge is completed.

34 Press **Macro Define** (Ctrl-F10) and enter **print** to name the macro.

35 Press **Enter** to bypass entering a description.

Notice that you can either use a filename or a keystroke to name a macro.

36 Press **Print** (Shift-F7) and select Full Document (1) to print the memo form on the screen.

37 Press **Exit** (F7) and then type **n** twice to clear the screen.

38 Press **Macro Define** (Ctrl-F10) to end defining the macro.

Starting the Print Macro from the Memo Form

Now, let's use the ^G merge code to have WordPerfect start the Print macro when you finish filling in the memo form.

39 Press **Retrieve** (Shift-F10) and then enter **memo.2** to retrieve the primary file.

40 Press **Home** twice and then **Down Arrow** (↓) to place the cursor at the end of the memo.

41 Press **Enter** to add a new line, and then press **Merge Codes** (Shift-F9) and type **g** to insert a ^G.

42 Type **print** for the name of the macro, and then press **Merge Codes** (Shift-F9) and type **g** to insert another ^G.

Your memo form should now look like the one illustrated below.

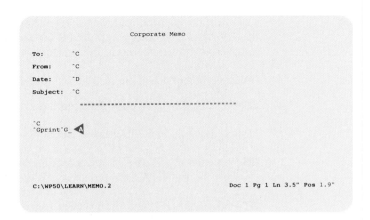

43 Press **Exit** (F7), type **y** to save the memo form, and then press **Enter** and type **y** to replace the original with the edited version.

44 Type **n** to clear the screen.

Starting the Merge with a Macro

You are now ready to test the automated memo form that you have created.

45 Hold down **Alt** and type **m** to start the memo form merge.

46 Fill in the memo with your own heading and message. Remember to press **Merge R** (F9) after typing the message to end the merge.

As soon as you finish filling in the memo, WordPerfect finds and starts the Print macro. The memo is then sent to the printer and your screen is cleared.

Summary

During this lesson you were introduced to the following tasks:

- Defining a simple macro.
- Ending or canceling a merge.
- Inserting text/codes from the keyboard during a merge (^C).
- Inserting the current date during a merge (^D).
- Merging a primary file only.
- Starting a macro from a primary file (^G).
- Starting a macro with Alt.
- Typing text to the right of the center position.

For a complete listing of all tasks introduced in the lessons, turn to *Feature Summary* at the end of the workbook.

Lesson 24: Lists

Lists provide a quick way to find information such as a full name, phone number, address, birth date, etc. Sometimes, though, the information changes as soon as the list is printed.

In this lesson, you use a primary and a secondary file to automate the task of creating and updating lists.

Retrieving the Primary File

Let's retrieve a primary file that you can use with the "Customer.wkb" secondary file to create a list.

1 Press **Retrieve** (Shift-F10) and enter **list.wkb** to retrieve the primary file.

The primary file uses ^F's to retrieve the information from field 1 (full name) and field 4 (phone number) for each record in the secondary file.

FULL NAME
PHONE NUMBER

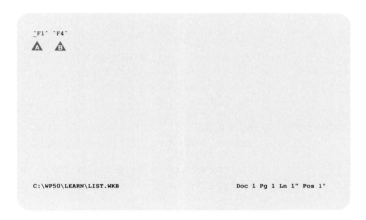

The two ^F's are separated by a tab, which means that each name and phone number will also be separated by a tab when the primary and secondary files are merged.

2 Press **Exit** (F7), type **y**, enter **list.pf** to create a new primary file, and then type **n** to clear the screen.

Merging the List

Now that you have been introduced to the primary file, let's start the merge and see what happens.

3 Press **Merge/Sort** (Ctrl-F9) and select Merge (1).

4 Enter **list.pf** for the name of the primary file, and then enter **customer.wkb** for the name of the secondary file.

When the merging is completed, the cursor is at the end of all the names and phone numbers.

5 Press **Home** twice and then **Up Arrow** (↑) to move to the beginning of the names and phone numbers.

Your screen should now look like the one illustrated below.

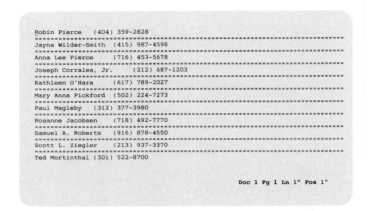

Replacing a Code with a Code

Notice that a page break has been added between each name and phone number, just like a page break separates each record in the secondary file.

You can quickly delete the page breaks and replace them with hard returns by using Replace.

6 Press **Replace** (Alt-F2) and type **n** to have WordPerfect replace each page break without stopping.

7 Press **Hard Page** (Ctrl-Enter) to have WordPerfect search for a Hard Page [HPg] code, and then press ◆**Search** (F2).

8 Press **Enter** to have WordPerfect replace the [HPg] code with a Hard Return [HRt] code, and then press ◆**Search** (F2) to start the replacing.

When replacing is completed, all the names and phone numbers should end with a Hard Return.

```
Robin Pierce    (404) 359-2828
Jayna Wilder-Smith  (415) 987-4598
Anna Lee Pierce     (716) 453-5678
Joseph Corrales, Jr.    (212) 687-1203
Kathleen O'Hara     (617) 789-2027
Mary Anna Pickford  (502) 224-7273
Paul Magleby   (312) 377-3980
Rosanne Jacobsen    (718) 492-7770
Samuel A. Roberts   (916) 878-4550
Scott L. Ziegler    (213) 937-3370
Ted Mortinthal (301) 522-8700
```

                                                  Doc 1 Pg 1 Ln 2.66" Pos 1"

Setting a Tab Stop

Because there is only one tab separating the names from the phone numbers, the phone numbers are not all lined up on the same tab stop.

A tab setting code could have been placed in the primary file to keep each phone number at the same tab stop, but then the same tab setting code would have been placed at the beginning of the line for *each person* in the list.

9 Press **Page Up** (PgUp) to move to the top of the list.

10 Press **Format** (Shift-F8), select Line (1), and then select Tab Set (8).

11 Press **Delete to End of Line** (Ctrl-End) to erase all the tabs from the left margin to the end of the tab ruler.

By checking the list against the tab ruler, it seems like 3.5 inches would be a good place to set a tab stop for the phone number.

▲ PHONE NUMBER TAB STOP

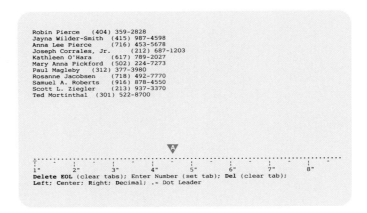

```
Robin Pierce   (404) 359-2828
Jayna Wilder-Smith  (415) 987-4598
Anna Lee Pierce   (716) 453-5678
Joseph Corrales, Jr.   (212) 687-1203
Kathleen O'Hara   (617) 789-2027
Mary Anna Pickford  (502) 224-7273
Paul Magleby  (312) 377-3980
Rosanne Jacobsen   (718) 492-7770
Samuel A. Roberts   (916) 878-4550
Scott L. Ziegler   (213) 937-3370
Ted Mortinthal  (301) 522-8700
```

```
                                    ▼
: . . . | . . . | . . . | . . . | . . . | . . . | . . . | . . . :
1"      2"      3"      4"      5"      6"      7"      8"
Delete EOL (clear tabs); Enter Number (set tab); Del (clear tab);
Left; Center; Right; Decimal; .= Dot Leader
```

12 Type **3.5** and then press **Enter** to set the tab stop at three inches.

13 Press **Exit** (F7) twice to save the tab setting and return to the list.

The phone numbers are now lined up at the same tab stop, 3.5 inches from the left margin.

```
Robin Pierce              (404) 359-2828
Jayna Wilder-Smith        (415) 987-4598
Anna Lee Pierce           (716) 453-5678
Joseph Corrales, Jr.      (212) 687-1203
Kathleen O'Hara           (617) 789-2027
Mary Anna Pickford        (502) 224-7273
Paul Magleby              (312) 377-3980
Rosanne Jacobsen          (718) 492-7770
Samuel A. Roberts         (916) 878-4550
Scott L. Ziegler          (213) 937-3370
Ted Mortinthal            (301) 522-8700




                                    Doc 1 Pg 1 Ln 1" Pos 1"
```

In most cases, it is a good idea to save formatting until the merging is done. The merged text may not look exactly the way you want, but that can be changed quickly by inserting the correct format codes (just once) at the beginning of the merged list.

14 Press **Exit** (F7) and type **n** twice to clear the screen.

Starting the Merge with a Macro

One of the most important reasons for using Merge is to help automate the process of creating documents. However, as you learned in the Memorandums lesson (22), macros let you automate the *entire task* of starting the merge and printing.

By using Alt, you can create a macro that starts the merge with a single keystroke.

15 Press **Macro Define** (Ctrl-F10), hold down **Alt** and type **L** to create an Alt-L macro, and then press **Enter** to bypass entering a description.

With the macro named, WordPerfect is ready to start recording keystrokes in the macro file. However, before starting the merge (which stops the macro definition), you should have the macro clear the screen.

16 Press **Exit** (F7) and type **n** twice to clear the screen.

You can also have the macro set the tab stop for the phone numbers *before* starting the merge, as the tab setting will remain at the top of the list when the merging is done.

17 Press **Format** (Shift-F8), select Line (1), and then select Tab Set (8).

18 Press **Delete to End of Line** (Ctrl-End) to erase the tab stop settings, and then enter **3** to set a tab stop at three inches.

19 Press **Exit** (F7) twice to return to the document screen.

20 Press **Merge/Sort** (Ctrl-F9) and select Merge (1).

21 Enter **list.pf** for the primary file, and then enter **customer.wkb** for the secondary file.

The merge starts, signaling WordPerfect to end recording keystrokes.

22 Press **Exit** (F7) and type **n** twice to clear the screen.

Editing the Print Macro

Now that you've created a macro to start the merge, you can add a macro to the primary file that will send the list to the printer.

A macro has already been provided for you that not only prints the merged list and clears the screen, but also pauses WordPerfect to let you select your own printer (or any other listed). However, before the list is printed, each page break needs to be replaced with a Hard Return.

You could define the entire macro over again to include the replacing; however, you can also use WordPerfect's macro editor to change the contents of the macro.

23 Press **Macro Define** (Ctrl-F10) and enter **printa** for the name of the macro.

Because the macro already exists, WordPerfect asks if you want to replace the macro by recording new keystrokes, or edit the contents of the macro.

24 Select Edit (2) to display the contents of the "Printa" macro.

As soon as you select Edit, the macro contents are displayed in a special editing window.

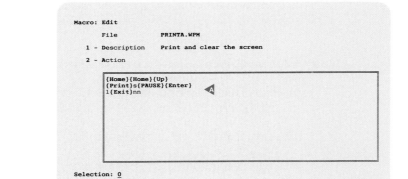

▲ MACRO CONTENTS

```
Macro: Edit

        File          PRINTA.WPM
   1 - Description    Print and clear the screen
   2 - Action

        {Home}{Home}{Up}
        {Print}s{PAUSE}{Enter}
        1{Exit}nn



Selection: 0
```

Above the window are the name of the macro and a description. In the window are three lines of keystrokes that have been recorded in the macro.

The first line moves the cursor to the beginning of the list by using Home and Up Arrow. The second line displays the list of printers, pauses to let you select your own printer, and then returns you to the Print menu. The last line selects the Full Document option (1), and then uses Exit to clear the screen.

Inserting Keystrokes in the Macro

Let's try adding the keystrokes that will replace the page breaks with Hard Returns.

25 Select Action (2) to edit the macro contents.

26 Press **Down Arrow** (↓) to place the cursor at the beginning of the {Print} line.

27 Press **Replace** (Alt-F2) and then type **n** to have WordPerfect replace without stopping.

Your macro should now include the following two new keystrokes.

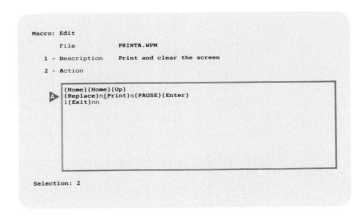

▲ NEW KEYSTROKES

```
Macro: Edit

        File            PRINTA.WPM

  1 - Description     Print and clear the screen

  2 - Action

      {Home}{Home}{Up}
   ▲  {Replace}n{Print}s{PAUSE}{Enter}
      1{Exit}nn




Selection: 2
```

As you add keystrokes to the macro, feature names ({Replace}) and characters (n) are added to the macro contents.

However, no messages or menus appear to let you know exactly what to select or type. For this reason, you may want to start using the macro editor on your own only after becoming more familiar with WordPerfect.

28 Press **Hard Page** (Ctrl-Enter) to search for a Hard Page break, and then press ◆**Search** (F2).

29 Press **Enter** to have the page break replaced with a Hard Return.

Inserting a Hard Return in the Macro

Notice that WordPerfect ended the line instead of inserting an {Enter} keystroke.

 HARD RETURN

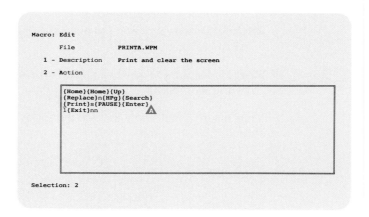

In order to have keystrokes inserted for the editing keys (Home, arrows, Enter, etc.), you need to switch to a special editing method that puts in a keystroke name for *every* key on the keyboard.

30 Press **Backspace** to erase the line ending.

31 Press **Macro Define** (Ctrl-F10) to insert keystroke names for all keys on the keyboard.

32 Press **Enter** to insert an {Enter} keystroke name.

33 Press **Macro Define** (Ctrl-F10) to return to normal editing.

34 Press ◆**Search** (F2) to have the macro begin replacing.

35 Press **Enter** to end the line of keystrokes.

Your edited macro should now look like the one illustrated below.

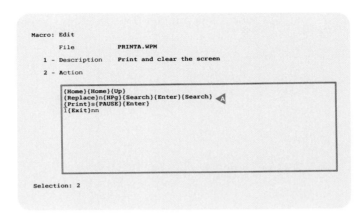

```
Macro: Edit

        File            PRINTA.WPM

   1 - Description      Print and clear the screen

   2 - Action

        {Home}{Home}{Up}
        {Replace}n{HPg}{Search}{Enter}{Search}
        {Print}s{PAUSE}{Enter}
        1{Exit}nn




Selection: 2
```

36 Press **Exit** (F7) twice to save the edited macro and return to the document screen.

Adding the Macro to the Primary File

The edited macro can now be added to the primary file to have WordPerfect print the list and clear the screen when the merge is completed.

37 Press **Retrieve** (Shift-F10) and enter **list.pf** to retrieve the primary file.

38 Press **End**, and then press **Merge Codes** (Shift-F9) and type **g** to insert a ^G merge code.

39 Type **printa** for the name of the macro.

40 Press **Merge Codes** (Shift-F9) and type **g** to insert a second ^G merge code.

Your edited primary file should now look like the one illustrated below.

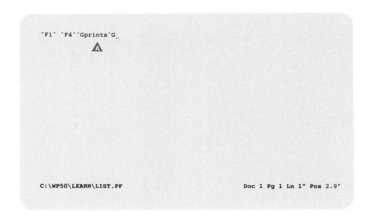

```
˜F1˜ ˜F4˜˜Gprinta˜G_
          ▲




C:\WP50\LEARN\LIST.PF                    Doc 1 Pg 1 Ln 1" Pos 2.9"
```

41 Press **Exit** (F7), type **y**, press **Enter** and then type **y** to replace the primary file.

42 Type **n** to clear the screen.

Starting the List Merge

With the primary file and macros in place, you are ready to use the Alt-L macro to start the merge and print out the list.

43 Hold down **Alt** and type **l** to create and print the list of names and phone numbers.

After a few moments, WordPerfect should pause for you to select your printer.

44 Place the reverse video cursor on the name of your printer, and then press **Enter** to continue the "Printa" macro.

The list is printed, the screen is cleared, and you have entirely automated the process of creating and printing a list.

If there are problems with the list printing, the screen being cleared, the phone numbers lining up on a tab stop, etc., you may want to start the lesson over from the point where you begin creating macros to make sure that they have been created and edited correctly.

Merging lists by using tabs to separate the information into columns only works if each item merged (e.g., full name, phone number) is one line in length. If you want to merge an item several lines long (e.g., an address), then you should set up the primary file in Parallel Columns. For an example of merging in Parallel Columns, turn to the Multiple-Column Labels heading in the Special Techniques lesson at the end of Merging Documents.

Summary

During this lesson, you were introduced to the following tasks:

- Defining a simple macro.
- Editing a macro.
- Inserting a field in a primary file (^F).
- Merging a primary and secondary file.
- Replacing text and codes.

For a complete listing of all tasks introduced in the lessons, turn to *Feature Summary* at the end of the workbook.

Lesson 25: Printed Forms

Merge is often used to print out invoices, billings, receipts, checks, and other pre-printed forms. For example, the addresses and terms printed in the heading of the following invoice form could be inserted from a secondary file during a merge.

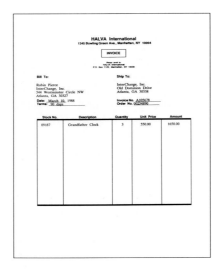

The merge could then pause for information about the invoice number, order number, and merchandise ordered by using ^C merge codes.

The Printed Forms lesson in Formatting Documents *takes you through the fundamental steps of setting up WordPerfect to fill in a pre-printed form. You may want to review the lesson before continuing with the exercise below.*

Editing the Secondary File

The first step in setting up the merge is to make sure that only the records you want to merge are included in the secondary file. The records also need to contain the correct information.

1 Press **Retrieve** (Shift-F10) and enter **customer.wkb** to retrieve the secondary file of customers.

Notice the information in the first record of the secondary file.

```
Robin Pierce~R
InterChange, Inc.
544 Westminster Circle NW
Atlanta, GA 30327~R
Robin~R
(404) 359-2828~R
~E
===========================================================================
Jayna Wilder-Smith~R
8611 Market St.
San Francisco, CA 94102~R
Jayna~R
(415) 987-4598~R
~E
===========================================================================
Anna Lee Pierce~R
P.O. Box 1392
Central Park Station
Buffalo, NY 14215~R
Anna~R
(716) 453-5678~R
~E
===========================================================================
Joseph Corrales, Jr.~R
C:\WP50\LEARN\CUSTOMER.WKB                        Doc 1 Pg 1 Ln 1" Pos 1"
```

The name and address can be used for the billing address, but the terms and a shipping address need to be added to the record.

2 Place the cursor to the left of the ^E at the end of the first record (below the phone number).

3 Type **90 days** for the terms, and then press **Merge R** (F9) to end the field.

If you pressed Merge R after the terms, your cursor should be at the left margin and in place for typing the shipping address.

```
Robin Pierce^R
InterChange, Inc.
544 Westminster Circle NW
Atlanta, GA 30327^R
Robin^R
(404) 359-2828^R
90 days^R
^E
▲ ========================================================================
Jayna Wilder-Smith^R
8611 Market St.
San Francisco, CA 94102^R
Jayna^R
(415) 987-4598^R
^E
========================================================================
Anna Lee Pierce^R
P.O. Box 1392
Central Park Station
Buffalo, NY 14215^R
Anna^R
(716) 453-5678^R
^E
========================================================================
C:\WP50\LEARN\CUSTOMER.WKB                    Doc 1 Pg 1 Ln 2.16" Pos 1"
```

Because the shipping address is to the right of the billing address in the middle of the form, each line of the shipping address needs to be merged separately into the primary file. You can do this by creating a field for each line.

4 Type the following address, pressing **Merge R** (F9) at the end of each line to create a separate field:

> **InterChange, Inc.**
> **Old Dominion Drive**
> **Atlanta, GA 30338**

The InterChange address has three lines, but other addresses may have four lines. Because each record in a secondary file needs to have the same number of fields, an extra ^R should be added below the last line of the Interchange address.

5 Press **Merge R** (F9) to add an empty field below the last line of the address.

You should now have five new fields added to the first record in the secondary file, with a ^R at the end of each line.

```
Robin Pierce^R
InterChange, Inc.
544 Westminster Circle NW
Atlanta, GA 30327^R
Robin^R
(404) 359-2828^R
90 days^R
InterChange, Inc.^R
Old Dominion Drive^R
Atlanta, GA 30338^R
^R
^E
====================================================================
Jayna Wilder-Smith^R
8611 Market St.
San Francisco, CA 94102^R
Jayna^R
(415) 987-4598^R
^E
====================================================================
Anna Lee Pierce^R
P.O. Box 1392
Central Park Station
Buffalo, NY 14215^R
C:\WP50\LEARN\CUSTOMER.WKB                    Doc 1 Pg 1 Ln 2.83" Pos 1"
```

Deleting a Block of Text

The same fields should be added to each record in the secondary file when doing your own merge; however, for this lesson you only need the first record. The rest can be deleted.

6 Press **Page Down** (PgDn) to place the cursor at the beginning of the second record.

7 Press **Block** (Alt-F4), and then press **Home** twice and **Down Arrow** (↓) to move to the end of the file.

8 Press **Backspace** and type **y** to delete all but the first record in the secondary file.

9 Press **Save** (F10) and enter **customer.1** to create a new file for the record.

Creating the Primary File

With the edited record still on the screen for reference, you can switch to the second document screen and retrieve "Invoice.wkb" to create a primary file.

10 Press **Switch** (Shift-F3) to open up the second document screen.

11 Press **Retrieve** (Shift-F10) and enter **invoice.wkb** to retrieve the primary file.

The comments in the primary file are used to indicate information to be filled in, while Advance codes below the comments print the information in the correct places on the form.

Inserting the Fields

For the information from the secondary file to be merged into the primary file, ^F merge codes need to be placed below each comment to the *right* of the Advance codes.

12 Press **End** to make sure that the cursor is to the right of the Advance codes in the empty line below the Bill To comment.

13 Press **Merge Codes** (Shift-F9), type **f**, enter **1** for the first field in the record, and then press **Enter** to return the cursor to the left margin.

14 Press **Merge Codes** (Shift-F9), type **f**, and then enter **2** for the second field in the record.

Your primary file should now look like the one illustrated below.

 ^F MERGE CODES

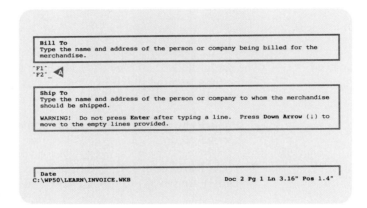

15 Press **Down Arrow** (↓) to place the cursor in the first empty line below the Ship To comment.

Notice that there are four empty lines below the comment. Advance codes have been placed at the beginning of each line so that each line of the shipping address is printed in the correct position on the form.

Because the shipping address in the secondary file is separated into individual fields, all you need to do is insert a ^F at the beginning of each empty line to insert the address into the primary file.

16 Press **Switch** (Shift-F3) to display the record in the first document screen.

Counting the Fields

Count and write down the field numbers for the shipping address and the terms. Your results should match those indicated in the screen below.

17 Press **Switch** (Shift-F3) to return to the primary file.

18 Press **Merge Codes** (Shift-F9), type **f**, and then enter **6** to insert a ^F6^ for the first line of the shipping address.

19 Press **Down Arrow** (↓) to move to the next empty line.

20 Insert the following ^F codes in the last three empty lines below the Ship To comment. Remember to press **Down Arrow** (↓) instead of Enter after inserting a ^F code:

^F7^
^F8^
^F9^

21 Press **Down Arrow** (↓) to move the cursor to the empty line below the Date comment (if it is not already there).

22 Press **Merge Codes** (Shift-F9) and type **d** to insert a ^D below the Date comment.

The ^D code will fill in the current date automatically when merging the primary and secondary files.

23 Press **Down Arrow** (↓) to move the cursor to the empty line below the Terms comment.

Your primary file should now look like the one illustrated below.

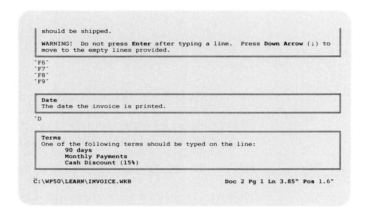

24 Press **Merge Codes** (Shift-F9), type **f**, and then enter **5** to insert an ^F5^ code for the terms.

Because the invoice and order numbers change from one form to the next, you can use ^C merge codes to type the numbers from the keyboard.

25 Press Down Arrow (↓) to place the cursor below the Invoice No. comment.

26 Press **Merge Codes** (Shift-F9) and then type **c** to insert a ^C merge code.

27 Press **Down Arrow** (↓) to place the cursor below the order No. comment.

28 Press Merge Codes (Shift-F9), type c to insert a ^C merge code, and then press Down Arrow (↓) to place the cursor below the last comment.

For details on using the Paragraph Numbering feature to automatically number the invoices, turn to Auto-Incrementing Numbers in the Special Techniques *lesson at the end of* Merging Documents.

If you pressed Down Arrow after inserting the second ^C code, your cursor should now be on the empty line below the comment for the merchandise ordered.

 ▲ CURSOR POSITION

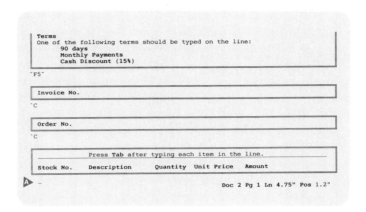

Because the merchandise also varies from invoice to invoice, a ^C can be placed below the comment to stop the merge and let you enter the required information.

29 Press **Merge Codes** (Shift-F9) and type **c** to insert a ^C code.

Deleting the Comments

Now that the ^F and ^C merge codes have been inserted into the invoice document, only the comments for the invoice number, order number, and merchandise ordered are needed. The rest of the comments can be deleted by using Replace.

30 Press **Page Up** (PgUp) to move the cursor above the first comment in the document.

31 Press **Replace** (Alt-F2) and type **y** to have WordPerfect stop at each comment.

32 Press **Text In/Out** (Ctrl-F5) and press ◆**Search** (F2) to have WordPerfect look for [Comment] codes.

At this point, the "Replace with:" message is displayed on the screen. If you simply press ◆Search to start the replacement, then WordPerfect will replace the comment with *nothing*. In other words, the comment will be deleted.

33 Press ◆**Search** (F2) to start the replacing.

WordPerfect stops below the Bill To comment and asks if you want the comment replaced.

A CURSOR POSITION

B CONFIRM REPLACEMENT MESSAGE

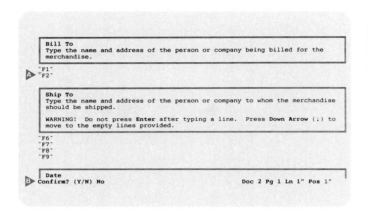

34 Type **y** to have the Bill To comment deleted.

WordPerfect stops below the Ship To comment and asks if you want the comment replaced.

35 Type **y** to have the Ship To comment deleted.

WordPerfect then stops below the Date comment. Only the Date and Terms Comments should be deleted. The comments above the ^C's need to stay as a guide for filling in the information.

36 Type **y** twice to delete the next two comments.

37 Type **n** three times to keep the last three comments, and then press **Page Up** (PgUp).

Your primary file should now look like the one illustrated below.

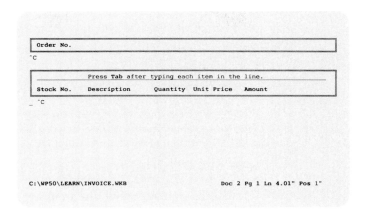

```
┌────────────────────────────────────────────────────────────┐
│ Order No.                                                    │
└────────────────────────────────────────────────────────────┘
˜C

  ┌──────────────────────────────────────────────────────────┐
  │           Press Tab after typing each item in the line.  │
  ├──────────────────────────────────────────────────────────┤
  │ Stock No.    Description      Quantity Unit Price   Amount│
  └──────────────────────────────────────────────────────────┘
_  ˜C




C:\WP50\LEARN\INVOICE.WKB                    Doc 2 Pg 1 Ln 4.01" Pos 1"
```

Inserting a Print Macro

As a final touch to the primary file, you can add a macro like the one used in the Lists lesson (24) to have WordPerfect send the information to the printer and clear the screen.

38 Press **Page Down** (PgDn) to move past the last ^C.

39 Press **Enter** to start a new line.

40 Press **Merge Codes** (Shift-F9) and type **g** to insert a ^G merge code.

41 Type **printb** for the name of the macro, and then press **Merge Codes** (Shift-F9) and type **g** to insert a second ^G merge code.

Your primary file should now look like the one illustrated below.

 MERGE MACRO

```
˜F7˜
˜F8˜
˜F9˜
˜D
˜F5˜

┌────────────────────────────────────────────────────────────┐
│ Invoice No.                                                  │
└────────────────────────────────────────────────────────────┘
˜C

┌────────────────────────────────────────────────────────────┐
│ Order No.                                                    │
└────────────────────────────────────────────────────────────┘
˜C

  ┌──────────────────────────────────────────────────────────┐
  │           Press Tab after typing each item in the line.  │
  ├──────────────────────────────────────────────────────────┤
  │ Stock No.    Description      Quantity Unit Price   Amount│
  └──────────────────────────────────────────────────────────┘
  ˜C
˜Gprintb˜G_
C:\WP50\LEARN\INVOICE.WKB                    Doc 2 Pg 1 Ln 4.91" Pos 2.2"
```

42 Press **Exit** (F7), type **y**, and enter **invoice.pf** to create a new file.

43 Type **y** to exit the document 2 screen.

44 Press **Exit** (F7) and type **n** twice to clear the document 1 screen.

Merging the Form

With both the secondary and primary files edited, you are ready to start a merge to fill in the invoice. An Alt-I macro has already been provided for you to automatically start the merge.

For details on laying out the keyboard to perform the tasks of starting merges, etc., turn to the Organizing the Keyboard heading in the Special Techniques section at the end of Merging Documents.

45 Hold down **Alt** and type **i** to start the invoice merge.

The addresses, date, and terms are inserted automatically for you. WordPerfect then stops at the ^C below the Invoice No. comment.

46 Type **A105678** for the invoice number, and then press **Merge R** (F9) to continue the merge.

47 Type **00254890** for the order number, and then press **Merge R** (F9) to continue the merge.

48 Type the following information for the merchandise ordered. As indicated in the comment, press **Tab** after typing an item to move to the next column:

09187 (stock no.)
Grandfather Clock (description)
3 (quantity)
550.00 (unit price)
1650.00 (amount)

Your primary file should now look like the one illustrated below.

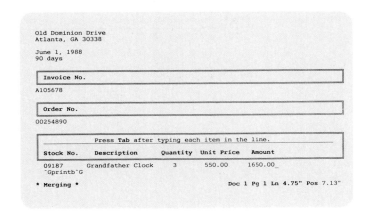

```
Old Dominion Drive
Atlanta, GA 30338

June 1, 1988
90 days
┌─────────────────────────────────────────────────────────────┐
│  Invoice No.                                                  │
└─────────────────────────────────────────────────────────────┘
A105678
┌─────────────────────────────────────────────────────────────┐
│  Order No.                                                    │
└─────────────────────────────────────────────────────────────┘
00254890
┌─────────────────────────────────────────────────────────────┐
│           Press Tab after typing each item in the line.      │
│                                                               │
│  Stock No.    Description     Quantity  Unit Price   Amount   │
   09187        Grandfather Clock    3       550.00    1650.00_
   ^Gprintb^G

* Merging *                            Doc 1 Pg 1 Ln 4.75" Pos 7.13"
```

49 Make sure that your cursor is in the line above the ^G macro (or the printb macro will not be started).

50 Press **Merge R** (F9) to continue the merge.

WordPerfect starts the macro, which then pauses for you to select your printer.

51 Highlight the name of your printer, and then press **Enter** to continue the macro.

The macro then sends the information to your printer and clears the screen. Your printed page should look similar to the one illustrated below.

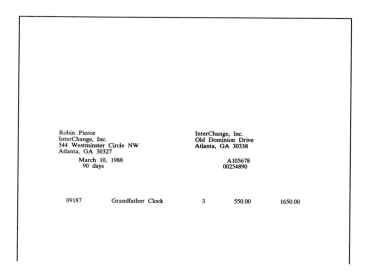

If you had placed an invoice form in your printer before starting the merge, then the information would have printed in the correct position on the form.

With more than one record in the secondary file, the same merge creates an invoice document for each record (stopping for the ^C merge codes), and then sends all the merged documents to the printer at the same time.

Summary

During this lesson, you were introduced to the following tasks:

- Erasing a block of text.
- Merging a primary and secondary file.
- Merging a primary file only.
- Replacing text and codes.

For a complete listing of all tasks introduced in the lessons, turn to *Feature Summary* at the end of the workbook.

Lesson 26: Sorting Records

As you discovered while merging business letters (Lesson 21), merged documents are created in the same order as the records in the secondary file. But what if you want to change the order in which the letters are merged?

For example, when mailing hundreds of letters at a time, the post office normally offers a discount bulk rate if the letters are pre-sorted by ZIP code.

1 Press **Retrieve** (Shift-F10), and then enter **customer.wkb** to display the customer records.

2 Press **Page Down** (PgDn) several times to check the ZIP codes in the customer list.

As you can immediately see, the records are *not* listed by ZIP code. In fact, they seem to have been entered randomly, instead of in any particular order.

Sorting to the Screen

By using the Sort feature, you can list the records by ZIP code, taking advantage of the bulk rate discount.

3 Press **Merge/Sort** (Ctrl-F9), and then select Sort (2).

A message at the bottom of the screen requests the name of the input file to sort. Notice that the word "(Screen)" follows the request.

WordPerfect is asking for the name of the file on disk you would like to sort. However, because the records you want sorted are already retrieved, you can use the name "(Screen)" to tell WordPerfect that the file is on the screen.

4 Press **Enter** to use the "(Screen)" name.

A second message requests an output file for the sorted document. If you press Enter to use the "(Screen)" name, WordPerfect will replace the records currently on the screen with the sorted records. Entering a filename leaves the records on the screen undisturbed, and saves the sorted records on disk.

5 Press **Enter** to have WordPerfect save the sorted records to the screen.

Selecting the Sort Type

The screen is now divided in half with the records displayed in the top half of the screen and the Sort menu displayed in a window in the bottom half of the screen.

A RECORDS

B SORT MENU

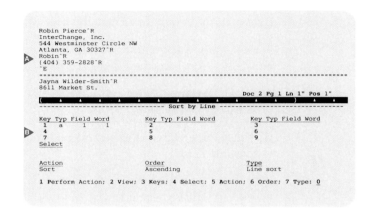

Sort is quite flexible, and includes several options for sorting *and* selecting records. The title at the top of the menu lets you know the type of sorting that WordPerfect will be doing.

6 Select Type (7), and then select Merge (1) to indicate that you want to sort a secondary merge file.

Creating a Key

Directly below the title are the keys (up to 9) that you can use for sorting the records. A *key* identifies the information by which you want the records sorted.

For example, to sort the records by ZIP code, you need to create a key that tells WordPerfect where the ZIP code is located in each record. Notice that a key for a secondary merge file includes the type, field, line, and word.

7 Select Keys (3) to create a key for sorting the records by ZIP code.

The cursor moves up to the "a" in the first key under the Type title. A message at the bottom of the screen indicates that you can type "a" or "n" to select an alphanumeric or numeric sort. The only time you need to do a numeric sort is if you are sorting numbers of unequal lengths such as dates (e.g. 12/1/89, 5/6/89). Most of the time, you will simply be doing an alphanumeric sort.

8 Press **Right Arrow** (→) to leave the "a" and move to the field number.

Because the fields in each record are counted from top to bottom, the ZIP code is at the end of the second field.

▲ END OF SECOND FIELD

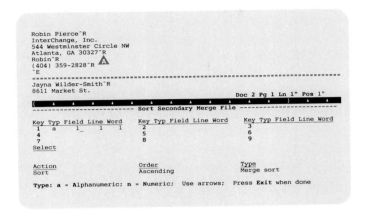

9 Type **2** for the field number, and then press **Right Arrow** (→) to move to the line number.

Using Negative Numbers

A field can have several lines, so WordPerfect needs to know in which line of the field the ZIP code is located. The lines in a record are also counted from top to bottom. Robin Pierce's address has three lines, but do all the addresses have three lines?

10 Press **Exit** (F7) to leave the key for a moment, select View (2), and then press **Down Arrow** (↓) until Jayna Wilder-Smith's address scrolls onto the screen.

While Robin's address is three lines, Jayna's address is only two lines in length.

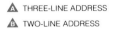 THREE-LINE ADDRESS

 TWO-LINE ADDRESS

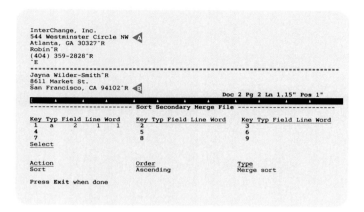

If you use "3" for the line number in the key, then WordPerfect will not find the ZIP code in line 2 of Jayna's record. However, if you use "2" for the line number, then WordPerfect will not find the ZIP code in Robin's record.

Fortunately, Sort provides a way of solving the problem by using *negative* numbers. If you count the lines from the top of the field to the bottom, then the line number for the ZIP code will vary. However, if you count the lines from *bottom to top*, then the ZIP code will always be in the first line.

By using the negative sign, you can tell WordPerfect to count the lines in the opposite direction (bottom to top), and always make sure that WordPerfect is looking in the correct line for the ZIP code.

11 Press **Exit** (F7), and then select Keys (3) to return to the first key.

12 Press **Right Arrow** (→) twice to move to the line number, and then type **-1** to indicate the first line from the bottom of the field.

Now that you've identified the correct line, the final step is to identify which word in the line is the ZIP code. However, notice that Robin's address (city, state and ZIP code) is three words in length, while Jayna's address is four words in length.

A THREE WORDS
B FOUR WORDS

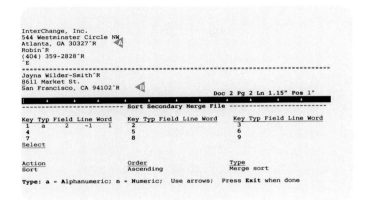

```
InterChange, Inc.
544 Westminster Circle NW
Atlanta, GA 30327^R          A
Robin^R
(404) 359-2828^R
^E
==================================================================
Jayna Wilder-Smith^R
8611 Market St.
San Francisco, CA 94102^R    B
                                    Doc 2 Pg 2 Ln 1.15" Pos 1"

------------------------- Sort Secondary Merge File -------------------------

Key Typ Field Line Word   Key Typ Field Line Word   Key Typ Field Line Word
 1   a     2    -1    1     2                          3
 4                          5                          6
 7                          8                          9
Select


Action                    Order                     Type
Sort                      Ascending                 Merge sort

Type: a = Alphanumeric;  n = Numeric;   Use arrows;  Press Exit when done
```

Because the words in a line are counted from left to right, you also need to use a negative number to tell WordPerfect to count the words from *right to left* in the line. The ZIP code is always the first word in from the right, so you can use a "-1" to identify the correct word.

13 Press **Right Arrow** (→), type **-1** for the word number, and then press **Exit** (F7) to save the key.

Sorting by ZIP Code

With the position of the ZIP code identified for each record, WordPerfect can now sort the records by ZIP code.

14 Select Perform Action (1) to begin the sort.

A counter at the bottom of the screen keeps you updated on the progress of the sort. When sorting is completed, WordPerfect replaces the original records on your screen with those that are sorted by ZIP code.

▲ EMPTY ADDRESS FIELD

```
Ted Mortinthal^R
^R
Ted^R
(301) 522-8700^R
^E
================================================================
Kathleen O'Hara^R
678 Forestvale Road
Boston, MA 02136^R
Kathy^R
(617) 789-2027^R
^E
================================================================
Joseph Corrales, Jr.^R
Kensington House, #312
176 West 45th
Manhattan, NY 10036^R
Joe^R
(212) 687-1203^R
^E
================================================================
Rosanne Jacobsen^R
555 Lafayette Ave.
Brooklyn, NY 11205^R
C:\WP50\LEARN\CUSTOMER.WKB                     Doc 1 Pg 1 Ln 1" Pos 1"
```

Notice that WordPerfect placed Ted Mortinthal's record at the top of the secondary file. Any records that WordPerfect cannot sort because the field is empty are placed at the top of the file. In this case, Ted's record is missing an address.

Sorting on a field is a good way of finding out which records in a secondary file are missing information in that field.

Sorting to a File

Let's try sorting the records again, but this time save the sorted records to a file on disk.

15 Press **Merge/Sort** (Ctrl-F9), select Sort (2), and press **Enter** to sort the records on the screen.

16 Enter **customer.2** for the output filename.

When the Sort menu appears, notice that the settings have not changed for the type of sort or the key being used to sort the record. This feature makes it convenient to sort several files using the same key.

Changing the Order

Another sorting feature lets you change the order in which the records are sorted.

17 Select Order (6) from the menu at the bottom of the screen.

Notice that you can sort the records in ascending or descending order.

▲ ASCENDING OR DESCENDING

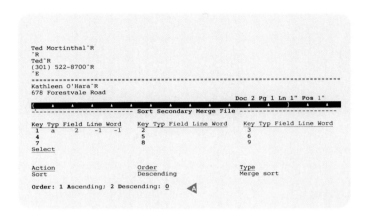

```
Ted Mortinthal˜R
˜R
Ted˜R
(301) 522-8700˜R
˜E
=================================================================
Kathleen O'Hara˜R
678 Forestvale Road
                                              Doc 2 Pg 1 Ln 1" Pos 1"
[   ▲    ▲    ▲    ▲    ▲    ▲    ▲    ▲    ▲   )  ▲  ▲--------
---------------------- Sort Secondary Merge File ----------------------

Key Typ Field Line Word    Key Typ Field Line Word    Key Typ Field Line Word
 1   a     2    -1   -1      2                          3
 4                           5                          6
 7                           8                          9
Select

Action                     Order                      Type
Sort                       Descending                 Merge sort

Order: 1 Ascending; 2 Descending: 0     ◀A
```

Ascending means that words are sorted from A to Z, while numbers are sorted from lowest to highest. *Descending* means that words are sorted from Z to A, while numbers are sorted from highest to lowest.

The records in the customer list were sorted in an ascending order, which means that the record with the lowest ZIP code number was placed at the top of the list (Kathleen O'Hara), while the record with the highest ZIP code number was placed at the bottom of the list (Samuel A. Roberts).

Let's sort the records in descending order before saving them in the customer file on disk.

18 Select Descending (2), and then select Perform Action (1) to begin sorting the records.

19 Press **Switch** (Shift-F3) to open the second document screen.

20 Press **Retrieve** (Shift-F10) and enter **customer.2** to retrieve the sorted records.

LESSON 26 **239**

As you can see, the first record is Samuel A. Roberts, while the rest of the list is in descending ZIP code order.

```
Samuel A. Roberts^R
6120 Cottage Way, Suite #456
Sacramento, CA 95825^R
Sam^R
(916) 878-4550^R
^E
--------------------------------------------------------------------------
Jayna Wilder-Smith^R
8611 Market St.
San Francisco, CA 94102^R
Jayna^R
(415) 987-4598^R
^E
--------------------------------------------------------------------------
Scott L. Ziegler^R
Merchants Exchange
450 S. Flower St.
Los Angeles, CA 90014^R
Scott^R
(213) 937-3370^R
^E
--------------------------------------------------------------------------
Paul Magleby^R
1820 Harbor Ave S.
C:\WP50\LEARN\CUSTOMER.2                       Doc 2 Pg 1 Ln 1" Pos 1"
```

Merging the Letters

Let's clear both editing screens and try merging the announcement letter with the newly-sorted secondary file.

21 Press **Exit** (F7), type **n**, and then type **y** to exit the document 2 screen.

22 Press **Exit** (F7) and type **n** twice to clear the document 1 screen.

23 Press **Merge/Sort** (Ctrl-F9), select Merge (1), enter **stores.wkb** for the primary file, and then enter **customer.2** for the secondary file.

When the merge is completed, the first record in the secondary file (Samuel A. Roberts) should be the first letter in the merged document.

24 Press **Home** twice and then press **Up Arrow** (↑) to move to the first letter.

```
Samuel A. Roberts
6120 Cottage Way, Suite #456
Sacramento, CA 95825

Dear Sam,

We are proud to announce the grand opening of several HALVA
International retail stores throughout the country.  Stores are
scheduled to open in the following cities during the first
quarter of the year:

     Manhattan, New York          January 18
     Boston, Massachusetts        January 26
     San Francisco, California    February 10
     Los Angeles, California      February 24
     Atlanta, Georgia             March 9
     Chicago, Illinois            March 17

As a preferred customer, you will be receiving a special
invitation, and I personally look forward to meeting you at the
opening.

Sincerely,

                                   Doc 1 Pg 1 Ln 1" Pos 1"
```

Sorting by Name

Another common way of sorting records is by last name. However, in case there is more than one person with the same last name, you need to create two keys.

25 Press **Exit** (F7) and type **n** twice to clear the document screen.

26 Press **Merge/Sort** (Ctrl-F9) and then select Sort (2).

27 Enter **customer.2** for the file you want sorted, and then press **Enter** to have the records sorted to the screen.

28 Select Keys (3), and then type the following for the first key (key1):

a 1 1 -1

The first key tells WordPerfect to sort the records by the last name, which is the first word from the right (-1) in the first line (1) of the first field (1). Like the ZIP code sort, you needed to use a negative number because some customers have a first and last name only, while others include a middle name or initial.

Because there may be more than one customer with the same last name, you need to tell WordPerfect to also sort by first name the customers with the same last name. You can do this by creating a second key.

29 Press **Right Arrow** (→) to move to the second key (key2), and then press **Right Arrow** again to fill in the key with "a 1 1 1."

After sorting the records by last name (key1), WordPerfect makes a second pass through the records. Any records with identical last names will then be sorted by first name (key2).

30 Press **Exit** (F7) to save the two keys, select Order (6), and then select Ascending (1) to have the records sorted alphabetically from A to Z.

31 Select Perform Action (1) to begin sorting the records.

When the sorting is completed, the records are displayed on your screen.

```
Joseph Corrales, Jr.^R
Kensington House, #312
176 West 45th          ◄A
Manhattan, NY 10036^R
Joe^R
(212) 687-1203^R
^E
==================================================
Rosanne Jacobsen^R
555 Lafayette Ave.     ◄B
Brooklyn, NY 11205^R
Rosanne^R
(718) 492-7770^R
^E
==================================================
Paul Magleby^R
1820 Harbor Ave S.
Chicago, IL 60617^R
Paul^R
(312) 377-3980^R
^E
==================================================
Ted Mortinthal^R
^R
                              Doc 1 Pg 1 Ln 1" Pos 1"
```

Notice that the record for "Joseph Corrales, Jr." has been sorted before the record for "Rosanne Jacobsen." Normally, WordPerfect would have seen "Jr." as the last name, and sorted "Corrales, Jr." *after* "Jacobsen" in the list.

However, a special Hard Space (Home-Spacebar) has been placed between "Corrales," and "Jr." to have WordPerfect treat both as one word. The Hard Space can be seen in Reveal Codes as a space between two brackets.

▲ HARD SPACE

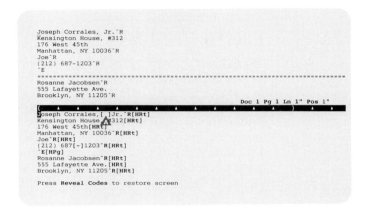

```
      Joseph Corrales, Jr.˜R
      Kensington House, #312
      176 West 45th
      Manhattan, NY 10036˜R
      Joe˜R
      (212) 687-1203˜R
      ˜E
      ==========================================================================
      Rosanne Jacobsen˜R
      555 Lafayette Ave.
      Brooklyn, NY 11205˜R
                                                       Doc 1 Pg 1 Ln 1" Pos 1"
      [    ▲    ▲    ▲    ▲   ▲   ▲    ▲    ▲    ▲    ▲    ▲   ▲    )   ▲    ▲
      Joseph Corrales,[ ]Jr.˜R[HRt]
      Kensington House,▲#312[HRt]
      176 West 45th[HRt]
      Manhattan, NY 10036˜R[HRt]
      Joe˜R[HRt]
      (212) 687[-]1203˜R[HRt]
      ˜E[HPg]
      Rosanne Jacobsen˜R[HRt]
      555 Lafayette Ave.[HRt]
      Brooklyn, NY 11205˜R[HRt]

      Press Reveal Codes to restore screen
```

By using a Hard Space, WordPerfect sorts "Corrales, Jr." instead of "Jr." and the record is placed in the correct order in the customer list.

Selecting and Sorting

Now let's introduce the other half of the sorting process—selecting records.

Unless you indicate otherwise, WordPerfect sorts *all* the records in the secondary file each time you use Sort. However, there may be times when you only want to select part of the records from the file and then sort them. For example, letters need to be sent immediately to customers in Boston and Manhattan, informing them of a January grand opening in their cities. The rest of the letters can be sent later in the month.

The customers in Boston and Manhattan need to be selected, and then sorted by ZIP code to get the bulk mailing discount.

32 Press **Merge/Sort** (Ctrl-F9), select Sort (2), and then press **Enter** twice to select and sort the records already on the screen.

You can select records by defining a key (or keys), and then identifying a word (or words) for each key in a select statement. When you start the sort with Perform Action, WordPerfect compares the word you identified to the defined key and selects only those records that match.

For example, you can create a "key1=smith" select statement for key1 (a 1 1 –1) to have WordPerfect select only those records with the last name of "Smith" before sorting.

However, you can also use a special "keyg" (global) when creating a select statement to have WordPerfect ignore the defined keys and compare *every* word in the record to the word you identify.

For example, you can tell WordPerfect to ignore the defined keys and match "boston" and "manhattan" against *every* word in the record by creating a "keyg =boston + keyg=manhatten" statement.

33 Type **4** for Select, type **keyg=boston + keyg=manhattan** for the select statement, and then press Exit (F7).

The plus sign (+) between the keys tells WordPerfect to select all records that have the word "Boston" *or* the word "Manhattan." The plus sign is one of several symbols that can be used to create a select statement. The available symbols are listed at the bottom of your screen (if you have not pressed Enter).

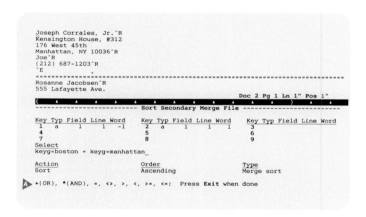

```
Joseph Corrales, Jr.^R
Kensington House, #312
176 West 45th
Manhattan, NY 10036^R
Joe^R
(212) 687-1203^R
^E                        .
===========================================================================
Rosanne Jacobsen^R
555 Lafayette Ave.
                                          Doc 2 Pg 1 Ln 1" Pos 1"
( ▲    ▲    ▲    ▲    ▲    ▲    ▲    ▲    ▲    ▲ ) ▲    ▲    ▲
------------------------ Sort Secondary Merge File -----------------------

Key Typ Field Line Word    Key Typ Field Line Word    Key Typ Field Line Word
 1   a    1     1   -1      2   a    1     1    1       3
 4                          5                           6
 7                          8                           9
Select
keyg=boston + keyg=manhattan_

Action                     Order                      Type
Sort                       Ascending                  Merge sort

▲ +(OR), *(AND), =, <>, >, <, >=, <=;  Press Exit when done
```

For a detailed explanation of all the select symbols, turn to the WordPerfect reference manual.

34 Select Keys (3), and then enter the following for key1 to sort the selected records by ZIP code:

a 2 -1 -1

35 Press **Right Arrow** (→) to move to key2, and then press **Delete to End of Line** (Ctrl-End) to erase the key information (the "a" will still be there).

36 Press **Exit** (F7) to save key1.

The settings below the keys should now read "Select and sort" for the Action, "Ascending" for the Order, and "Merge sort" for the Type of Sort.

37 Select Perform Action (1) to begin selecting and sorting the records.

When the selecting and sorting is completed, you should have the records for Kathleen O'Hara and Joseph Corrales, Jr. on the screen, with Kathleen's record before Joseph's.

```
Kathleen O'Hara˜R
678 Forestvale Road
Boston, MA 02136˜R
Kathy˜R
(617) 789-2027˜R
˜E
===================================================================================
Joseph Corrales, Jr.˜R
Kensington House, #312
176 West 45th
Manhattan, NY 10036˜R
Joe˜R
(212) 687-1203˜R
˜E
===================================================================================
_




                                        Doc 1 Pg 3 Ln 1" Pos 1"
```

38 Press **Exit** (F7) and type **n** twice to clear the screen.

Sorting and selecting increases the efficiency of mass mailings. After using Sort a few times, you'll begin to see a variety of ways in which sorting can help you at the office or at home.

During this lesson, you were introduced to the following tasks:

- Creating a key for sorting.
- Selecting records from a secondary merge file (global).
- Sorting in descending order.
- Sorting from the screen to a file (and vice versa).

For a complete listing of all tasks introduced in the lessons, turn to *Feature Summary* at the end of the workbook.

Lesson 27: Special Techniques

Now that you have completed *Merging Documents*, we'd like to take a moment to give you some insights and special techniques that many people have found to be valuable when automating the process of creating and printing documents.

While not all the special methods discussed below are included in *Feature Summary* at the end of the workbook, you can find them listed in the index.

Auto-Incrementing Numbers

Forms such as checks and invoices are often numbered in sequence to help when filing and locating the form. If you are merging a form with a secondary file, you can have WordPerfect automatically insert numbers in the correct sequence by including a paragraph number in the secondary file.

Paragraph numbers automatically update sequentially, and can be defined to start at any number. By including a paragraph number as a field in the secondary file, and defining the starting number after merging is completed, the merged forms will be numbered in the correct order.

For example, the invoice form used in Lessons 16 and 25 has a place for an invoice number.

 INVOICE NUMBER

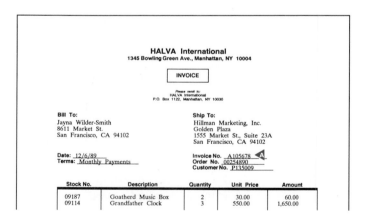

Adding Paragraph Numbers to the Secondary File

Let's add a paragraph number to three of the records in the secondary file (Customer.wkb), insert the field number in the primary file (Invoice.wkb), and then merge the files to number the invoices.

1 Press **Retrieve** (Shift-F10) and enter **customer.wkb** to retrieve the secondary file.

2 Press **Page Down** (PgDn) and then **Up Arrow** (↑) to place the cursor before the ^E merge code at the end of the first record.

3 Type **F** to begin each invoice number with an "F."

4 Press **Date/Outline** (Shift-F5), select Paragraph Number (5), and then enter **1** to insert a paragraph number.

The number that is inserted and the style of numbering will be changed after you merge the invoices.

5 Press **Merge R** (F9) to end the field.

By using steps 3 through 5 as a guide, you can add a paragraph number field to the next two records. When you finish,

6 Press **Home** twice and then **Up Arrow** (↓) to move to the beginning of the records.

The first three records should look similar to the following screen.

```
Robin Pierce^R
InterChange, Inc.
544 Westminster Circle NW
Atlanta, GA 30327^R
Robin^R
(404) 359-2828^R
FI.^R
^E
=========================================================================
Jayna Wilder-Smith^R
8611 Market St.
San Francisco, CA 94102^R
Jayna^R
(415) 987-4598^R
FII.^R
^E
=========================================================================
Anna Lee Pierce^R
P.O. Box 1392
Central Park Station
Buffalo, NY 14215^R
Anna^R
(716) 453-5678^R
FIII.^R
C:\WP50\LEARN\CUSTOMER.WKB                    Doc 1 Pg 1 Ln 1" Pos 1"
```

7 Press **Page Down** (PgDn) three times to place the cursor at the beginning of the fourth record.

8 Press **Block** (Alt-F4) and then press Home twice and **Down Arrow** (↓) twice to highlight records 4 through 11.

9 Press **Backspace** and then type **y** to delete the records.

10 Press **Exit** (F7), type **y**, and then enter **customer.3** to create a new file for the customer records.

11 Type **n** to clear the screen.

Adding a ^F Merge Code to the Primary File

Now that the secondary file is ready, let's create a primary file that inserts the paragraph number during a merge.

12 Press **Retrieve** (Shift-F10) and enter **invoice.wkb** to retrieve the information document for the invoice.

13 Press **Page Down** (PgDn) and then press **Up Arrow** (↑) twice to place the cursor below the Invoice No. comment.

14 Press **Merge Codes** (Shift-F9), type **f**, and then enter **5** to insert ^F5^ for the paragraph number.

After inserting the ^F merge code, your document should look like the one illustrated below.

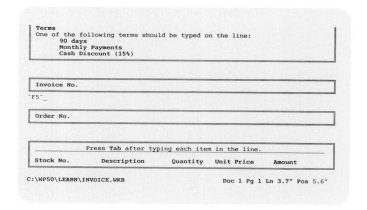

15 Press **Exit** (F7), type **y**, and then enter **invoice.3** to create a new primary file.

16 Type **n** to clear the screen.

Merging the Paragraph Numbers

With the primary and secondary files created, you are ready to begin merging.

17 Press **Merge/Sort** (Ctrl-F9), select Merge (1), enter **invoice.3** for the primary file, and then enter **customer.3** for the secondary file.

When the merge is completed, you should see the third invoice on your screen with a paragraph number inserted.

```
Terms
One of the following terms should be typed on the line:
        90 days
        Monthly Payments
        Cash Discount (15%)


Invoice No.

FIII.

Order No.


        Press Tab after typing each item in the line.

Stock No.      Description       Quantity   Unit Price    Amount


—                                  Doc 1 Pg 3 Ln 4.75" Pos 1.2"
```

Defining the Paragraph Numbers

Assuming that the first invoice number needs to be "F950," let's move to the beginning of the merged invoices and define the style and starting number.

18 Press **Home** three times and then **Up Arrow** (↑) to place the cursor at the beginning of the merged invoices.

19 Press **Date/Outline** (Shift-F5) and then select Define (6).

20 Select Starting Paragraph Number (1) and then enter **950** for the number of the first invoice.

The first digit of the starting number cannot be zero (0), and the highest number allowed is 65535.

21 Select User-defined (6) and then enter **1** to use digits without punctuation for the numbering style.

22 Press **Exit** (F7) three times to return to the merged invoices.

23 Press **Home** twice and then **Down Arrow** (↓) to display the last invoice.

Notice that the invoice number for the third invoice is "F952."

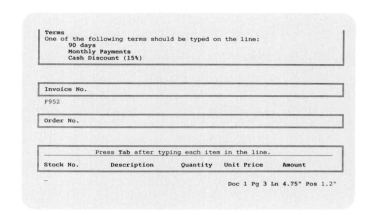

```
Terms
One of the following terms should be typed on the line:
       90 days
       Monthly Payments
       Cash Discount (15%)


Invoice No.

F952

Order No.


           Press Tab after typing each item in the line.
Stock No.        Description      Quantity   Unit Price     Amount

-                                      Doc 1 Pg 3 Ln 4.75" Pos 1.2"
```

Now that you have tried using Paragraph Numbers in a secondary file, you may want to try merging other features from a secondary file. However, remember to limit the secondary file to only those features that will be used frequently.

Form Types

Whenever you select a paper size from the Page Format menu, you are also asked to select a paper type.

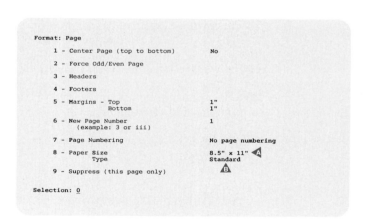

A PAPER SIZE
B PAPER TYPE

```
Format: Page

       1 - Center Page (top to bottom)         No

       2 - Force Odd/Even Page

       3 - Headers

       4 - Footers

       5 - Margins - Top                       1"
                     Bottom                    1"

       6 - New Page Number                     1
           (example: 3 or iii)

       7 - Page Numbering                      No page numbering

       8 - Paper Size                          8.5" x 11"
           Type                                Standard

       9 - Suppress (this page only)

Selection: 0
```

By selecting a type, you are asking WordPerfect to check for the name (standard, envelope, label, etc.) in a list of types that have already been set up for your printer.

The list can be seen when editing the information for a selected printer.

1 Press **Print** (Shift-F7) and type **s** to select a printer.

2 Highlight the name of your printer, and then select Edit (3) to display a menu of information about the printer.

For example, the menu for the Standard Printer is illustrated below.

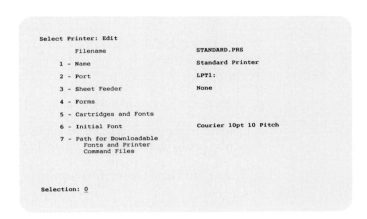

```
Select Printer: Edit

                Filename              STANDARD.PRS

        1 - Name                      Standard Printer

        2 - Port                      LPT1:

        3 - Sheet Feeder              None

        4 - Forms

        5 - Cartridges and Fonts

        6 - Initial Font              Courier 10pt 10 Pitch

        7 - Path for Downloadable
            Fonts and Printer
            Command Files



    Selection: 0
```

3 Select Forms (4) to display the list of form types set up for the Standard Printer.

A list of forms appears with the first form highlighted in the list. Unless you have already created other form types, there may only be a Standard (and possibly an Envelope) form type in the list.

A HIGHLIGHTED FORM

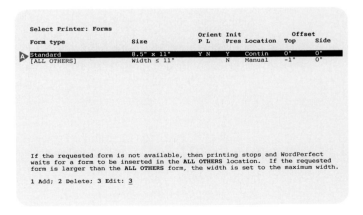

```
Select Printer: Forms
                                      Orient Init            Offset
    Form type            Size         P L    Pres Location  Top    Side

►   Standard             8.5" x 11"   Y N    Y    Contin    0"     0"
    [ALL OTHERS]         Width ≤ 11"       N Manual   -1"    0"






If the requested form is not available, then printing stops and WordPerfect
waits for a form to be inserted in the ALL OTHERS location.  If the requested
form is larger than the ALL OTHERS form, the width is set to the maximum width.

1 Add; 2 Delete; 3 Edit: 3
```

Notice that the form type (Standard) and the form size (8.5" x 11") match the options listed in the paper size and type menus. When you select a type, WordPerfect looks for it in the list. If it is not there, then the closest match is used for the type.

For example, after selecting "Envelope" in the Envelopes and Labels lesson (22), WordPerfect looked through the form types list for "Envelope". If "Envelope" was found, then you saw "Envelope" displayed in the Page Format menu. Otherwise, the Standard form type was selected and displayed with an asterisk (*) noting that the form was not available.

While in the list of forms, let's try adding a form type for envelopes. If one already exists, then you may want to try the same steps, but create one for labels.

4   Select Add (1) to add a form to the list.

A menu of paper types appears on your screen, exactly like the menu displayed when you select Paper Size/Type from the Page Format menu.

5   Select Envelope (5) for the form type.

The definition menu displayed lists all the preset information for the Envelope form type.

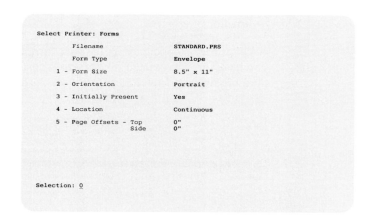

```
Select Printer: Forms

           Filename                STANDARD.PRS

           Form Type               Envelope

      1 - Form Size                8.5" x 11"

      2 - Orientation              Portrait

      3 - Initially Present        Yes

      4 - Location                 Continuous

      5 - Page Offsets - Top       0"
                        Side       0"




Selection: 0
```

6   Select Form Size (1), and then select Envelope (5) to indicate a standard 9.5" x 4" legal business envelope.

If you are setting up a form type for labels, you will need to select Other (O) and enter the width and height of the label.

You are returned to the definition menu to edit the rest of the information. Orientation refers to the way the envelope is inserted into the printer. For most printers, the envelope is fed in the same way as a normal sheet of paper, and "Portrait" is the correct setting. However, most laser printers use the "Landscape" setting.

Assuming that you will be inserting the envelope before sending an address to the printer, the "Yes" setting for Initially Present is correct. If you are inserting the envelope into the printer *after* sending the address, then you should select "Manual" (in most cases) for the location.

7 Select Location (4), and then select Manual (3).

The page offsets let you make adjustments to the top and side of the envelope in case the printer is not allowing for the correct margin spacing.

8 Press **Exit** (F7) to return to the list of forms.

You should have a form for an envelope (or label) added to the list. Now, whenever you select Envelope from the Page Size/Form menus, WordPerfect will use the information for "Envelope" in the list to help with the printing of your envelope.

9 Press **Exit** (F7) four times to return to the document screen.

The possibilities for setting up form types are quite varied. You can set up a type for each form listed, create your own form types, or even have several types set up for the same form. For details on creating and using form types, turn to Forms in the WordPerfect reference manual.

Multiple-Column Labels

Labels for printing are available in 8.5" x 11" sheets that can be fed continuously through a printer (e.g., dot matrix, daisy wheel), fed from a sheet feeder bin, or fed a sheet at a time through a laser printer. The labels fill the sheet and are usually two or three across.

You can set up a merge to automatically create addresses for the 8.5" x 11" sheets by using a primary and secondary file and Text Columns. However, the primary file for continuous forms and sheet feeder bins is different from that used for a laser printer.

Continuous Forms and Sheet Feeder Bins

The primary file for continuous forms or a sheet feeder bin simply contains the ^F codes to merge the address. For example, the primary file for the customer records ("Labela.wkb" file) contains a ^F1^ and ^F2^ code.

All you need to do is merge the primary file with the secondary file, and then set Text Columns to place the labels across the page.

1 Press **Merge/Sort** (Ctrl-F9) and select Merge (1).

2 Enter **labela.wkb** for the primary file, and then enter **customer.wkb** for the secondary file.

3 Press **Home** twice and then **Up Arrow** (↑) when the merge is completed to move to the beginning of the addresses.

There should be a page break between each address on your screen.

A PAGE BREAK

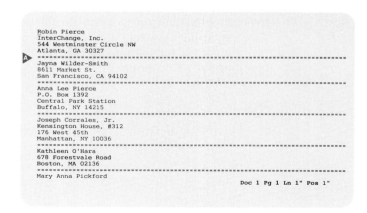

You can now set Text Columns to place the addresses across the page for printing in multiple columns. For example, let's set the columns to print on 1" x 2 3/4" standard labels. The labels are placed in rows of three across the page, so three columns need to be defined.

4 Press **Math/Columns** (Alt-F7) and select Column Define (4).

5 Select Number of Columns (2) and enter **3** to place three labels across the page.

6 Select Distance Between Columns (3) and enter **0** to give the maximum room possible for each line of an address.

WordPerfect calculates the margins for each column. However, the margins need to be adjusted for printing labels. If you start the first left margin at .25 inches, then add 2.75" for each label, the addresses should print on the labels correctly.

7 Select Margins (4) to enter margins for each column.

8 Enter **.25** for the left margin and **3** for the right margin of the first column.

9 Enter **3** for the left margin and **5.75** for the right margin of the second column.

10 Enter **5.75** for the left margin and **8.5** for the right margin of the third column.

The settings on your Column Definition menu should match those illustrated below.

```
Text Column Definition

     1 - Type                              Newspaper

     2 - Number of Columns                 3

     3 - Distance Between Columns          0"

     4 - Margins

     Column   Left    Right    Column    Left     Right
       1:     0.25"   3"         13:
       2:     3"      5.75"      14:
       3:     5.75"   8.5"       15:
       4:                        16:
       5:                        17:
       6:                        18:
       7:                        19:
       8:                        20:
       9:                        21:
      10:                        22:
      11:                        23:
      12:                        24:

Selection: 0
```

11 Press **Exit** (F7) to save the settings, and then select Column On/Off (3).

12 Press **Home** twice and then **Down Arrow** (↓) to place the addresses in columns.

13 Press **Home** twice and then **Up Arrow** (↑) to return to the beginning of the addresses.

The labels are now displayed three across the page with a hard page break between each set of three.

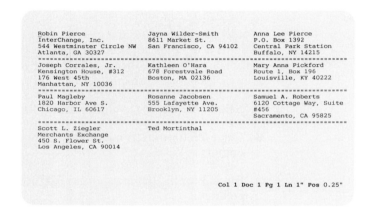

```
Robin Pierce            Jayna Wilder-Smith       Anna Lee Pierce
InterChange, Inc.       8611 Market St.          P.O. Box 1392
544 Westminster Circle NW  San Francisco, CA 94102  Central Park Station
Atlanta, GA 30327                                Buffalo, NY 14215
============================================================================
Joseph Corrales, Jr.    Kathleen O'Hara          Mary Anna Pickford
Kensington House, #312   678 Forestvale Road      Route 1, Box 196
176 West 45th           Boston, MA 02136         Louisville, KY 40222
Manhattan, NY 10036
============================================================================
Paul Magleby            Rosanne Jacobsen         Samuel A. Roberts
1820 Harbor Ave S.      555 Lafayette Ave.       6120 Cottage Way, Suite
Chicago, IL 60617       Brooklyn, NY 11205       #456
                                                 Sacramento, CA 95825
============================================================================
Scott L. Ziegler        Ted Mortinthal
Merchants Exchange
450 S. Flower St.
Los Angeles, CA 90014



                                     Col 1 Doc 1 Pg 1 Ln 1" Pos 0.25"
```

14 Press **Replace** (Alt-F2), type **n**, and then press **Hard Page** (Ctrl-Enter) *twice* to search for any double [HPg] codes.

15 Press ◆**Search** (F2), press **Hard Page** (Ctrl-Enter), and then press ◆**Search** again to replace the double codes with a single [HPg] code.

The addresses are now ready to send to the printer. If you want to print the addresses on your screen, you need to select your own printer before selecting Full Document from the Print menu. After printing,

16 Press **Exit** (F7) and type **n** twice to clear the screen.

Laser printers

Whenever a laser printer receives a hard page break that can be seen on the screen, the printer starts printing on a new sheet of paper. In order to eliminate the visible hard page breaks, the column definition needs to be in the primary file and a set of ^F's in each column to create the labels.

1 Press **Retrieve** (Shift-F10) and enter **labelb.wkb** to retrieve a primary file for laser printers.

The "Labelb.wkb" is ready for you to merge and print labels. While many of the merge codes are not displayed, you can see them in Reveal Codes.

2 Press **Reveal Codes** (Alt-F3) to see the column and formatting codes in the file.

▲ FORMATTING CODES

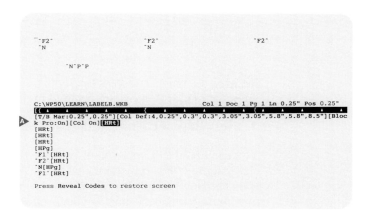

The ^F's in each column insert the addresses, and the ^N's at the end of the file make sure that the address is inserted for the next record in the secondary file. The ^P's (also at the end of the file) simply start the merge over using the same primary file.

The margins are set to .25" for the top and bottom, as a minimum of .25" is required for the margins for most laser printers. The columns are defined as Parallel with Block Protect Columns so that no visible hard page breaks will be placed between the addresses.

Even though there are only three labels across the page, four columns are set. The first column is only .05" wide and is used to make sure there are enough lines available for the longest address.

▲ FIRST COLUMN

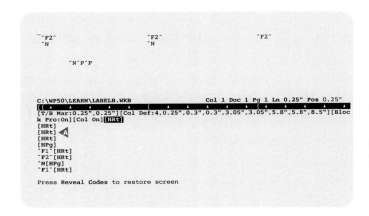

Because the longest address (including the name) in the secondary file is 4 lines, four Hard Returns are inserted into the first column.

3 Press **Reveal Codes** (Alt-F3) to return to the full document screen.

You can edit the "Labelb.wkb" primary file for your own secondary file by changing the ^F's to insert the address (you can have more or fewer ^F's), and changing the number of hard returns in the first column to match the maximum number of lines in your longest address.

Let's merge the primary file with the secondary file, and see what happens.

4 Press **Exit** (F7) and type **n** twice to clear the screen.

5 Press **Merge/Sort** (Ctrl-F9) and select Merge (1).

6 Enter **labelb.wkb** for the primary file, and then enter **customer.wkb** for the secondary file.

7 Press **Home** twice and **Up Arrow** (↑) to move to the beginning of the labels, and then press **Down Arrow** (↓) to rewrite the screen.

```
Robin Pierce
InterChange, Inc.
544 Westminster Circle NW
Atlanta, GA 30327

Joseph Corrales, Jr.
Kensington House, #312
176 West 45th
Manhattan, NY 10036

Paul Magleby
1820 Harbor Ave S.
Chicago, IL 60617


Scott L. Ziegler
Merchants Exchange
450 S. Flower St.
Los Angeles, CA 90014




                                    Col 1 Doc 1 Pg 1 Ln 0.41" Pos 0.25"
```

Now there are no visible hard page breaks, and the file can be sent to a laser printer. If you want to print the merged addresses, you need to select your own printer before selecting Full Document from the Print menu. Otherwise,

8 Press **Exit** (F7) and type **n** twice to clear the screen.

Because the labels are so close on a sheet of 1" x 2 3/4" labels, you may need to make some adjustments to the top and bottom margin settings in the "Labelb.wkb" file to print an address on each label.

Organizing the Keyboard

While automating the process of merging the memo, list, and invoice (Lessons 23-25) you used the Alt-M, Alt-L, and Alt-I macros to merge with a single keystroke.

WordPerfect also provides an impressive Keyboard Layout feature that lets you create and assign a task to *any key* on the keyboard, as well as create several keyboard layouts from which to select when editing in WordPerfect.

1 Press **Setup** (Shift-F1) and select Keyboard Layout (6).

A list of keyboard layouts similar to the following illustration is displayed on your screen.

The list of predefined keyboard layouts may vary, depending on the date your copy of WordPerfect was packaged.

Keyboard layouts can be created to simulate the keystrokes of another software program, the design of another typing system (e.g., AZERTY), or assign the WordPerfect features you use most to more convenient function keys.

Let's create a keyboard layout to organize the merge macros you created in *Merging Documents*.

2 Select Create (4) and then enter **merges** for the name of the file where the keystrokes and tasks will be stored.

A keystroke definition menu is displayed from which you can create and assign tasks to keystrokes. You can also assign macros that have already been created to the Merges keyboard layout.

3 Select Retrieve (6) to retrieve and assign the Alt-I macro (invoice) to the Merge keyboard layout.

A "Key:" message on the status line indicates that WordPerfect wants you to press the key(s) to which you want the macro assigned.

4 Hold down **Ctrl** and type **i** to assign the macro to the Ctrl-I keystroke.

A "Macro:" message on the status line indicates that WordPerfect needs the name of the macro.

5 Enter **alti.wpm** to retrieve the Alt-I macro.

You are returned to the keystroke menu, where the Ctrl-I keystroke now appears in the list.

▲ CTRL-I KEYSTROKE

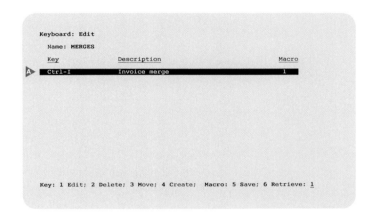

```
Keyboard: Edit
   Name: MERGES

   Key                   Description                          Macro
▶  Ctrl-I                Invoice merge                            1




   Key: 1 Edit; 2 Delete; 3 Move; 4 Create;  Macro: 5 Save; 6 Retrieve: 1
```

While the Alt-I macro is still available, you can press Ctrl-I when using the Merges keyboard layout to start the invoice merge.

If you are using a keyboard layout with tasks assigned to the Alt key, those tasks will be performed instead of the Alt key macros you have created.

Now that you have added the Alt-I macro to the Merges keyboard layout, you can also add the Alt-L and Alt-M macros by using steps 3 through 5 as a guide. Remember that you can assign the macros to any key on the keyboard.

Not only can a macro be assigned to the keyboard layout, but you can also create a task and assign it to a key.

6 Select Create (4) to create a Ctrl-E keystroke that will start the envelope merge from Lesson 22.

7 Hold down **Ctrl** and type **e** to assign the task to the Ctrl-E keystroke.

An editing menu appears that looks similar to the macro editing menu you used in the Lists lesson (24).

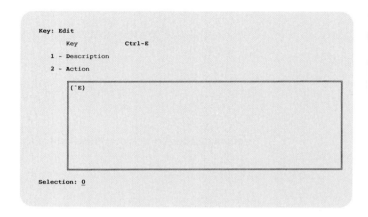

```
Key: Edit
        Key             Ctrl-E
 1 - Description
 2 - Action

     {^E}




Selection: 0
```

You can enter a description that will be displayed in the keystroke menu, and enter the keystrokes for the tasks in the editing window.

8 Select Description (1) and enter **Envelope merge** for the description.

9 Select Action (2) to insert the keystrokes into the editing window.

The {^E} keystroke indicates that the task is assigned to the Ctrl-E keystroke.

10 Press **Right Arrow** (→) to move past the {^E} keystroke, and then press **Enter** to start a new line.

11 Press **Merge/Sort** (Ctrl-F9) and select Merge (1).

Like the macro editing window, you do not see menus or messages to guide you through the keystrokes.

12 Press **Enter** to start a new line.

13 Type **envelope** for the name of the primary file.

14 Press **Macro Define** (Ctrl-F10), press **Enter**, and then press **Macro Define** again to insert an {Enter} keystroke.

15 Press **Enter** to start a new line, and then type **customer.wkb** for the name of the secondary file.

16 Press **Macro Define** (Ctrl-F10), press **Enter**, and then press **Macro Define** again to insert an {Enter} keystroke.

17 Press **Exit** (F7) twice to return to the Keyboard menu.

Now you have at least two keystrokes defined for the Merges keyboard layout.

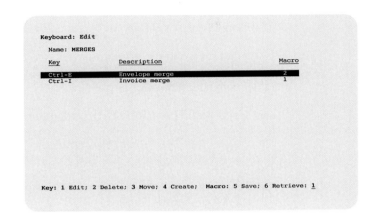

```
Keyboard: Edit

   Name: MERGES

   Key                Description                        Macro
   Ctrl-E             Envelope merge                       2
   Ctrl-I             Invoice merge                        1




   Key: 1 Edit; 2 Delete; 3 Move; 4 Create;  Macro: 5 Save; 6 Retrieve: 1
```

18 Press **Exit** (F7) to return to the list of keyboard layouts.

19 Place the reverse video cursor on the Merges keyboard layout (if it is not already there), and press **Enter** to select the keyboard layout.

20 Press **Exit** (F7) to return to the document screen.

At this point you can use the Ctrl-I or Ctrl-E keystrokes to start a merge for the invoice or the envelope. When you want to return to the original keyboard mapping,

21 Press **Setup** (Shift-F1) and select Keyboard Layout (6).

22 Select Original (6) and then press **Exit** (F7) to return to the document screen.

After creating one keyboard layout, you may now want to create one for you own use, or try using one of the keyboard layouts provided by WordPerfect.

For details on creating and using keyboard layouts, turn to Keyboard Layout in WordPerfect's reference manual.

Merging to the Printer

During a merge, WordPerfect stores all the documents it creates in the computer's memory. If there is not enough room in memory, then temporary files are created on disk to hold the rest of the documents.

If merged documents run into hundreds or thousands, many companies choose to handle a merge by having each document sent to the printer as it is created. This process of merging to the printer saves memory space because only one document (e.g., letter) is in memory at one time. In addition, you can save valuable printer time by merging and printing during off hours (e.g., evenings and weekends).

You can merge to the printer in WordPerfect by simply adding four codes to the end of the primary file. For example, they can be added to the end of the announcement letter.

1 Press **Retrieve** (Shift-F10) and enter **stores.wkb** to retrieve the letter.

2 Press **Page Down** (PgDn) to move to the end of the letter, and then press **Enter** to start a new line.

3 Hold down **Control** (Ctrl) while typing the letters **tnpp** to insert the ^T^N^P^P merge codes.

You can also use Merge Codes (Shift-F9) to insert the same four codes, but it will take a few more keystrokes.

▲ MERGE CODES

```
International retail stores throughout the country.  Stores are
scheduled to open in the following cities during the first
quarter of the year:

      Manhattan, New York          January 18
      Boston, Massachusetts        January 26
      San Francisco, California    February 10
      Los Angeles, California      February 24
      Atlanta, Georgia             March 9
      Chicago, Illinois            March 17

As a preferred customer, you will be receiving a special
invitation, and I personally look forward to meeting you at the
opening.

Sincerely,


Bryan Metcalf
President
HALVA International
^T^N^P^P_ ◀

C:\WP50\LEARN\STORES.WKB                    Doc 1 Pg 1 Ln 5.66" Pos 1.8"
```

The ^T^N^P^P merge codes tell WordPerfect to send the current document to the printer (^T), clear the screen, go to the next record in the secondary file (^N), and then merge the record with the same primary file (^P^P).

Notice that once you begin using merge codes other than the standard ^R, ^E, and ^F, the control of the merge is turned over to you. WordPerfect will not automatically merge with the next record in the secondary file unless you tell it to do so.

While the ^T^N^P^P works well with merging letters and continuous forms, you may want to use a ^G macro with other merges to send the merged document(s) to the printer.

4 Press **Exit** (F7) and type **n** twice to clear the screen.

For references to other applications of Merge in the workbook, turn to Merge in the index.

Summary

During this lesson, you were introduced to the following tasks:

- Adding a keystroke to the keyboard layout.
- Creating a form type.
- Creating a keyboard layout.
- Defining Newspaper and Parallel columns.
- Defing a Paragraph numbering style.
- Inserting a paragraph number.

For a complete listing of all tasks introduced in the lessons, turn to *Feature Summary* at the end of the workbook.

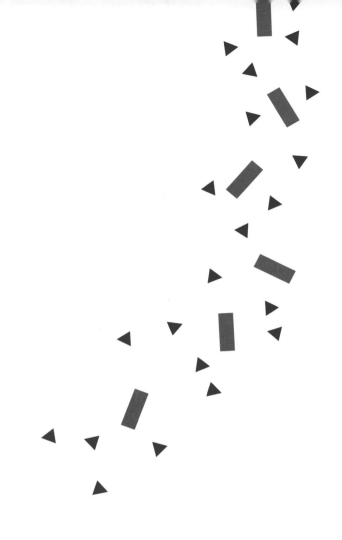

Lesson 28: Financial Statements

Budgets, comparison charts, income statements, and other financial documents are an important part of a company's records. Because they are often included in reports, WordPerfect provides a Math feature that calculates the figures needed for timely and accurate evaluations.

In this lesson you are introduced to a comparison table and an income statement that both use Math. The comparison table is part of a corporate report, while the income statement is kept as a separate document.

The Printed Forms lesson (16) includes an exercise in using Math to calculate an invoice.

Calculating a Total

Before retrieving either statement, let's show you how Math can be used to quickly calculate totals.

1 Press **Math/Columns** (Alt-F7) and select Math On (1).

A "Math" message on the status line indicates that Math is on and ready to calculate a total.

2 Press **Tab**, type **150.00** for the first number, and then press **Enter** to start a new line.

3 Press **Tab**, type **300.00** for the second number, and then press **Enter** to start a new line.

4 Press **Tab** and type a plus sign (+) to have the figures totalled.

Because Math is on, the numbers are automatically aligned at the decimal point, and the plus sign is inserted as a code that actually calculates the

Because the plus sign is a code, it is bolded in the Reveal Codes screen to help you distinguish it from a normal plus sign character.

5 Press **Math/Columns** (Alt-F7) and select Calculate (2) to add the figures.

The calculated total should appear on your screen next to the plus sign.

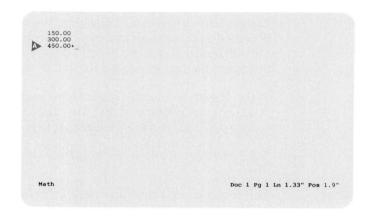

▲ CALCULATED TOTAL

```
150.00
300.00
450.00+_
```

Math   Doc 1 Pg 1 Ln 1.33" Pos 1.9"

Calculating Subtotals

The plus sign is called a *math operator*, and is similar to the plus sign you use on a hand calculator to add numbers. However, it also indicates a subtotal, and can be used with an equal sign (=) to calculate a total.

6 Press **Enter** twice to insert some extra spacing.

7 Press **Tab**, type **75.00** for the first number, and then press **Enter** to start a new line.

8 Press **Tab**, type **25.00** for the second number, and then press **Enter** to start a new line.

9 Press **Tab** and type a plus sign (+) for a subtotal, and then press **Enter** four times to insert some extra spacing.

10 Press **Tab** and type an equal sign (=) for a total.

11 Press **Math/Columns** (Alt-F7) and select Calculate (2) to calculate the two subtotals (+) and the total (=).

The subtotals should appear next to the plus signs, while a total should appear next to the equal sign.

SUBTOTAL
TOTAL

Notice that a subtotal operator (+) only adds the numbers above it to the next subtotal operator. For example, the subtotal of "100" does not include the "150" and "300" at the top of the column. The total operator (=) adds all the subtotals above it to the next total operator. For example, the subtotals of "450" and "100" are added at the equal sign.

Inserting an Extra Subtotal

Whenever you want to insert an extra subtotal, you can type a lowercase "t," and the number is treated exactly like a calculated subtotal.

12 Press **Up Arrow** (↑) twice to place the cursor at the beginning of an empty line above the total operator.

13 Press **Tab** and type **t650.00** to insert an extra subtotal.

14 Press **Math/Columns** (Alt-F7) and select Calculate (2).

Notice that the total has increased by "650," and that WordPerfect automatically inserts a comma into the new total.

 EXTRA SUBTOTAL

 NEW TOTAL

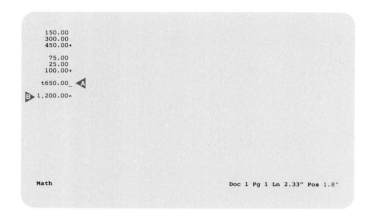

Adjusting the Math Columns

Because tab stops are used for Math columns, you can easily adjust the spacing for the columns by setting new tab stops.

15 Press **Page Up** (PgUp) to place the cursor at the very beginning of the math document.

16 Press **Format** (Shift-F8), select Line (1), and then select Tab Set (8).

17 Press **Delete to End of Line** (Ctrl-End), and then enter **4** to set a tab stop at 4 inches.

18 Press **Exit** (F7) twice to return to the math document.

Your math column should now be displayed close to the center of the screen.

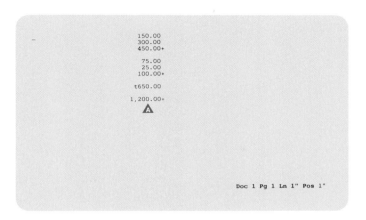

```
                        150.00
                        300.00
                        450.00+

                         75.00
                         25.00
                        100.00+

                       t650.00

                      1,200.00=
                          ▲



                                        Doc 1 Pg 1 Ln 1" Pos 1"
```

Updating the Figures

Whenever a number needs to be updated, simply type the new figure and then calculate.

19 Press **Right Arrow** (→) until the cursor is on the "1" of "150.00."

20 Press **Delete** (Del) three times to erase "150," and then type **25000** for the new number.

21 Press **Math/Columns** (Alt-F7) and select Calculate (2).

Even though you did not type a comma for the "25000," WordPerfect still inserted a comma for you in the first subtotal.

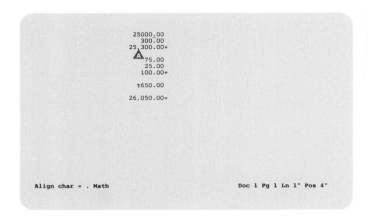

As you can see, one of the major advantages of using Math is that WordPerfect does all the calculating for you. All you need to do is enter the numbers and calculate.

22 Press **Exit** (F7) and type **n** twice to clear the screen.

The comma and period are often reversed (or other characters used) to indicate a decimal point and the thousands separator. Changing these characters can be done from the Other Format menu (Shift-F8,4). For details, turn to the WordPerfect reference manual.

Retrieving the Corporate Report

Now that you have been introduced to some basics of Math, let's see how the feature is used in a report.

23 Press **Retrieve** (Shift-F10) and enter **present.wkb** to retrieve the second part of a corporate report.

24 Press **Page Down** (PgDn) to place the cursor at the top of the second page.

A table is included in the report that compares the operating expenses of the last two quarters of the year.

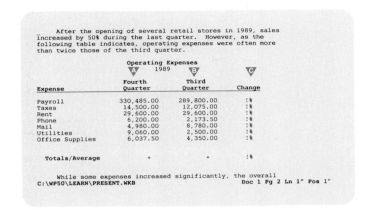
The first column includes figures for the fourth quarter, the second column includes figures for the third quarter, and the third column calculates the change as a percent figure. Because the expense titles (Payroll, Taxes, etc.) are at the left margin, they are not counted as a Math column.

Displaying the Codes

The calculating in the last column is done by setting up a formula in a Math definition.

25 Press ◆**Search** (F2), press **Math/Columns** (Alt-F7), and then select Def (1) to find the Math definition.

26 Press ◆**Search** (F2) to begin the search.

27 Press **Reveal Codes** (Alt-F3) to display the codes for the comparison table.

Notice the codes that are being used to set up Math for the comparison table.

```
increased by 50% during the last quarter.  However, as the
following table indicates, operating expenses were often more
than twice those of the third quarter.

                         Operating Expenses
                               1989

                      Fourth          Third
Expense               Quarter         Quarter        Change

Payroll                  330,485.00      289,800.00       !%
C:\WP50\LEARN\PRESENT.WKB                     Doc 1 Pg 2 Ln 2.83" Pos 1"
[                          ▲               ▲             ]
[BOLD][UND]Expense[Cntr]Quarter[C/A/Flrt][Cntr]Quarter[C/A/Flrt][Cntr]Change[C/A
/Flrt]     [bold][und][HRt]
[HRt]
[Tab Set:0",0.5",3.8",5.3",6.4"][Math Def][Math On]Payroll[Align]330,485[C/A/Flr
t].00[Align]289,800[C/A/Flrt].00[Align][!][C/A/Flrt]%[HRt]
Taxes[Align]14,500[C/A/Flrt].00[Align]12,075[C/A/Flrt].00[Align][!][C/A/Flrt]%[H
Rt]
Rent[Align]29,600[C/A/Flrt].00[Align]29,600[C/A/Flrt].00[Align][!][C/A/Flrt]%[HR
t]
Phone[Align]6,200[C/A/Flrt].00[Align]2,173[C/A/Flrt].50[Align][!][C/A/Flrt]%[HRt

Press Reveal Codes to restore screen
```

The tab code sets the spacing for the three columns, the Math definition code includes the formula, and the Math On code activates the Math feature for inserting numbers, operators, and calculating.

A Math Off code (not displayed) is inserted at the beginning of the paragraph below the comparison table. By turning Math on and off you can keep the special features of Math limited to the area between the on and off codes.

Displaying the Math Definition

You can see the formula by selecting Math Define from the Math/Columns menu.

28 Press **Math/Columns** (Alt-F7) and select Math Define (2) to display the Math definition menu.

The menu includes options for defining columns by type, negative number display, and digits to the right of the decimal point. You can define up to 24 columns (A-X).

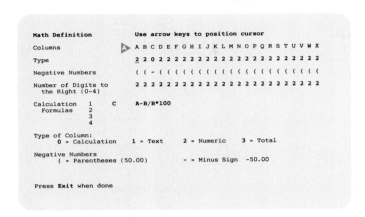

▲ TWENTY-FOUR COLUMNS

When you first start WordPerfect, all columns are already set for the numeric type. As soon as you turn on Math (as you did at the beginning of the lesson), you can enter numbers and operators to begin calculating subtotals and totals.

However, if you want to create a formula that calculates the numbers in one or more of the columns, you need to define a column for calculating, and then create a formula. For example, column C is defined as a calculation column.

🄰 CALCULATION COLUMN

🄱 FORMULA

```
Math Definition          Use arrow keys to position cursor

Columns                  A B C D E F G H I J K L M N O P Q R S T U V W X

Type                     2 2 0 2 2 2 2 2 2 2 2 2 2 2 2 2 2 2 2 2 2 2 2 2

Negative Numbers         ( ( 🄰 ( ( ( ( ( ( ( ( ( ( ( ( ( ( ( ( ( ( ( ( (

Number of Digits to      2 2 2 2 2 2 2 2 2 2 2 2 2 2 2 2 2 2 2 2 2 2 2 2
  the Right (0-4)

Calculation   1    C     A-B/B*100
  Formulas    2
              3
              4

Type of Column:
     0 = Calculation    1 = Text     2 = Numeric    3 = Total

Negative Numbers 🄱
     ( = Parentheses (50.00)         - = Minus Sign  -50.00


Press Exit when done
```

The formula subtracts the third quarter figure (Column B) from the fourth quarter figure (Column A), and then divides the result by the third quarter figure (Column B) to calculate the percentage.

The Printed Forms lesson (16) includes an exercise in creating a Math formula.

Editing the Math Definition

Notice that the number of digits to the right of the decimal point is set to "2" for the calculation column. Negative numbers in the column are also set to be displayed with a minus sign (-) instead of parenthesis.

⚠ DIGITS TO RIGHT OF DECIMAL POINT

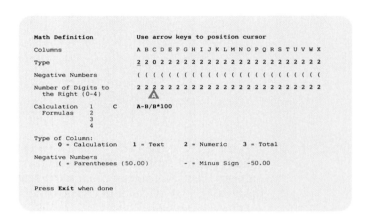

To display the calculated percentages as a whole number, you need to set the number of digits to zero.

29 Place the cursor on the "2" below Column C in the menu.

30 Type **0** to display the percentages as whole numbers.

31 Press **Exit** (F7) twice to return to the comparison table.

Notice that there are *two* math definition codes displayed in the Reveal Codes screen.

```
increased by 50% during the last quarter.  However, as the
following table indicates, operating expenses were often more
than twice those of the third quarter.

                    Operating Expenses
                          1989

                   Fourth         Third
                   Quarter        Quarter        Change
Expense

Payroll             330,485.00    289,800.00        !%
C:\WP50\LEARN\PRESENT.WKB                      Doc 1 Pg 2 Ln 2.83" Pos 1"
[                         ▲             ▲             ▲        ]
[BOLD][UND]Expense[Cntr]Quarter[C/A/Flrt][Cntr]Quarter[C/A/Flrt][Cntr]Change[C/A
/Flrt]    [bold][und][HRt]
[HRt]
[Tab Set:0",0.5",3.8",5.3",6.4"][Math Def][Math Def][Math On]Payroll[Align]330,4
85[C/A/Flrt].00[Align]289,800[C/A/Flr▲].00[Align▲[!][C/A/Flrt]%[HRt]
Taxes[Align]14,500[C/A/Flrt].00[Align▲2,075[C/▲Flrt].00[Align][!][C/A/Flrt]%[H
Rt]
Rent[Align]29,600[C/A/Flrt].00[Align]29,600[C/A/Flrt].00[Align][!][C/A/Flrt]%[HR
t]
Phone[Align]6,200[C/A/Flrt].00[Align]2,173[C/A/Flrt].50[Align][!][C/A/Flrt]%[HRt

Press Reveal Codes to restore screen
```

Whenever you edit the settings in the Math definition menu, a new Math definition is inserted into your document. As with all formatting codes, it is a good idea to erase the original code before you continue editing.

32 Place the cursor on the first (original) Math Definition code, and press **Delete** (Del) to erase the code.

Math can be turned on and off as many times as you want in a document using the same Math definition. However, the on and off codes need to come *after* the definition code for the definition to be used by WordPerfect.

33 Press **Reveal Codes** (Alt-F3) to display the full document screen.

34 Press **Right Arrow** (→) until the "Math" message is displayed on the status line.

Calculating the Table

The "Math" message indicates that the cursor has moved past the Math On code, and WordPerfect is ready to calculate the formulas and subtotals. In fact, the Calculate option only appears on the Math/Columns menu when the "Math" message is displayed.

35 Press **Math/Columns** (Alt-F7) and select Calculate (2).

The formulas and subtotals are calculated and displayed on your screen.

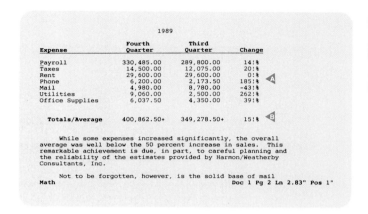

▲ FORMULAS

▲ SUBTOTALS

```
                               1989

                         Fourth        Third
Expense                  Quarter       Quarter      Change

Payroll                330,485.00    289,800.00      14!%
Taxes                   14,500.00     12,075.00      20!%
Rent                    29,600.00     29,600.00       0!%
Phone                    6,200.00      2,173.50     185!%   ◄▲
Mail                     4,980.00      8,780.00     -43!%
Utilities                9,060.00      2,500.00     262!%
Office Supplies          6,037.50      4,350.00      39!%


  Totals/Average       400,862.50+   349,278.50+     15!%   ◄▲

     While some expenses increased significantly, the overall
average was well below the 50 percent increase in sales.  This
remarkable achievement is due, in part, to careful planning and
the reliability of the estimates provided by Harmon/Weatherby
Consultants, Inc.

     Not to be forgotten, however, is the solid base of mail
Math                                   Doc 1 Pg 2 Ln 2.83" Pos 1"
```

Notice that the formulas calculated *across* the columns, while the subtotals calculated *down* the columns. The formula being used for Payroll is the same formula being used for Taxes, Rent, etc. Although you can only create one formula for a calculation column, you can define up to four calculation columns—each with its own formula.

The Mail percentage figure is displayed with a minus sign, which indicates that it is a negative number. You can change the display of calculated negative numbers to parenthesis sign in the Math Definition menu.

Editing the Table

Once you have the columns defined, you can quickly insert or delete items from the math document.

36 Place the cursor on the "T" in the "Taxes" title.

37 Press **Delete to End of Line** (Ctrl-End), and then press **Delete** (Del) to erase the empty line.

38 Place the cursor on the "Office Supplies" title, press **End**, and then press **Enter** to insert a new line.

39 Type **Miscellaneous** for the title of a new expense category.

40 Press **Tab** and type **16,760.00** for the fourth quarter figure, and then press **Tab** and type **3,480.00** for the third quarter figure.

41 Press **Tab** to move to the last column.

WordPerfect inserts a formula operator (!) to indicate that the percentage formula will be calculated for miscellaneous expenses.

If you do not want a formula calculated in a column, then simply erase the formula operator.

42 Press **End** to place the cursor at the very end of the line (beyond the alignment codes).

43 Type **%** to have a percent sign added to the calculated figure.

If you want to add a character to a calculated figure, it should be placed *outside* the alignment codes, or the character may not be displayed correctly.

Calculating the Table

You are now ready to calculate the comparison table for the final time.

44 Press **Math/Columns** (Alt-F7) and select Calculate (2).

A NEW FORMULA RESULTS
B NEW SUBTOTALS

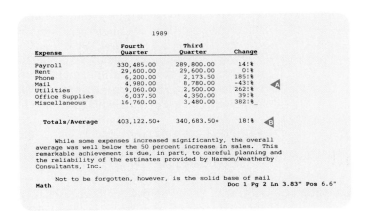

If you want to print the table, make sure that you select your own printer before selecting Full Document. While the operators are displayed on the screen for your convenience, they will not be printed.

45 Press **Exit** (F7) and type **n** twice to clear the screen.

Retrieving the Income Statement

While Math can be included as part of a document, there are times when you may want to create an entire document using Math. For example, an income statement is often created and printed as a separate document.

46 Press **Retrieve** (Shift-F10) and enter **income.wkb** to retrieve an income statement.

Text, Numeric, and Total Columns

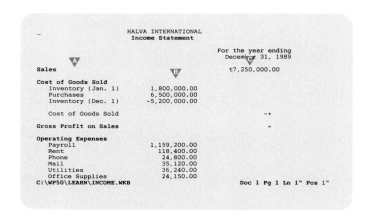

A TEXT COLUMN

B NUMERIC COLUMN

C TOTAL COLUMN

The income statement is defined using three different types of columns.

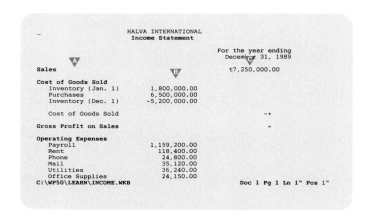

The *text* column is used for typing the unbolded titles (Inventory, Purchases, etc.) and the *numeric* column is used for entering numbers.

The *total* column is a special type designed especially for accounting documents like the income statement. Subtotal operators (+) in the total column calculate numbers *from the column* to the left. The calculated subtotal figures are then displayed in the total column.

47 Press **Down Arrow** (↓) until the "Math" message is displayed at the bottom of the screen, and then press **Math/Columns** (Alt-F7) and select Calculate (2).

Negative Values and Grand Totals

A INVENTORY AND PURCHASE NUMBERS

B SUBTOTAL

Although the inventory and purchases numbers are entered in column B, the subtotal (cost of goods sold) is calculated in column C.

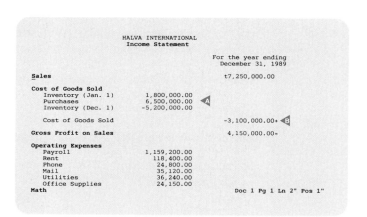

A negative sign is used whenever a number (like the Dec. 1 inventory) needs to be subtracted from the calculation. However, unlike the percent sign in the comparison table, the negative sign needs to be placed between the Alignment codes for the calculating to work correctly.

48 Press **Page Down** (PgDn) to display the lower half of the income statement.

Notice that a grand total operator (*) is being used to calculate the net profit figure.

A GRAND TOTAL OPERATOR

```
Cost of Goods Sold
   Inventory (Jan. 1)      1,800,000.00
   Purchases               6,500,000.00
   Inventory (Dec. 1)     -5,200,000.00

   Cost of Goods Sold                        -3,100,000.00+

Gross Profit on Sales                         4,150,000.00=_

Operating Expenses
   Payroll                 1,159,200.00
   Rent                      118,400.00
   Phone                      24,800.00
   Mail                       35,120.00
   Utilities                  36,240.00
   Office Supplies            24,150.00
   Miscellaneous              67,040.00

   Total Expenses                            -1,464,950.00+

Net Profit (before taxes)                     4,150,000.00*   ◄A


Math                                      Doc 1 Pg 1 Ln 5.66" Pos 7.3"
```

The grand total operator simply adds all the total figures above it to the next grand total operator. The net profit is calculated by subtracting the total expenses from the gross profit. However, notice that even though a negative sign is being used with the total expenses figure, the figure is not being subtracted from the gross profit on sales.

A NEGATIVE TOTAL EXPENSES FIGURE
B CALCULATED GRAND TOTAL

```
Cost of Goods Sold
   Inventory (Jan. 1)      1,800,000.00
   Purchases               6,500,000.00
   Inventory (Dec. 1)     -5,200,000.00

   Cost of Goods Sold                        -3,100,000.00+

Gross Profit on Sales                         4,150,000.00=_

Operating Expenses
   Payroll                 1,159,200.00
   Rent                      118,400.00
   Phone                      24,800.00
   Mail                       35,120.00
   Utilities                  36,240.00
   Office Supplies            24,150.00
   Miscellaneous              67,040.00

   Total Expenses                            -1,464,950.00+ ◄A

Net Profit (before taxes)                     4,150,000.00* ◄B


Math                                      Doc 1 Pg 1 Ln 5.66" Pos 7.3"
```

Because the plus sign (+) to the right of the total expenses figure indicates a subtotal, and the grand total only adds totals (=), the total expenses figure is being ignored.

Extra Total Figures

This situation can be quickly corrected by deleting the plus sign, and typing a "T" next to the total expenses figure. The "T" identifies the total expense figure as a total.

49 Press **Up Arrow** (↑) twice to place the cursor to the right of the plus sign.

50 Press **Backspace** to delete the plus sign.

51 Press **Word Left** (Ctrl-Left Arrow) and then **Right Arrow** (→) to place the cursor on the "1".

52 Type **T** to indicate that the figure is a total.

The "T" should be inserted between the negative sign and the first "1" of the figure.

▲ "T" FOR EXTRA TOTAL

```
Cost of Goods Sold
    Inventory (Jan. 1)        1,800,000.00
    Purchases                 6,500,000.00
    Inventory (Dec. 1)       -5,200,000.00

    Cost of Goods Sold                        -3,100,000.00+

Gross Profit on Sales                          4,150,000.00=

Operating Expenses
    Payroll                   1,159,200.00
    Rent                        118,400.00
    Phone                        24,800.00
    Mail                         35,120.00
    Utilities                    36,240.00
    Office Supplies              24,150.00
    Miscellaneous                67,040.00

    Total Expenses                            -T1,464,950.00

Net Profit (before taxes)               ▲     ,150,000.00*


Align char = . Math                     Doc 1 Pg 1 Ln 5.33" Pos 6"
```

53 Press **Math/Columns** (Alt-F7) and select Calculate (2).

The recalculated net profit should now include the total expense figure.

△ RECALCULATED GRAND TOTAL

```
Sales                                        t7,250,000.00

Cost of Goods Sold
    Inventory (Jan. 1)      1,800,000.00
    Purchases               6,500,000.00
    Inventory (Dec. 1)     -5,200,000.00

    Cost of Goods Sold                       -3,100,000.00+

Gross Profit on Sales                         4,150,000.00=

Operating Expenses
    Payroll                 1,159,200.00
    Rent                      118,400.00
    Phone                      24,800.00
    Mail                       35,120.00
    Utilities                  36,240.00
    Office Supplies            24,150.00
    Miscellaneous              67,040.00

    Total Expenses                           -T1,464,950.00  ◁

Net Profit (before taxes)                     2,685,050.00*  ◁
Align char = . Math                          Doc 1 Pg 1 Ln 5.33" Pos 6"
```

Recalculating the Subtotal

Whenever you want the total expenses subtotal recalculated, all you need to do is erase the line (except the title) and insert a new negative sign and subtotal operator.

54 Press **Left Arrow** (←) until the cursor is on the space immediately after the "s" in the "Total Expenses" title.

55 Press **Delete to End of Line** (Ctrl-End) to clear the line.

56 Press **Tab** twice to move to the last column, and then type a negative sign (-) followed by a plus sign (+) for the subtotal operator.

The negative sign and subtotal operator should be in place for calculating the total expenses figure.

△ NEGATIVE SIGN AND SUBTOTAL
   OPERATOR

```
Sales                                        t7,250,000.00

Cost of Goods Sold
    Inventory (Jan. 1)      1,800,000.00
    Purchases               6,500,000.00
    Inventory (Dec. 1)     -5,200,000.00

    Cost of Goods Sold                       -3,100,000.00+

Gross Profit on Sales                         4,150,000.00=

Operating Expenses
    Payroll                 1,159,200.00
    Rent                      118,400.00
    Phone                      24,800.00
    Mail                       35,120.00
    Utilities                  36,240.00
    Office Supplies            24,150.00
    Miscellaneous              67,040.00

    Total Expenses                           ▷-+_

Net Profit (before taxes)                     2,685,050.00*
Math                                         Doc 1 Pg 1 Ln 5.33" Pos 7.1"
```

57 Press **Math/Columns** (Alt-F7) and select Calculate (2).

The subtotal is calculated and can be used to update the grand total by erasing the "+" and inserting a "T" again between the minus sign and the number.

58 Press **Exit** (F7) and type **n** twice to clear the screen.

While there are limitations to Math in WordPerfect, there are many features which make it ideal for calculating documents such as the comparison table and the income statement. For details on Math, turn to Math in the WordPerfect reference manual.

Summary

During this lesson, you were introduced to the following tasks:

- Calculating totals.
- Defining Math columns.
- Searching for text and codes.

For a complete listing of all tasks introduced in the lessons, turn to *Feature Summary* at the end of the workbook.

Lesson 29: Legal Documents

While the required format of legal documents varies from one office to another (and from one court to another), the demands of accuracy, content, and organization are rigorous. WordPerfect helps you meet these demands by providing powerful features for formatting and assembling documents.

Retrieving the Legal Brief

A *brief* is an argument written by an attorney that lists the legal issues of a case. Some briefs are long and include a table of contents and table of authorities. Other briefs may be short and include the basic points of the case.

The tutorial in your Learn directory (or on your Learning diskette) includes a lesson on WordPerfect's Table of Authorities feature. For an exercise that includes WordPerfect's Table of Contents feature, turn to the Reports lesson in Special Applications.

1 Press **Retrieve** (Shift-F10) and enter **brief.wkb** to retrieve a legal brief.

Setting the Line Numbering

The brief includes a title page and four pages of text. Because the lines on all pages of the brief are usually numbered in the left margin, WordPerfect includes a Line Numbering feature that takes care of the numbering for you.

2 Press **Format** (Shift-F8), select Line (1), and then select Line Numbering (5) and type **y** for yes.

The menu displayed on your screen includes options for positioning and setting the line numbers.

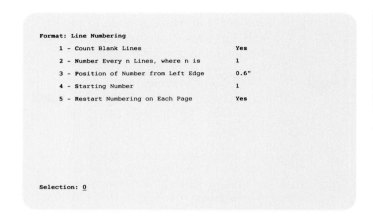

```
Format: Line Numbering
     1 - Count Blank Lines                          Yes
     2 - Number Every n Lines, where n is           1
     3 - Position of Number from Left Edge          0.6"
     4 - Starting Number                            1
     5 - Restart Numbering on Each Page             Yes




Selection: 0
```

3 Select Number Every n Lines (2) and enter **2** to have WordPerfect number every other line.

4 Press **Exit** (F7) twice to return to the legal brief.

Line Numbering is now set for numbering every other line, .6 inches from the left edge of the page, with the numbering restarting on each page.

5 Press **Print** (Shift-F7) and select View Document (6) to see the line numbering.

The page on your screen is the title page, and includes numbering down the left margin for every other line.

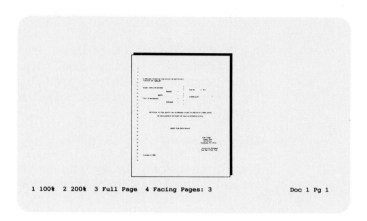

6 Press **Page Down** (PgDn) to display the first page of the brief contents.

The first page of the brief also includes much of the information displayed on the title page. Although the numbering starts over on the first page of the brief, you may want the numbering to continue on the second, third, and fourth pages *without* starting over.

7 Press **Exit** (F7) to return to the document screen.

8 Press **Format** (Shift-F8), select Line (1), select Line Numbering (5), and then type **y** to display the menu of options.

9 Select Restart Numbering on Each Page (5) and type **n** for no.

10 Press **Exit** (F7) to return to the first page of the legal brief.

Using Paragraph Numbering

Paragraph numbering is also important in many legal documents. In the legal brief on your screen, each paragraph, beginning with the jurisdiction paragraphs, is numbered.

11 Press **Page Down** (PgDn) to move to the top of the jurisdiction page.

Digits are being used to number the paragraphs. Because each digit is actually a paragraph numbering code, the numbers automatically update whenever you add or delete paragraphs.

12 Press **Page Down** twice to move to the top of the last page.

Adding a Paragraph

Let's add a final paragraph to the legal brief using Paragraph Numbering.

13 Press **Tab** twice to indent the first line of the paragraph.

14 Press **Date/Outline** (Shift-F5) and select Paragraph Number (5).

A message on the status line indicates that you can enter the paragraph level, or press Enter to insert an automatic paragraph number. There are 8 levels of numbering available for paragraphs, each with its own numbering style. The left margin is the first level, with levels 2 through 8 at the tab stop settings.

15 Press **Enter** to insert an automatic paragraph numbering code.

Because the cursor is already at the third level (two tabs in from the left margin), a digit (10) with a trailing period (.) is used for the style.

▲ THIRD LEVEL NUMBERING STYLE

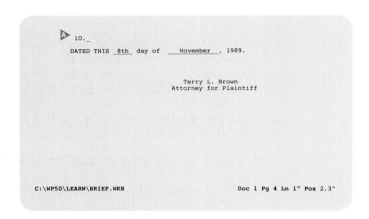

```
▷  10._
    DATED THIS _8th_ day of ___November___, 1989.



                            Terry L. Brown
                            Attorney for Plaintiff







C:\WP50\LEARN\BRIEF.WKB                    Doc 1 Pg 4 Ln 1" Pos 2.3"
```

16 Press **Tab** to add some spacing after the number, and then type the following paragraph:

For costs of suit herein incurred, and for such other relief as the court deems proper.

Resetting the Numbering

While there are ten paragraphs of text in the legal brief, the last three paragraphs should be numbered separately from the rest of the brief.

17 Press **Home** and **Up Arrow** (↑), and then **Escape (Esc)** and **Up Arrow** to display the "WHEREFORE" sentence on your screen.

18 Place the cursor at the beginning of the "WHEREFORE" line.

CURSOR POSITION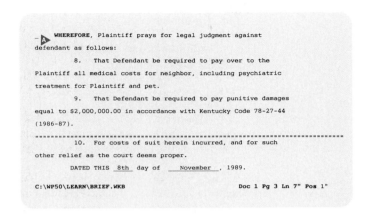

```
  ᐅ  WHEREFORE, Plaintiff prays for legal judgment against
defendant as follows:
          8.   That Defendant be required to pay over to the
Plaintiff all medical costs for neighbor, including psychiatric
treatment for Plaintiff and pet.
          9.   That Defendant be required to pay punitive damages
equal to $2,000,000.00 in accordance with Kentucky Code 78-27-44
(1986-87).
================================================================================
          10.  For costs of suit herein incurred, and for such
other relief as the court deems proper.
          DATED THIS _8th_ day of ___November__ , 1989.

C:\WP50\LEARN\BRIEF.WKB                    Doc 1 Pg 3 Ln 7" Pos 1"
```

When you want to change the paragraph numbering style, or start numbering over, you can use the Paragraph Numbering Definition menu.

19 Press **Date/Outline** (Shift-F5) and then select Define (6).

A menu of numbering styles appears on your screen with several preset styles, as well as an option that lets you create a style of your own.

NUMBERING STYLES FOR LEVELS
LEGAL NUMBERING STYLE

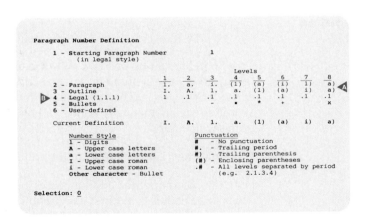

```
Paragraph Number Definition

     1 - Starting Paragraph Number        1
         (in legal style)

                                             Levels
                          1    2    3    4    5    6    7    8
     2 - Paragraph        1.   a.   i.  (1)  (a)  (i)  1)   a)  ᐊ
     3 - Outline          I.   A.   1.   a.  (1)  (a)  i)   a)
     4 - Legal (1.1.1)    1    .1   .1   .1   .1   .1   .1   .1
     5 - Bullets          -    -    -    •    *    +         x
     6 - User-defined

     Current Definition   I.   A.   1.   a.  (1)  (a)  i)   a)

         Number Style              Punctuation
         1 - Digits               #   - No punctuation
         A - Upper case letters   #.  - Trailing period
         a - Lower case letters   #)  - Trailing parenthesis
         I - Upper case roman     (#) - Enclosing parentheses
         i - Lower case roman     .#  - All levels separated by period
         Other character - Bullet       (e.g.  2.1.3.4)

     Selection: 0
```

Notice the format used for each level in a style. There is even a style set for legal numbering (1, 1.1, 1.1.1, etc.).

20 Select Starting Paragraph Number (1) and enter **1** to start the numbering over at one.

21 Press **Exit** (F7) twice to return to the legal brief.

22 Press **Screen** (Ctrl-F3) and then press **Enter** to update the last three paragraph numbers.

The paragraph numbers should start numbering at "1" below the "WHEREFORE" sentence.

 NEW PARAGRAPH NUMBERS

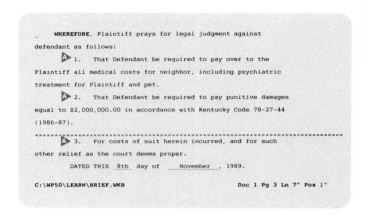

For details on using Paragraph Numbering and creating a paragraph numbering definition, turn to the WordPerfect reference manual.

Editing with Redline and Strikeout

Because a legal document must be very accurate in wording and format, it may be edited several times before a final draft is ready to print.

To help in the editing process, WordPerfect provides Redline and Strikeout features that let you highlight text to be included (Redline) and text to be deleted (Strikeout). Once the final draft is ready, you can then have WordPerfect automatically remove all redline markings and strikeout text from the document.

23 Press **Page Up** (PgUp) to return to the top of the Jurisdiction page.

For example, during the editing process, an attorney decides that a sentence needs to be added to the first jurisdiction paragraph, while the second jurisdiction paragraph should be deleted.

24 Place the cursor at the end of the first paragraph and press the **Space Bar** twice.

25 Press **Font** (Ctrl-F8), select Appearance (2), and then select Redline (8).

26 Type the following sentence:

Plaintiff has expressed no desire to relocate to any other state in the Union.

27 Place the cursor in the first line of the second paragraph, and then press **Home** twice and **Left Arrow** (←) to place the cursor at the beginning of the line.

28 Press **Block** (Alt-F4), and then press **Down Arrow** (↓) six times to place the cursor at the beginning of the third paragraph.

29 Press **Font** (Ctrl-F8), select Appearance (2), and then select Strikeout (9).

30 Press **Go To** (Ctrl-Home) and then **Up Arrow** (↑) to return to the top of the page.

Like all other font attributes, selecting Redline and Strikeout places on and off codes at the beginning and end of the new sentence and the second paragraph.

When the text is printed, redlined text is normally printed in a different font, or with a mark in the left margin next to each line. Strikeout text is normally printed in a different font, or with a dash printed over every character.

Depending on the type of screen attributes you have set for your computer (the Setup key), redline and strikeout text may be displayed in reverse video, as a different size, with a line running through the text, etc.

31 Press **Print** (Shift-F7), type **s** to display the list of printers, highlight the name of your printer, and then press **Enter** to select the printer.

If you have a graphics monitor, you can see what your printer is using for redline and strikeout by displaying the text in the Preview screen. If not, go to step 33.

32 Select View Document (6), and then select 100% (1) to see the redline and strikeout text.

Printing the Edited Page

A REDLINE TEXT

B STRIKEOUT TEXT

Your redline and strikeout text should look similar to that displayed below.

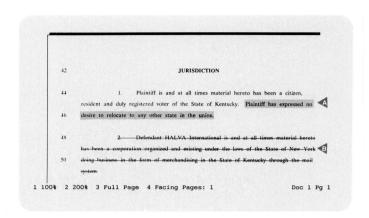

33 Select Full Page (3) and then press **Cancel** (F1) to return to the Print menu.

34 Select Page (2) to print the edited page.

Removing Redline and Strikeout

Once the final editing decisions have been made on the text of the legal document, you can then have WordPerfect automatically remove all Redline on and off codes, and delete all the strikeout text.

35 Press **Mark Text** (Alt-F5) and select Generate (6).

36 Select Remove Redline Markings and Strikeout Text from Document (1) and then type **y** to begin the process.

37 Press **Page Up** (PgUp) twice to return to the Jurisdiction page.

When WordPerfect is finished, the Redline marks are gone from the new sentence, and the second paragraph is removed from the legal brief. The paragraph numbers are also updated automatically.

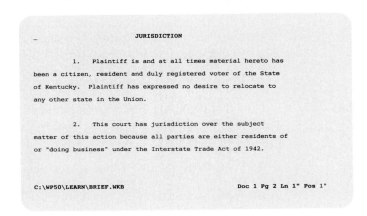

```
                       JURISDICTION

        1.   Plaintiff is and at all times material hereto has
been a citizen, resident and duly registered voter of the State
of Kentucky.  Plaintiff has expressed no desire to relocate to
any other state in the Union.

        2.   This court has jurisdiction over the subject
matter of this action because all parties are either residents of
or "doing business" under the Interstate Trade Act of 1942.



C:\WP50\LEARN\BRIEF.WKB                    Doc 1 Pg 2 Ln 1" Pos 1"
```

For an example of using Document Compare to automatically insert Redline and Strikeout codes, turn to the Reports lesson at the end of Special Applications.

Adding a Vertical Line

The legal paper on which you print your documents may include a vertical line that separates the line numbering from the text of the document.

 VERTICAL LINE

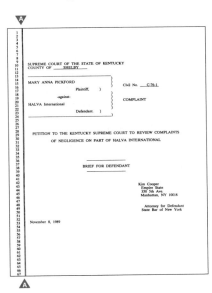

If your printer can handle graphics, then you may want to add your own vertical line to the printed page.

38 Press **Home** three times and then **Up Arrow** (↑) to move to the very beginning of the legal brief.

39 Press **Graphics** (Alt-F9), select Line (5), and then select Vertical Line (2).

40 Select Horizontal Position (1), select Set Position (4), and then enter **.8** to place the line slightly to the left of the left margin.

41 Press **Exit** (F7) to return to the legal brief.

Printing the Final Version

Now that the vertical line has been added to the title page, you can view it it in the Preview screen (if you have a graphics card), and then send the brief to the printer.

42 Press **Print** (Shift-F7) and select View Document (6).

43 When you are ready, press **Cancel** (F1) to return to the Print menu, and then select Full Document (1).

44 Press **Exit** and type **n** twice to clear the screen.

You can create a Header that includes the vertical line if you want it printed on every page.

Creating a Will

Many legal documents use the same paragraphs, with minor changes, for different clients or cases. By using WordPerfect's Merge feature, you can automate the process of assembling a legal document, saving hours of time in typing and editing.

Reviewing the Primary File

For example, a will can be created quickly by using a primary and secondary file. The primary file contains a menu that lets you choose from a variety of clauses, while the secondary file contains the text of the clauses.

45 Press **Retrieve** (Shift-F10) and enter **willpf.wkb** to retrieve the primary file.

Notice that a menu of standard clauses for a will has been created between a pair of ^O's.

▲ PAIR OF ^O MERGE CODES

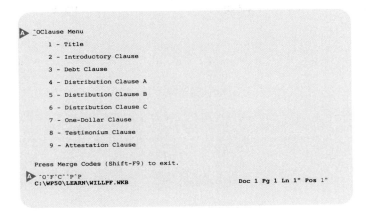

```
▲ ^OClause Menu
        1 - Title
        2 - Introductory Clause
        3 - Debt Clause
        4 - Distribution Clause A
        5 - Distribution Clause B
        6 - Distribution Clause C
        7 - One-Dollar Clause
        8 - Testimonium Clause
        9 - Attestation Clause

    Press Merge Codes (Shift-F9) to exit.
▲ ^O^F^C^^P^P
  C:\WP50\LEARN\WILLPF.WKB                          Doc 1 Pg 1 Ln 1" Pos 1"
```

A ^F and ^C at the bottom of the menu actually stop the merge to let you enter a field number. The field you enter is then retrieved from the secondary file, and the pair of ^P's display the menu again to let you select another field.

The menu numbers are the field numbers in the secondary file where the clauses are located.

46 Press **Switch** (Shift-F3) to open up the second document screen.

47 Press **Retrieve** (Shift-F10) and enter **willsf.wkb** for the name of the secondary file.

Reviewing the Secondary File

The secondary file contains the text and codes needed for each clause to create the will.

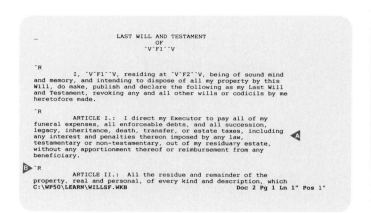

Each clause is a field (ending with ^R), and there is a field for each item in the menu. The clauses are in the same order as the menu items, and are all contained in one record.

48 Press **Home** twice and then **Down Arrow** (↓) to move to the end of the clauses.

The clauses end with a ^E and a hard page break, just like a normal record.

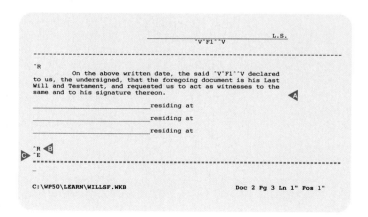

Because there is only one record in the secondary file, WordPerfect only retrieves one field (clause) when you enter a field number from the menu.

49 Press **Home** twice and then **Up Arrow** (↑) to move to the beginning of the clauses.

Notice that the ^V merge code surrounds each ^F (and ^C) in the text.

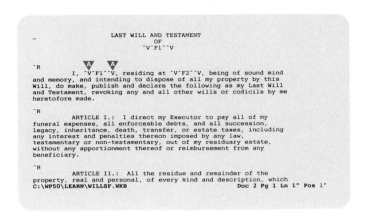

The ^V tells WordPerfect to ignore the merge code and simply retrieve it with the field.

For example, if the ^F1^ in the introductory clause (I, ^F1^, residing at. . .) had no ^V codes, then WordPerfect would actually retrieve field 1 (the title) into the clause during the merge.

50 Press **Exit** (F7), type **n**, and then type **y** to exit the second document screen.

51 Press **Exit** (F7) and type **n** twice to clear the first document screen.

Assembling the Will

Now that you have been introduced to the primary and secondary files, let's try using them to assemble a will.

52 Press **Merge/Sort** (Ctrl-F9), and then select Merge (1).

53 Enter **willpf.wkb** for the primary file, and then enter **willsf.wkb** for the secondary file.

The menu of clauses scrolls onto your screen and a "Field:" message appears on the status line.

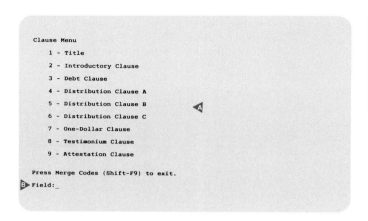

A MENU OF CLAUSES
B FIELD MESSAGE

```
Clause Menu
    1 - Title
    2 - Introductory Clause
    3 - Debt Clause
    4 - Distribution Clause A
    5 - Distribution Clause B                   ◁
    6 - Distribution Clause C
    7 - One-Dollar Clause
    8 - Testimonium Clause
    9 - Attestation Clause

Press Merge Codes (Shift-F9) to exit.
▷ Field:_
```

54 Enter **1** to select the title (field 1) from the secondary file.

The title is retrieved (but not displayed), and the menu scrolls onto your screen again.

55 Enter **2** to select the introductory clause (field 2) from the secondary file.

The menu scrolls onto the screen again, ready for the next selection. You can select any clause, as many times as you wish, to build the will.

56 Enter the following numbers to assemble the rest of the will:

   3 (debt clause)
   5 (distribution clause B)
   7 (one-dollar clause)
   8 (testimonium clause)
   9 (attestation clause)

57 Press **Merge Codes** (Shift-F9) to end the merge.

58 Press **Home** twice and then **Up Arrow** (↑)to move to the beginning of the assembled will.

Reviewing the Assembled Will

You should now see the title and several clauses on your screen.

```
                    LAST WILL AND TESTAMENT
                             OF
                            ^F1^

        I, ^F1^, residing at ^F2^, being of sound mind and
memory, and intending to dispose of all my property by this Will,
do make, publish and declare the following as my Last Will and
Testament, revoking any and all other wills or codicils by me
heretofore made.

        ARTICLE I.:  I direct my Executor to pay all of my
funeral expenses, all enforceable debts, and all succession,
legacy, inheritance, death, transfer, or estate taxes, including
any interest and penalties thereon imposed by any law,
testamentary or non-testamentary, out of my residuary estate,
without any apportionment thereof or reimbursement from any
beneficiary.

        ARTICLE II.:  In the event that ^F3^, shall not survive
me, then all the interest in and share of my inheritance
hereinbefore devised shall pass to any children who may survive
me.

                                    Doc 1 Pg 1 Ln 1" Pos 1"
```

The article numbers are paragraph numbers set to level 1, and use the outline numbering style.

59 Press **Down Arrow** (↓) until Article III and the "IN WITNESS WHEREOF" clauses are on your screen.

Besides the ^F's in the title, introductory clause, and Article II, there are also ^C's in Article III (and in the Testimonium clause) to stop a merge and let you enter information.

A ^F MERGE CODE

B ^C MERGE CODE

```
        ARTICLE I.:  I direct my Executor to pay all of my
funeral expenses, all enforceable debts, and all succession,
legacy, inheritance, death, transfer, or estate taxes, including
any interest and penalties thereon imposed by any law,
testamentary or non-testamentary, out of my residuary estate,
without any apportionment thereof or reimbursement from any
beneficiary.
                                  ▼A
        ARTICLE II.:  In the event that ^F3^, shall not survive
me, then all the interest in and share of my inheritance
hereinbefore devised shall pass to any children who may survive
me.
                          ▼B
        ARTICLE III.:  If ^C, whose name has been intentionally
omitted from this Last Will and Testament, shall contest the
articles hereinbefore stated, I direct my Executor to pay said
person the sum of One Dollar (U.S Currency) as an expression of
good faith and settlement.

        IN WITNESS WHEREOF, I have hereunto set my hand and
seal on this  ^C  day of  ^C  19^C.

                                               L.S.
      _                           _____
                                    Doc 1 Pg 1 Ln 6.5" Pos 1"
```

Reviewing the Client File

What you have created by assembling the will from the primary file (menu) and the secondary file (clauses) is another primary file that can be merged with client information kept in a secondary file.

60 Press **Switch** (Shift-F3) to open the second document screen.

61 Press **Retrieve** (Shift-F10) and enter **clients.wkb** to retrieve the client information.

A secondary file appears with a record for each client that includes the name (uppercase), the address, and the executor (or executrix). A comment is also included at the top of the file.

A INSTRUCTIONS IN COMMENT

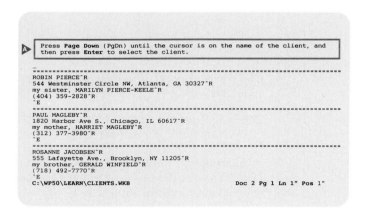

Creating Two Files

A macro has been created for you that saves the assembled will (in the document 1 screen) in a "Will" file, clears the screen, retrieves the client file (the one on your screen), and then pauses to let you select a client by following the instructions in the comment.

The macro continues by creating a secondary file ("Client") that contains the selected client record, and then merging the assembled will with the client record.

You can see the actual keystrokes of the macro by viewing them in the macro editing window. For details on editing a macro, turn to Feature Summary *at the end of the workbook.*

Before using the macro for the first time, you need to create a "Will" file and a "Client" file that can be replaced while the macro is running. If the files are not created before starting the macro the first time, then the macro will not work correctly.

62 Press **Save** (F10) and enter **will** to create a "Will" file.

63 Press **Save** (F10) and enter **client** to create a "Client" file.

Because both files are replaced during the macro, it does not matter what they contain when first creating the files.

64 Press **Exit** (F7), type **n**, and then type **y** to close the second document screen.

Starting the Will Macro

With the assembled will on your screen, you are now ready to start the macro.

65 Press **Macro** (Alt-F10) and enter **will** for the name of the macro.

After saving the assembled will, the macro retrieves the client file and pauses for you to select a record.

66 Press **Page Down** (PgDn) four times until the cursor stops on the record for Michael Grayson.

67 Press **Enter** to select the record and continue the macro.

Filling in the ^C Information

The "Client" file is created, the merge started, and then WordPerfect pauses at the ^C in the One-Dollar clause for a name.

68 Type **CHRIS GRAYSON** and then press **Merge R** (F9) to continue the merge.

WordPerfect then pauses in the Testimonium clause for the day, month, and year.

69 Type the following day, month, and year, pressing **Merge R** (F9) after typing each item:

SIXTH (day)
NOVEMBER (month)
89 (year)

70 Press **Home** twice and then **Up Arrow** (↑) to return to the beginning of the will.

The will should now look similar to the one illustrated below.

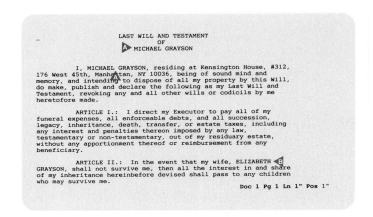

Replacing Executor with Executrix

Because the executor of the will is Michael Grayson's wife, the word "Executor" needs to be replaced with "Executrix."

71 Press **Replace** (Alt-F2), and type **n** to have WordPerfect replace without confirming.

72 Type **Executor** and press ◆**Search** (F2), and then type **Executrix** and press ◆**Search** to being replacing.

The completed will is ready for final approval and printing. You may also want to set the format for double spacing. If you want to print the will at this time, select your printer, and then check the page break before sending it to the printer. Otherwise,

73 Press **Exit** (F7) and type **n** twice to clear the screen.

Summary

During this lesson, you were introduced to the following tasks:

- Creating a menu in a primary file (^O).
- Creating a vertical line.
- Defining a paragraph numbering style.
- Ignoring merge codes in a secondary file (^V).
- Inserting a paragraph number.
- Numbering lines.
- Redlining text.
- Removing redline markings and strikeout text.
- Restarting line numbering.
- Striking out text.

For a complete listing of all tasks introduced in the lessons, turn to *Feature Summary* at the end of the workbook.

Lesson 30: Newsletters

As quality printers (and scanners) become less expensive each year, more people are beginning to publish their own papers, reports, newsletters, etc., instead of sending them out to be typeset and printed. This personal approach is called *desktop publishing*, and gives you more control over the printing process, as well as cutting publishing costs significantly.

While WordPerfect is not a desktop publishing program, it contains desktop publishing features that let you create many of the same documents in less time and with more editing flexibility.

You have already been introduced to some of these features (graphics, columns, styles, etc.) in other lessons. In this lesson, you are given some insights into how these features can be used to create and design the front page of a newsletter.

Evaluating Your Hardware

Before you begin using WordPerfect to create the newsletter, you should know what to expect from your computer and printer.

If you do not have a graphics card installed in your computer, you can still see text in the Preview screen, but it is very difficult to judge what a document will look like before it is printed. If you are planning on using WordPerfect to do desktop publishing, you should consider installing a graphics card.

Most dot matrix printers can print text in several different fonts, as well as print horizontal lines, vertical lines, and graphics figures. However, the quality of the printed text and graphics may not be satisfactory. If that is the case, you may want to consider investing in a laser printer.

A laser printer normally prints at 300 dpi (dots per inch), which produces high quality text characters and graphics figures. In addition, the large variety of fonts available for laser printers makes it much easier to design professional-looking documents.

This lesson is designed for those people who already have a graphics card installed and a printer that can produce graphics images. If you have a printer that can print graphics, but do not have a graphics card, then the lesson is still important. However, it will be more difficult to design the newsletter if you cannot see it taking shape in a graphics Preview screen.

Retrieving the Style List

The first time you create a document such as a newsletter, a lot of decisions are made about what fonts to use, what kind of masthead to design, how many columns for text, etc.

Once the decisions are made, you can then create a list of styles to be retrieved whenever you create the next newsletter.

1 Press **Style** (Alt-F8) and select Retrieve (7).

2 Enter **news.sty** to retrieve a list of styles created for a newsletter.

You should see the following styles listed on your screen.

 STYLES

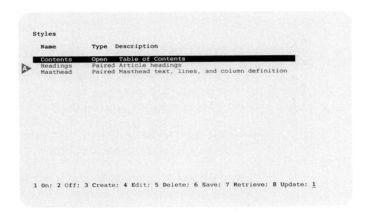

Inserting the Masthead Style

Let's begin creating the newsletter by inserting the Masthead style

3 Highlight the Masthead style and select On (1) to insert the style into the document screen.

4 Press **Reveal Codes** (Alt-F3) to display the masthead codes.

The Masthead style inserts a Style On and a Style Off code. Both codes contain several formats. For example, the Style Off code not only includes the masthead text, but horizontal lines and a Text Columns definition.

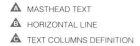
A MASTHEAD TEXT
B HORIZONTAL LINE
C TEXT COLUMNS DEFINITION

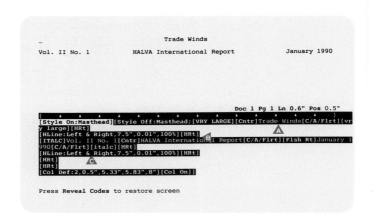

Many mastheads also include a figure or logo. Although a graphics figure cannot be included in a style, it can be retrieved between on and off style codes to be included as part of the masthead.

5 Press **Retrieve** (Shift-F10) and enter **compass.wkb** to retrieve a compass figure into the masthead.

Both a graphics option code and figure code are inserted between the on and off style codes as part of the masthead.

A FIGURE OPTIONS CODE
B FIGURE CODE

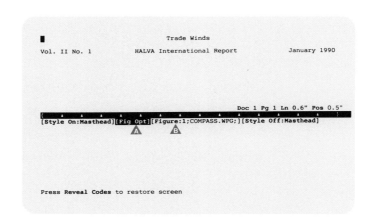

6 Press **Reveal Codes** (Alt-F3) to display the full document screen.

7 Press **Print** (Shift-F7) to display the Print menu (your printer should be selected).

8 Select View Document (6) and then 100% (1) to see the results of the graphics and formatting codes in the style.

The compass is included in the masthead, with the text enclosed in horizontal lines.

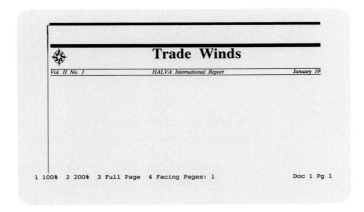

All the screens in this lesson were created with a laser printer selected, fonts assigned to each attribute, and a graphics card installed in the computer. While the text in the newsletter you create may be displayed in a different font style or size, you can still successfully complete the lesson.

9 Press **Exit** (F7) to return to the document screen, and then press **Page Down** (PgDn) to move the cursor below the masthead.

Retrieving the Articles

After retrieving the Masthead style and compass, the next step is to retrieve the articles for the newsletter. The articles are edited, spell-checked, and ready to insert into the newsletter.

Before retrieving the articles, notice that the status line includes a Column (Col) number.

◢ COLUMN NUMBER

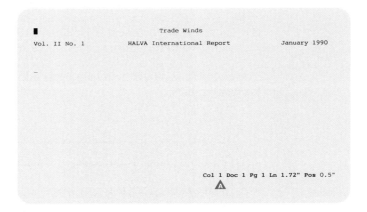

```
■                          Trade Winds

Vol. II No. 1         HALVA International Report      January 1990

  ─




                              Col 1 Doc 1 Pg 1 Ln 1.72" Pos 0.5"
                                       ◢
```

The Masthead style includes Text Column codes that automatically place the articles in columns when you retrieve the file.

10 Press **Retrieve** (Shift-F10) and enter **newstext.wkb** to retrieve three articles for the newsletter.

Formatting the Headings

The articles are simple text with no attributes (bold, large, small, etc.) or formatting codes. The heading for each article can be formatted by using the Heading style.

11 Place the cursor at the beginning of the "Product Boosts Sales. . ." heading (if it is not already there).

12 Press **Block** (Alt-F4) and then press **End** to highlight the title.

13 Press **Style** (Alt-F8), highlight the Headings style, and then select On (1) to format the heading.

Now that the heading for the first article is styled, you can follow the same three steps (11 through 13) to style the headings for the second and third articles.

14 Press **Down Arrow** (↓) until the following two headings are on the screen, and then format them with the Headings style.

> **Training Classes and Seminars** (second article)
> **HALVA Goes Retail** (third article)

Previewing the Newsletter

The Heading style formats the headings with the Large font attribute. Let's look at the headings in the Preview screen.

15 Press **Page Up** (PgUp), and then press **Print** (Shift-F7) and select View Document (6) to see the page at 100%.

The 100% displays the text in the same size as it will be printed. You should be able to see the text in the masthead and the heading for the first article.

A MASTHEAD

B HEADING FOR FIRST ARTICLE

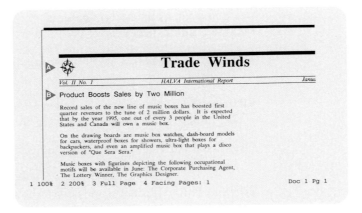

Besides the Large font attribute for the heading, the masthead (Trade Winds) is formatted with the Very Large attribute, while the volume numbers are formatted with the Italics attribute.

If you have a different font assigned to each attribute, then all three lines of text (masthead, volume numbers, and heading) should be displayed in different styles and sizes on the screen. If an attribute is not assigned a font, then it will be displayed in the same style and size as the text of the first article.

For example, the newsletter for this lesson was created using a laser printer with a Times Roman 18pt (point) Bold font selected for Very Large (masthead), a Times Roman 11pt Italic font selected for Italics (volume numbers), and a Helvetica 14pt Bold selected for Large (headings).

If your fonts are larger than those mentioned above, then the headings may wrap, and text may spill into column 2.

Because each of the font attributes (Very Large, Large, and Italics) had a font assigned to it, WordPerfect displayed the style and size of each font on the Preview screen.

WordPerfect displays Helvetica, Times Roman, and Courier in the Preview screen in any size and in normal, bold, or italic. If you are using another style (Garamond, Futura, etc.), then WordPerfect displays the font in the Preview style that is closest to the one you are using.

16 Press **Exit** (F7) to return to the document screen.

When you select a printer while installing WordPerfect, some fonts are assigned to the attributes. If you want to change the fonts for the attributes, you need to use the Printer program. For an explanation of the program, turn to the Printer Program heading in the Appendix of the WordPerfect reference manual.

Placing the Articles in Columns

There are two columns defined for the newsletter. The first column is twice as wide as the second column. Right now, all three articles are in the first column. Let's move the third article into the second column.

17 Press **Down Arrow** (↓) until the cursor is on the "HALVA Goes Retail" heading.

18 Press **Home** three times and then **Left Arrow** (←) to move to the beginning of the line (on the Style On code).

19 Press **Hard Page** (Ctrl-Enter) to move the third article to the top of the second column.

20 Press **Print** (Shift-F7) and select View Document (6).

21 Select Full Page (3) to see the layout of the page.

The third article should now be at the top of the third column, with the first two articles in the first column.

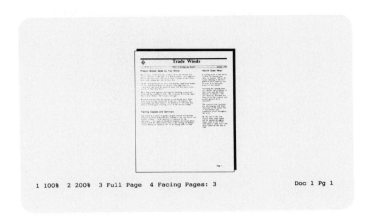

As you create a document for printing, you may want to use the 100% view for checking fonts and text, and the Full Page view for checking the design (layout) of the page.

22 Press **Exit** (F7) to return to the document screen.

Adding a Graphics Figure

A graph has been created as an illustration for the first article (Product Boosts Sales. . .), and needs to be placed below the first paragraph. However, in case the article is edited, the graph should stay with the first paragraph.

23 Press **Go To** (Ctrl-Home) and then **Left Arrow** (←) to return to the first column.

24 Place the cursor on the "R" of "Record" at the beginning of the first paragraph in the "Product Boosts Sales" article.

25 Press **Graphics** (Alt-F9), select Figure (1), and then select Create (1).

26 Select Filename (1) and then enter **graph.wpg** for the name of the graph file.

Creating a Caption

A caption can be added to the graph to help emphasize the importance of the graph information.

27 Select Caption (2) to enter a caption for the graph illustration.

A figure number is automatically inserted into the caption editing screen for you.

▲ FIGURE NUMBER

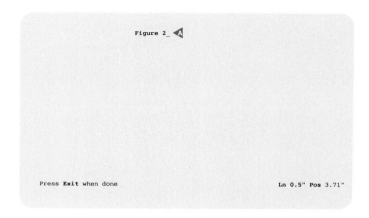

The number is actually a code (like a paragraph numbering code) that automatically updates as you add or delete other figures in the document.

Let's delete the caption number and type a caption for the graph.

28 Press **Backspace** to delete the figure number.

29 Press **♦Indent** (F4), press **Font** (Ctrl-F8), select Appearance (2), and then select Italics (4).

30 Type **Future Looks Bright for Music Box Sales.** and then press **Right Arrow** (→) to end the italics.

31 Press **Exit** (F7) to save the caption and return to the Figure Definition menu.

Setting the Position and Size

Because the graph needs to stay with the first paragraph, "Paragraph" is the correct setting for Type. However, the vertical position of "0" inches means that the top of the graph will be lined up evenly with the top of the paragraph.

32 Select Vertical Position (4) and enter **1** to have the graph offset (moved down) one inch from the top of the paragraph.

The Horizontal Position setting of "Right" means that the graph will be placed at the right margin. Because the paragraph is in a text column, WordPerfect automatically places the graph at the right margin of the *column* instead of the page.

Let's leave the graph at the right margin, but change the size of the graph.

33 Select Size (6), and then select Width (1) and enter **3** to change the size to a three inch square.

WordPerfect automatically calculates a height that is proportional to the new width.

34 Select Edit (8) to view the graph.

Because the figure options for the compass in the masthead are set for no border, there is no box drawn around the graph. However, as the graph itself is square, it does not need to be framed in a box.

35 Press **Exit** (F7) twice to return to the document screen.

36 Press **Screen** (Ctrl-F3) and then press **Enter** to rewrite the screen.

An empty box labeled "FIG 2" is displayed on the screen, and the second and third paragraphs of the article wrap around the box.

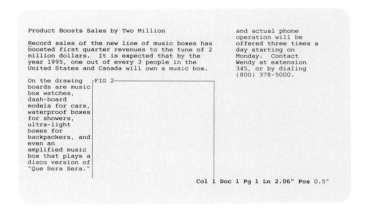

Inserting the Table of Contents

The final item that needs to be added to the front page of the newsletter is the table of contents.

37 Press **Page Up** (PgUp) and then press **Right Arrow** (→) four times to place the cursor at the beginning of the first heading.

38 Press **Style** (Alt-F8), place the cursor on the Contents style (if it is not already there), and then select On (1).

39 Press **Print** (Shift-F7) and select View Document (6) to see the layout of the first page of the newsletter.

Notice that the table of contents is displayed inside a box, while the compass and graph have no box. If your printer can do gray shading, then the table of contents is also shaded.

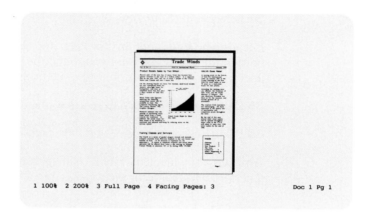

The Graphics menu includes four different categories of graphics—Figure, Table, Text Box, and User-Defined. While the menus and features available for each category are the same, you can set different options for each category.

For example, the Figure options for the newsletter are set for no border around the figure. However, the table was created as a Text Box, and the options for the Text Box category have been set for a box around the figure.

40 Press **Exit** (F7) to return to the document screen.

Adding a Horizontal Line

Now that the graph has been added to the newsletter, the second article has moved down the page. However, there is still room left to separate it from the first article by using a horizontal line.

41 Press **Down Arrow** (↓) until the cursor is on the "Training Classes and Seminars" heading.

42 Press **Home** three times and then **Left Arrow** (←) to move to the very beginning of the line.

43 Press **Enter** twice to add extra spacing between the articles, and then press **Up Arrow** (↑) twice to move two line above the heading.

44 Press **Graphics** (Alt-F9), select Line (5), and then select Horizontal Line (1).

The horizontal line is set to fill the space between the right and left margins of the column. The width is only one hundredth of an inch, but is all that is needed for a line separating the articles. The shading is 100%, which means that the line will be printed a solid black.

45 Press **Exit** (F7) to return to the document screen.

46 Press **Print** (Shift-F7) and select View Document (6).

Adjusting and Printing

The first page of the newsletter is formatted, styled, and ready to send to the printer.

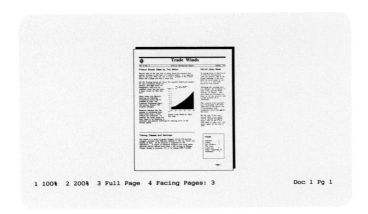

Because the fonts you are using are probably different from those used for the lesson, you may need to make some adjustments before your newsletter looks similar to the one illustrated above.

For example, you may need to change the vertical position of the graph. The graph settings can be edited by pressing Graph (Alt-F9), selecting Figure (1), selecting Edit (2), and then entering "2" for figure three.

You may also need to adjust the vertical spacing of the text to match the spacing illustrated. This can be quickly done by adding or deleting Hard Returns. For fine tuning, you can also use Advance.

47 Press **Cancel** (F1) to return to the Print menu.

48 Select Full Document (1) to send the newsletter page to the printer.

Adding a Vertical Line Between Columns

Sometimes vertical lines are used in a newsletter to separate the columns of text. Vertical Line lets you quickly insert lines between columns.

49 Press **Page Up** (PgUp) to move to the very beginning of the page.

Whenever you want the vertical lines to run the full length of the columns, place the cursor to the right of the Column On code.

50 Press **Right Arrow** (→) four times to display the Column (Col) number on the status line.

51 Press **Graphics** (Alt-F9), select Line (5), and then select Vertical Line (2).

```
Graphics: Vertical Line
        1 - Horizontal Position          Left Margin
        2 - Vertical Position            Full Page
        3 - Length of Line
        4 - Width of Line                0.01"
        5 - Gray Shading (% of black)    100%




    Selection: 0
```

The horizontal position for the line is preset for the left margin. However, the line needs to be placed between Columns 1 and 2.

52 Select Horizontal Position (1), select Between Columns (3), and then enter **1** to place the line to the right of Column 1.

The vertical position is set to print the line the full length of the page. However, the line needs to start at the top of the column.

53 Select Vertical Position (2), select Set Position (5), and then press **Enter** to use the displayed measurement.

Because the cursor is at the top of the first column, WordPerfect automatically enters a vertical measurement that starts at the top of the column. The length of the line is also set to stop at the bottom of the column.

▲ BOTTOM OF COLUMN

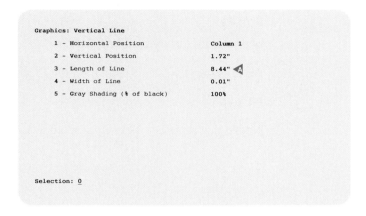

54 Press **Exit** (F7) to return to the document screen.

55 Press **Print** (Shift-F7) and select View Document (6).

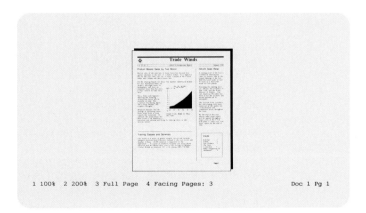

Changing the Page Layout

Now that a vertical line has been added between the columns, the layout of the page could be changed.

For example, the horizontal line above the second article and the box around the table of contents clutter the page with extra graphics that are not needed.

56 Press **Exit** (F7) to return to the document screen.

57 Press **Down Arrow** (↓) until the cursor is two lines above the "Training Classes and Seminars" heading.

58 Press **Backspace** and type **y** to delete the code for the horizontal line.

59 Press **Delete** (Del) to erase one empty line above the heading.

Changing the Border Style

Because the table of contents is in the Contents style, you need to edit the border from the style editing screen.

60 Press **Style** (Alt-F8) and then highlight the Contents style.

61 Type **4** twice to display the codes in the style.

Notice that there is a Text Options code and a Text Box code in the style.

▲ TEXT BOX OPTIONS CODE
▲ TEXT BOX CODE

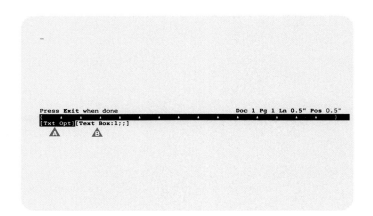

62 Press **Delete** (Del) to erase the Text Options code.

Now that the options code has been deleted, let's check the initial option settings for text boxes.

63 Press **Graphics** (Alt-F9), select Text Box (3), and then select Options (4).

Text boxes are initially set for a thick top and bottom border with no sides to the box.

```
Options:    Text Box

    1 - Border Style
            Left                            None
            Right                           None
            Top                             Thick
            Bottom                          Thick
    2 - Outside Border Space
            Left                            0.16"
            Right                           0.16"
            Top                             0.16"
            Bottom                          0.16"
    3 - Inside Border Space
            Left                            0.16"
            Right                           0.16"
            Top                             0.16"
            Bottom                          0.16"
    4 - First Level Numbering Method        Numbers
    5 - Second Level Numbering Method       Off
    6 - Caption Number Style                [BOLD]1[bold]
    7 - Position of Caption                 Below box, Outside borders
    8 - Minimum Offset from Paragraph       0"
    9 - Gray Shading (% of black)           10%

Selection: 0
```

This style is known as a "call out," and is often used for tables and quotes from an article.

There are also options for spacing around the border, spacing inside the border of the box, caption numbering and styling, and an option that lets you shade the contents of the box. The shading is initially set at 10 percent, which is a good percentage for shading text without losing legibility.

If your printer can do shading, then the text in the table of contents will be shaded when you print the newsletter. If your printer cannot do shading, then the percentage setting is ignored.

64 Press **Exit** (F7) to return to the Style editing screen.

Updating the Table of Contents

After assembling the newsletter, the table of contents should be updated to indicated any new page numbers or articles.

65 Press **Graphics** (Alt-F9), select Text Box (3), select Edit (2), and then enter **1** to display the settings for the table of contents figure.

66 Select Edit (8) to display the text inside the table of contents figure.

```
                                            Inside

                                            Editorial. . . . . 2
                                            Letters. . . . . . 3
                                            New Products. . 5
                                            The Swiss
                                            Connection. . . .6
                                            What's Happening In
                                            Manhattan. . . . 8

Press Exit when done, Graphics to rotate text              Ln .5" Pos 4.76"

[LARGE]Inside[large][HRt]
[HRt]
[ITALC]Editorial. . . . . 2[HRt]
Letters. . . . . . 3[HRt]
New Products. . 5[HRt]
The Swiss[SRt]
Connection. . . .6[HRt]
What's Happening In[HRt]
Manhattan. . . . 8[italc]
```

Besides graphics images, you can also type, format, and edit text inside a figure, table, text box, or user-defined box, by simply selecting Edit instead of entering a filename to retrieve a graphics image.

You can also retrieve and edit a WordPerfect document by selecting Filename (1), entering the filename of the document, and then selecting Edit (8) to view and edit the text.

67 Place the cursor on the "L" of the "Letters" title, press **Enter** to add an extra line, and then press **Up Arrow** (↑) to return to the extra line.

68 Type **Holidays** for the article title, press **Tab**, and then type **4** for the page number.

The setting for the dot leader tab stop is in the text box.

69 Press **Exit** (F7) five times to return to the newsletter in the document screen.

Previewing and Printing

With the horizontal line erased above the second article, and the box style and contents of the table of contents edited, the newsletter is ready to be previewed and then printed.

70 Press **Print** (Shift-F7) and select View Document (6).

Notice the cleaner look of the newsletter layout with the editing changes to the second article and table of contents.

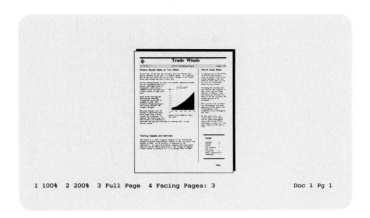

While WordPerfect includes some powerful features for creating professional-looking documents, it is a good idea to use only 3 or 4 fonts per page, and to use graphics in a meaningful way.

71 Press **Cancel** (F1) to return to the Print menu.

72 Select Full Document (1) to print the newsletter.

73 Press **Exit** (F7) and then type **n** twice to clear the screen.

After creating and printing the newsletter, you probably have a few questions, as well as a few ideas about what you would like to do to create your own documents with WordPerfect's desktop publishing features.

Many of the answers you need can be found by turning to the WordPerfect reference manual. However, the more you learn about design and layout of documents, the better you will understand how WordPerfect can help you to do your own desktop publishing.

Summary

During this lesson, you were introduced to the following tasks:

- Creating a caption.
- Creating a horizontal line.
- Creating a graphics figure.
- Creating a vertical line between columns.
- Editing text in a graphics box.
- Moving between text columns.
- Previewing a document.
- Setting options for a graphics figure.

For a complete listing of all tasks introduced in the lessons, turn to *Feature Summary* at the end of the workbook.

Lesson 31: Presentation Graphics

Preparing materials for a presentation has become much easier in the past few years with the introduction of presentation graphics software that helps you produce overheads, handouts, and even 35mm slides. The software may include word processing, outlining, drawing tools, and a *slide show* feature to help you rehearse your presentation.

While WordPerfect is not designed as a presentation graphics package, the printing and graphics features of WordPerfect can help you produce professional-looking handouts and overheads for any presentation.

In this lesson, you are guided through preparing a presentation that includes an outline, an organizational chart, and a graph. You are then introduced to a macro that helps when rehearsing or displaying the presentation.

The introduction to the Newsletter lesson (30) provides an explanation of what you can expect from WordPerfect and your printer when using attributes, graphics, and the Preview screen. If you have not completed Lesson 30, take a moment to read through the introduction to the lesson before continuing below.

Presentation Materials

There are three basic types of presentation materials that WordPerfect can help you prepare—transparencies, handouts, and large screen displays.

Transparencies are the sheets of clear acetate (plastic) that you use with an overhead projector. Transparencies can be prepared by printing the document (outline, chart, etc.), and then using a copier to copy the document on to the sheet of acetate.

If you have a laser printer, you can print the document directly on a sheet of acetate. However, check your printer manual before purchasing any transparencies for limitations on the type and quality of the acetate film that can be used.

If you have the correct equipment, you can also take slides of the presentation materials as they are displayed in the Preview screen. For details on creating a macro that displays the graphics without displaying the Preview menu, see the Slide Macro heading at the end of this lesson.

Once you have created the overheads, you can print the same presentation materials as handouts. If you have a laser printer (or a high quality dot matrix printer), you may want to print one copy, and then have them reproduced at a print shop. Otherwise, you may want to print originals for each participant in the audience.

Because the quality of large screen displays has increased significantly over the past few years, using the displays for presentations to large or small groups has become a standard alternative to transparencies or slides. We'll introduce a macro at the end of this lesson that can help you take advantage of large screen displays by organizing the graphics images like a slide show.

While there are other ways in which WordPerfect can help you prepare materials for a presentation, this introductory lesson should give you some basic ideas that can be expanded to meet your needs.

Preparing the Outline

An outline is an important way of organizing a presentation. After it is created, the outline can be used for display and/or as a handout.

1 Press **Retrieve** (Shift-F10) and enter **outline.wkb** to retrieve an outline for a presentation.

The outline on your screen is for a presentation on the growth of HALVA International in the 1990's.

```
                              A Time For Growth
                             HALVA in the 1990's


         I. The First Fifty Years
                A. The Roots of Mail Order
                B. The European Connection

         II. The Organizational Question
                A. Direction vs. Management
                B. Maximizing the Organization

         III. The Retail Question
                A. Mail Order in the 1990's


         IV. The Next Fifty Years



         C:\WP50\LEARN\OUTLINE.WKB                    Doc 1 Pg 1 Ln 1" Pos 1"
```

Editing the Outline

The outline was created using Outline in WordPerfect. Let's finish the outline by adding another topic under "The Retail Question" heading.

2 Press **Date/Outline** (Shift-F5) and then select Outline (4) to turn on the feature.

Notice that an "Outline" message is displayed on the status line at the bottom of your screen.

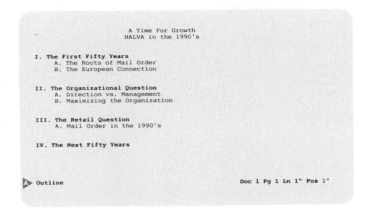

```
                              A Time For Growth
                            HALVA in the 1990's

        I. The First Fifty Years
              A. The Roots of Mail Order
              B. The European Connection

        II. The Organizational Question
              A. Direction vs. Management
              B. Maximizing the Organization

        III. The Retail Question
              A. Mail Order in the 1990's

        IV. The Next Fifty Years



     ▲ Outline                              Doc 1 Pg 1 Ln 1" Pos 1"
```

In the Legal Documents lesson (29), you inserted paragraph numbers that automatically updated whenever a paragraph was added or deleted.

Now that Outline is on, these same paragraph numbers are inserted automatically to help you build or edit an outline.

3 Place the cursor on the "Mail Order in the 1990's" line below "The Retail Question."

4 Press **End** to place the cursor at the end of the line.

5 Press **Enter** to insert a new line.

As soon as you press Enter, WordPerfect inserts a paragraph number at the left margin.

▲ PARAGRAPH NUMBER

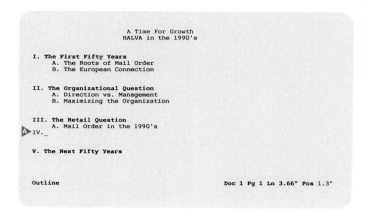

```
                              A Time For Growth
                            HALVA in the 1990's

                I. The First Fifty Years
                       A. The Roots of Mail Order
                       B. The European Connection

                II. The Organizational Question
                       A. Direction vs. Management
                       B. Maximizing the Organization

                III. The Retail Question
                       A. Mail Order in the 1990's
              ▷ IV. _

                V. The Next Fifty Years


                Outline                          Doc 1 Pg 1 Ln 3.66" Pos 1.3"
```

Because the paragraph number WordPerfect inserts is an automatic number, it updates to the correct style of level numbering as soon as you press Tab.

6 Press **Tab**, press the **Space Bar**, and then type **Expanding Markets** for the topic.

7 Press **Enter** to insert a new line and paragraph number, and then press **Tab** twice to move to the third level of the outline.

8 Press the **Space Bar**, type **Music Boxes** for the first subtopic, and then press **Enter**.

9 Press **Tab** twice to move to the third level, press the **Space Bar**, and then type **Oriental Furniture** for the second subtopic.

10 Press **Date/Outline** (Shift-F5) and select Outline (4) to turn off the feature.

Your completed outline should look like the one illustrated below.

▲ NEW TOPIC AND SUBTOPICS

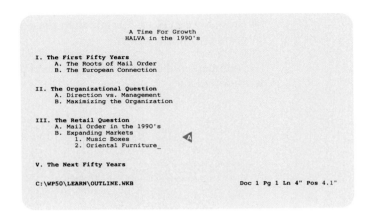

Changing the Style

Not only is creating an outline quick and easy using Outline, but there are several styles of numbering from which you can choose.

11 Press **Page Up** (PgUp) to place the cursor at the top of the page.

12 Press **Date/Outline** (Shift-F5) and select Define (6).

A menu appears from which you can select one of several preset styles, or even create one of your own.

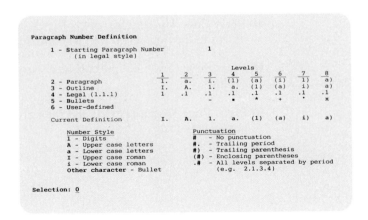

A popular style for presentation graphics is the use of the Paragraph style for numbering an outline.

13 Select Paragraph (2) and then press **Exit** (F7) twice to return to the outline.

14 Press **Screen** (Ctrl-F3) and then press **Enter** to rewrite the paragraph numbers on the screen.

The numbers immediately change to the Paragraph style you selected in the definition menu.

```
                              A Time For Growth
                            HALVA in the 1990's


       1. The First Fifty Years
              a. The Roots of Mail Order
              b. The European Connection


       2. The Organizational Question
              a. Direction vs. Management
              b. Maximizing the Organization


       3. The Retail Question
              a. Mail Order in the 1990's
              b. Expanding Markets
                    i. Music Boxes
                    ii. Oriental Furniture


       4. The Next Fifty Years


       C:\WP50\LEARN\OUTLINE.WKB              Doc 1 Pg 1 Ln 1" Pos 1"
```

Organizing the Presentation

Once an outline is completed, the entire outline may be shown at the beginning of a presentation, with parts of the outline shown during the presentation to emphasize the next point.

15 Press **Page Up** (PgUp), press **Block** (Alt-F4), and then move the cursor to the line below the "Maximizing the Organization" title.

16 Press **Save** (F10) and press **Enter** to save the highlighted part of the outline.

17 Press **Page Down** (PgDn) and then press **Hard Page** (Ctrl-Enter) to start a new page.

18 Press **Retrieve** (Shift-F10) and then press **Enter** to retrieve the saved part of the outline.

19 Press **Page Down** (PgDn) and then press **Hard Page** (Ctrl-Enter) to insert a new page.

With the cursor at the top of page 3, you are ready to retrieve an organizational chart to help illustrate "Maximizing the Organization." However, before continuing, let's save the outlines in a file that can be used later for printing or displaying the entire presentation.

20 Press **Save** (F10) and enter **slides** to create a file for saving the presentation.

Retrieving the Organizational Chart

Organizational charts are useful for presenting the management structure of a company at a glance. An organizational chart has been prepared for the "Maximizing the Organization" part of the presentation, and needs some final editing.

21 Press **Retrieve** (Shift-F10) and enter **chart.wkb** to retrieve an organizational chart.

22 Press **Escape** (Esc), type **24**, and then press **Down Arrow** (↓) to display the full chart on your screen.

What you see on your screen is a chart created using Graphics. There is a text box (TXT 1) at the top of your screen with several solid blocks below the box.

A TEXT BOX
B SOLID BLOCK

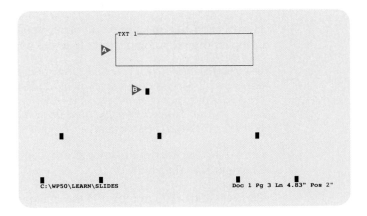

The box and the solid blocks are all text boxes. However, the box is a Paragraph type text box, while the blocks represent Character type text boxes.

What you *do not see* on your screen is the text in the boxes, and the horizontal and vertical lines connecting the boxes.

23 Press **Print** (Shift-F7) and select View Document (6).

24 Select 100% (1), press **Down Arrow** (↓) twice, and then press **Right Arrow** (→) to fill the screen with the chart.

Previewing the Chart

You should see the same chart as illustrated below.

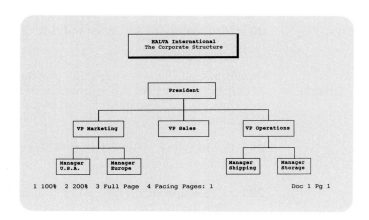

The horizontal and vertical lines are created using the Lines feature. Because each line is inserted separately into the chart (and not drawn), it takes some calculating to indicate exactly where the lines need to be placed, and exactly how long they need to be to intersect correctly.

However, with a little trial and error, you can soon create even more complex organizational charts than the one used for this lesson.

WordPerfect also provides a Line Draw feature that lets you quickly draw all the boxes and connecting lines that you need. However, the lines are created using the ASCII graphics characters, which may not be available for the fonts you are using. For an example of using Line Draw, turn to the Line Draw heading in the WordPerfect Reference manual.

Let's return to the organizational chart and insert the position of Accounts Manager into the chart.

25 Press **Exit** (F7) to return to the document screen.

Inserting a Text Box

The first step is to insert a text box that includes the "Manager Accounts" title. The manager needs to be placed in the middle of the last row of boxes.

⚠ CURSOR POSITION

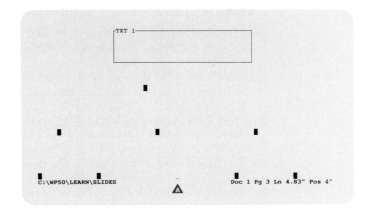

26 Place the cursor in the middle of the last row of boxes (as illustrated above).

27 Press **Reveal Codes** (Alt-F3) to see the codes in the chart.

Notice that tabs are being used to separate the text boxes in the line.

⚠ TABS

One advantage of using the Character style of a graphics box is that you can position it on the page by simply using tabs, spaces, and Hard Returns. This is especially useful for creating an organizational chart.

28 Place the cursor on the [Text Box:8;] code.

Copying the Box

Because all the boxes in the line are the same size, all you need to do is insert a copy of one of the boxes, and then edit the text in the box.

29 Press **Delete** (Del) to delete Text Box 8, and then press **Cancel** (F1) and select Restore (1) to undo the deletion.

30 Press **Left Arrow** (←) three times, press **Cancel** (F1), and then select Restore (1) to insert the same text box again.

31 Press **Left Arrow** (←), and then press **Backspace** twice to delete two tabs.

32 Press **Down Arrow** (↓) to rewrite the last line of text boxes.

Editing the Box Contents

Notice that Text Boxes 8 and 9 have been updated to 9 and 10, and that the new text box is now 8.

🔺A NEW TEXT BOX

🔺B UPDATED TEXT BOXES

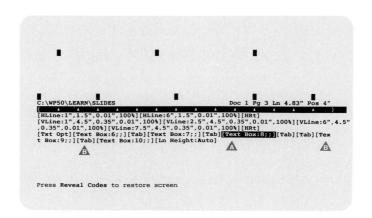

33 Press **Graphics** (Alt-F9), select Text Box (3), and then select Edit (2).

34 Enter **8** to edit the new text box, and then select Edit (8) to display the contents.

35 Erase the word "Shipping" from the title, and then type **Accounts** for the new title.

36 Press **Exit** (F7) twice to return to the document screen.

Adding a Vertical Line

The final step in editing the organizational chart is to add a vertical line to connect the Vice-President of Sales to the Accounts Manager.

37 Press **Up Arrow** (↑) five times, and then place the cursor on the second Vertical Line code in the line.

Your cursor should now be on the [VLine:6.74",4.15",0.38". . .] code in the Reveal Codes screen.

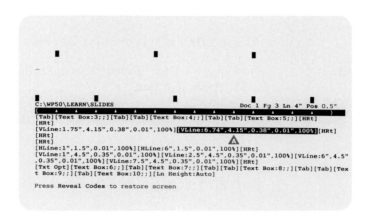

▲ VERTICAL LINE CODE

Notice that both vertical lines that connect the second and third row of boxes start 4.15" down the page (vertical position), and are .38" inches long. However, the vertical line for the Accounts Manager box needs to be a little longer because it does not branch out like the other two vertical lines.

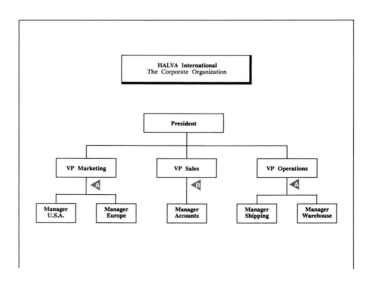

▲ EXISTING VERTICAL LINES

▲ NEW LINE NEEDED FOR ACCOUNTS MANAGER

38 Press **Graphics** (Alt-F9), select Line (5), and then select Vertical Line (2).

39 Select Horizontal Position (1), select Set Position (4), and then enter **4.25** to set the line in the center of the page.

40 Select Vertical Position (2), select Set Position (5), and then enter **4.15** to start the line 4.15 inches down from the top of the page.

41 Select Length of Line (3) and enter **.7** for a line 7/10 of an inch long.

42 Press **Exit** (F7) to return to the chart.

Previewing and Adjusting

Now that you have created the box and the vertical line, let's check the chart in the Preview screen.

43 Press **Print** (Shift-F7) and select View Document (6).

The vertical line is in position and the correct length, but the Accounts Manager box needs to be centered.

44 Press **Exit** (F7) to return to the document screen.

You can use spaces to help center the box in the line.

45 Place the cursor on the [Text Box:8;] code in the last line and press the **Space Bar** three times.

46 Press **Up Arrow** (↑) five times, press **Print** (Shift-F7) and then select View Document (6).

Saving the Edited Chart

The box is now centered in the line, and the chart is ready to save with the rest of the presentation.

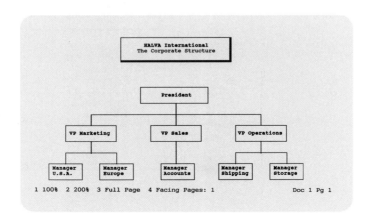

47 Press **Exit** (F7) to return to the chart.

48 Press **Reveal Codes** (Alt-F3) to display the full document screen.

49 Press **Save** (F10), press **Enter**, and then type **y** replace the "Slides" file.

50 Press **Page Down** (PgDn) and then press **Hard Page** (Ctrl-Enter) to start a new page for the next item in the presentation.

When creating an organizational chart with Graphics, remember to first create and position the text boxes. Once the boxes are in place, create all the horizontal lines, and then create the vertical lines.

If you set your status line to display inches, then you can use it to help with the measurements for the vertical lines. Simply place the cursor where you want the line to start, write down the Line number (Ln), move the cursor down to the line of boxes, and then write down the Line number. The first line number is the vertical position. Subtracting the first line number from the second line number also gives you the line length.

The measurements will be approximate, but close enough that you can adjust them to get the results you need. Remember to use the 100% Preview screen to see if the lines are connecting correctly.

Inserting the Music Box Outline

The next topic to emphasize in the presentation is the sales growth potential for music boxes. This can be done by inserting another part of the outline, followed by a graph.

51 Press **Home** three times and then **Up Arrow** (↑) to return to the beginning of the presentation.

52 Press **Block** (Alt-F4) and highlight the outline down to (and including) the "Music Boxes" topic.

53 Press **Save** (F10) and then press **Enter** to save the highlighted part of the outline.

54 Press **Home** twice and then press **Down Arrow** (↓) to return to the end of the document.

55 Press **Retrieve** (Shift-F10) and then press **Enter** to retrieve the "Music Boxes" outline.

56 Press **Save** (F10), press **Enter**, and then type **y** to replace the "Slides" file.

Preparing the Graph Box

The last item that needs to be prepared for the presentation is a graph showing the future sales potential for music boxes. The graph is already created, but needs to be retrieved and set up as a graphics figure in WordPerfect.

57 Press **Page Down** (PgDn) and then press **Hard Page** (Ctrl-Enter) to start a new page for the graph.

Before retrieving the graph, you can use the Figure options to design a border for the graph.

58 Press **Graphics** (Alt-F9), select Figure (1), and then select Options (4).

By setting a thick border for the right and bottom, you can create an effect similar to a shadow for the box.

59 Select Border Style (1), press **Enter** for the Left border, type **6** (Thick) for the Right border, press **Enter** for the Top border, and then type **6** for the Bottom border.

60 Press **Exit** (F7) to return to the document screen.

Retrieving the Graph

With the options set, you can create a graphics figure from the graph file.

61 Press **Graphics** (Alt-F9), select Figure (1), and then select Create (1).

62 Select Filename (1), and then enter **graph.wpg** for the name of the file.

63 Select Type (3) and then select Page (2).

64 Select Horizontal Position (5), select Margins (1), and then select Center (3) to center the graph between the left and right margins.

The measurements for the graph indicate that it is a little more than 3 inches square. Because the entire page is available for the graph, let's try creating a larger graph that is rectangular instead of square.

65 Select Size (6), and then select Both Width and Height (3).

66 Enter **6** for a width of six inches, and then enter **4.5** for a height of four and a half inches.

67 Select Edit (8) to display the graph.

**Changing the
Proportions**

While the box is rectangular, the graph is still in the shape of a square.

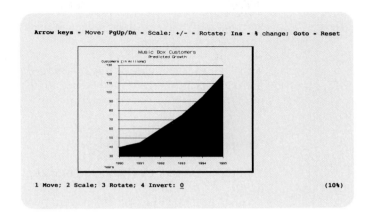

This can be corrected by *stretching* the graph horizontally with Scale.

68 Select Scale (2) and then enter **130** for the X value.

The X value is used for scaling horizontally, while the Y value is used for scaling vertically. When both are set to "100," then the figure is in the same proportions as when it was first retrieved into WordPerfect.

By increasing the X value to "130," the graph is stretched an extra 30 percent horizontally for a better fit in the box.

69 Press **Enter** to leave the Y value at 100 percent.

Now that the graph fills the box, let's reduce the entire graph proportionally (X and Y) to leave more space between the border of the box and the graph.

70 Press **Page Down** (PgDn) to scale down the entire graph by 10 percent.

71 Press **Exit** (F7) twice to return to the document screen.

**Displaying the
Presentation**

With the outlines (full and partial), chart, and graph prepared, the presentation is ready to be saved and displayed.

72 Press **Exit** (F7), type **y**, press **Enter** to use the "Slides" filename, and then type **y** to replace the file.

73 Type **n** to clear the screen and stay in WordPerfect.

Before giving the presentation, you may want to create a macro that automatically pauses to display each presentation graphic, then continues when you press Enter.

This feature is sometimes called a *slide show* in a presentation graphics package because it can also be used to display the graphics on a large screen monitor or display just like running a slide show.

To save you time, a macro has already been prepared that runs a slide show for you.

74 Press **Macro** (Alt-F10) and enter **show** for the name of the macro.

As each graphics figure is displayed, press **Enter** to continue on the next figure. After the last figure (the graph), the screen is cleared and the show is finished.

If you want to see the contents of the macro, turn to the Editing a Macro heading in Feature Summary *for details on displaying the macro keystrokes.*

Selecting a Base Font

The outline title is formatted with the Large and Italic font attributes, while the four major topics in the outline are bolded. Before printing or displaying the outline, you may want to change to a font that is larger or a different style.

75 Press **Retrieve** (Shift-F10) and then enter **slides** to retrieve the presentation.

76 Press **Print** (Shift-F7), type **s**, and highlight the name of your printer.

77 Press **Enter** to select the printer, and then press **Exit** (F7) to return to the document screen.

78 Press **Font** (Ctrl-F8) and select Base Font (4).

A list of all the available fonts is displayed on your screen. Each font listed has its own set of fonts assigned to the attributes. As soon as you select a font from the list, the attributes are adjusted for the new base font.

For example, the following outline was printed on a laser printer using Times Roman 11pt (point) as the base font for the document.

A Time For Growth
HALVA in the 1990's

1. **The First Fifty Years**
   a. The Roots of Mail Order
   b. The European Connection

2. **The Organizational Question**
   a. Direction vs. Management
   b. Maximizing the Organization

3. **The Retail Question**
   a. Mail Order in the 1990's
   b. Expanding Markets
      i. Music Boxes
      ii. Oriental Furniture

4. **The Next Fifty Years**

By selecting Helvetica 14pt for a new base font, WordPerfect automatically adjusted the font attributes, printing the text in a different style and size.

A Time For Growth
HALVA in the 1990's

1. **The First Fifty Years**
   a. The Roots of Mail Order
   b. The European Connection

2. **The Organizational Question**
   a. Direction vs. Management
   b. Maximizing the Organization

3. **The Retail Question**
   a. Mail Order in the 1990's
   b. Expanding Markets
      i. Music Boxes
      ii. Oriental Furniture

4. **The Next Fifty Years**

Before saving the presentation, you may want to choose a larger base font to increase the size or change the style of the text.

79 Highlight the base font you want to use (it may be the one you are using now), and then press **Enter** to select the font.

You can see the new font attributes in the Preview screen.

80 Press **Print** (Shift-F7), select View Document (6), and then select 100% (1) to see the style and size of the text in the outline.

81 Press **Exit** (F7) to return to the document screen.

82 Press **Exit** (F7), type **y**, and then press **Enter** and type **y** to use the "slides" filename.

83 Type **n** to clean the screen.

At this point you may want to use the "Show" macro again to display the fonts for the outline and organizational chart.

When the organizational chart is displayed, the vertical lines may be out of alignment because a larger or smaller font may be selected. You can adjust the vertical position by using Advance.

Summary

During this lesson, you were introduced to the following tasks:

- Creating an outline.
- Creating a vertical line.
- Changing the proportions of a graphics figure.
- Defining an outline style.
- Editing the graphics figure options.
- Previewing a document.
- Selecting a base font.

For a complete listing of all tasks introduced in the lessons, turn to *Feature Summary* at the end of the workbook.

Lesson 32: Reports

A report is a formal paper that informs people of your research, ideas, and predictions about a selected topic. Strict guidelines and standards require you to support your claims, adhere to the rules of grammar, and produce a polished document that looks professional.

WordPerfect helps you meet these challenges by providing features such as auto-referencing, footnotes, endnotes, and automatic creation of tables, lists, and indexes.

In this lesson, you are introduced to many of these features as you edit a corporate report for HALVA International. The report is divided into several files. After editing, you then use a master document to assemble the files, generate a table of contents, endnotes, and an index, and then save and print the report.

Because each feature is briefly introduced, you may want to turn to the WordPerfect reference manual for more details about a particular feature.

Retrieving the First Part of the Report

The text of the report is divided into files that contain information about the past, present, and future of the company. Let's begin by retrieving the information about the past.

1 Press **Retrieve** (Shift-F10) and enter **past.wkb** to retrieve the first part of the report.

Notice the number at the end of the quotation in the first paragraph.

▲ FOOTNOTE NUMBER

The First Fifty Years

A wise man once said that "Friends come and go, but enemies accumulate."1 The same can be said of the relationships that develop between a company and its customers.

The year 1989 marks the 50th anniversary of the founding of HALVA International. While many other import/export businesses have started in glory and ended in defeat, the HALVA International corporation continues to thrive.

While there are many theories surrounding the success of HALVA International, the truth lies in the careful cultivation of customer relationships and continued efforts to provide quality merchandise at affordable prices.

In this report, the past, present, and future status of HALVA International are reviewed, with an emphasis on these characteristics as being vital to the continued survival of the company.

The European Connection
The year was 1939, and the rumors of war had become a
C:\WP50\LEARN\PAST.WKB   Doc 1 Pg 1 Ln 1" Pos 1"

The number will be printed with the text and indicates that a footnote has been created for the quotation. The footnote will be printed at the bottom of the page.

Footnotes are displayed in the Preview screen. You may want to use the Preview screen to see the footnote before continuing the lesson.

Creating a Footnote

All you need to do to add a footnote to a document is type the text of the footnote. WordPerfect inserts the footnote number in the text and prints the footnote at the bottom of the page for you.

2 Press **Page Down** (PgDn) to move to the bottom of the page.

You should see an indented quotation in the middle of your screen.

▲ INDENTED QUOTATION

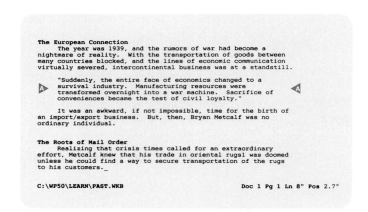

3 Place the cursor at the end of the quotation.

4 Press **Footnote** (Ctrl-F7), select Footnote (1), and then select Create (1).

An editing screen is displayed with a footnote number inserted. The footnote number is like a paragraph number, and automatically updates as footnotes are created or deleted in the document.

5 Type the following footnote text, using **Underline** (F8) to underline the title of the book:

Edith Steinhardt, "The War Remembered," in <u>The Economics of Survival</u>, ed. Lillian Holmes (New York: Harper Row, Ltd., 1986), p. 89.

6 When you finish, press **Exit** (F7) to save the footnote and return to the report.

Changing the Endnote Numbering Style

A footnote number (2) now appears on your screen at the end of the quote. However, notice that another number also appears in the last paragraph of the page.

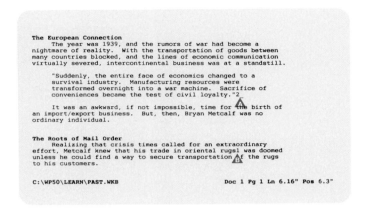

▲ FOOTNOTE NUMBER

⬛ ENDNOTE NUMBER

The number represents an endnote that has been created. Endnotes can be used instead of footnotes to document a report, and are printed at the end of your document (or wherever you want) instead of at the bottom of a page.

In this case, footnotes are being used to document the report, while endnotes are being used to add additional notes to the end of the report.

Because footnotes and endnotes are numbered separately by WordPerfect, the endnote number in the last paragraph did not update to "3" when you created a new footnote. However, to avoid confusion, you should probably change the endnote numbering style.

7 Press **Page Up** (PgUp) to place the cursor at the beginning of the page.

8 Press **Footnote** (Ctrl-F7), select Endnote (2), and then select Options (4).

The menu of endnote options displayed lets you change the spacing and numbering style of the endnotes in your document.

9 Select Endnote Numbering Method (5), and then select Letters (2).

10 Press **Exit** (F7) to return to the report, and then press **Page Down** (PgDn) to move to the end of the page.

Now the endnote numbering uses letters, while the footnote numbering uses numbers.

⚠ NUMBER

⚠ LETTER

```
The European Connection
      The year was 1939, and the rumors of war had become a
nightmare of reality.  With the transportation of goods between
many countries blocked, and the lines of economic communication
virtually severed, intercontinental business was at a standstill.

      "Suddenly, the entire face of economics changed to a
      survival industry.  Manufacturing resources were
      transformed overnight into a war machine.  Sacrifice of
      conveniences became the test of civil loyalty."2

      It was an awkward, if not impossible, time for the birth of
an import/export business.  But, then, Bryan Metcalf was no
ordinary individual.

The Roots of Mail Order
      Realizing that crisis times called for an extraordinary
effort, Metcalf knew that his trade in oriental rugsa was doomed
unless he could find a way to secure transportation of the rugs
to his customers._

C:\WP50\LEARN\PAST.WKB                         Doc 1 Pg 1 Ln 8" Pos 2.7"
```

The options menu for footnote numbering also contains options that let you change spacing, numbering style, etc., for footnotes.

11 Press **Page Up** (PgUp) to return to the beginning of the page.

Hyphenating the Text

When you finish editing a document, you can improve the printed appearance of some lines by using Hyphenation.

12 Press **Format** (Shift-F8), select Line (1), and then select Hyphenation (1).

13 Select Automatic (3) to have WordPerfect automatically hyphenate words for you, and then press **Exit** (F7) to return to the report.

As you scroll through the text, WordPerfect automatically hyphenates for you.

14 Press **Home** and then **Down Arrow** (↓) to move to the bottom of the screen.

If WordPerfect stops for help in hyphenating a word, simply press escape (Esc) to continue.

Notice that the word "International" has moved back up a line, and is now hyphenated.

▲ HYPHENATED WORD

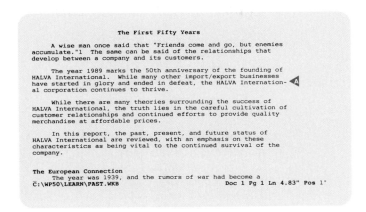

By letting WordPerfect hyphenate words, the lines can be adjusted to print a more exact number of characters in the line. This adjusting produces more evenly-spaced text when the document is printed.

You can adjust the frequency of hyphenation by increasing or decreasing the size of the Hyphenation Zone in the Line Format menu. See your WordPerfect reference manual for details.

15 Press **Exit** (F7), type **y**, and then enter **past** to save the first part of the report in a new file.

16 Type **n** to clear the screen.

Retrieving the Second Part of the Report

The next file that needs to be edited contains information about the present condition of the company.

17 Press **Retrieve** (Shift-F10) and then enter **present.wkb** to retrieve the second part of the report.

The second part of the report is ready to print, but some marking needs to be done so that the "Direction vs. Management" subtitle is included in the table of contents, and the word "personality" is included in the index.

18 Press **Down Arrow** (↓) until the cursor is at the beginning of the "Direction vs. Management" title.

Marking a Title for the Table of Contents

For WordPerfect to create a table of contents, you need to mark each title in your document that you want in that table. WordPerfect then uses the text of each title to create a table of contents, inserting the page number on which the text is located.

19 Press **Reveal Codes** (Alt-F3) to see the codes in the report.

20 Press **Block** (Alt-F4), press **End**, and then press **Left Arrow** (←) to place the cursor on the [bold] code.

21 Press **Mark Text** (Alt-F5), and then select Table of Contents (1).

You are now asked to type a level number. Like outline and paragraph numbering, you can define a numbering style for each level (up to five) of the table of contents.

The title for each report section (e.g., "A Time for Reflection") is marked for level 1, while the subtitles (e.g., "Direction vs. Management") are marked for level 2.

22 Type **2** for the level number.

After typing the level number, WordPerfect inserts marking codes around the title. Notice that only the text of the title is placed between the [Mark:ToC,2] and [End Mark:ToC,2] codes.

A BEGINNING CODE
B ENDING CODE

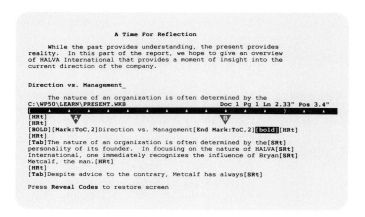

If you had included the Bold codes in the highlighted text, then they would have also been included in the table of contents. However, only the titles need bolding in the table of contents, so only the text of the subtitles should be included between the Mark and End Mark codes.

23 Press **Reveal Codes** (Alt-F3) to display the full document screen.

Marking a Word to Include in the Index

With the subtitle marked, you are ready to mark the word "personality" for inclusion in the index.

24 Press ♦**Search** (F2), type **personality**, and then press ♦**Search** to place the cursor next to the word.

25 Press **Mark Text** (Alt-F5) and select Index (3).

Notice that WordPerfect displays the word "Personality" for the index heading. If you use Block to highlight two or more words (before pressing Mark Text), WordPerfect will display the highlighted words for the heading.

26 Press **Enter** to use "Personality" for the heading.

27 Press **Enter** to bypass adding a subheading.

You can enter any text you want for the heading or subheading to be included in the index. However, by using the cursor and Block, you can have WordPerfect display the text you want for most index markings.

28 Press **Reveal Codes** (Alt-F3) to display the index marking code.

There is only one code for index marking, as WordPerfect uses the text in the code for creating the index.

▲ ONE INDEX MARKING CODE

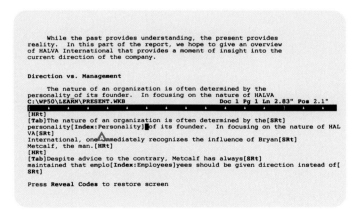

```
        While the past provides understanding, the present provides
reality.  In this part of the report, we hope to give an overview
of HALVA International that provides a moment of insight into the
current direction of the company.

Direction vs. Management

        The nature of an organization is often determined by the
personality of its founder.  In focusing on the nature of HALVA
C:\WP50\LEARN\PRESENT.WKB                    Doc 1 Pg 1 Ln 2.83" Pos 2.1"
[                                                                       ]
[HRt]
[Tab]The nature of an organization is often determined by the[SRt]
personality[Index:Personality] of its founder.  In focusing on the nature of HAL
VA[SRt]
International, one immediately recognizes the influence of Bryan[SRt]
Metcalf, the man.[HRt]
[HRt]
[Tab]Despite advice to the contrary, Metcalf has always[SRt]
maintained that emplo[Index:Employees]yees should be given direction instead of[
SRt]

Press Reveal Codes to restore screen
```

29 Press **Reveal Codes** (Alt-F3) to display the full document screen.

Marking an Automatic Reference

The second page of the document contains a table of operating expenses for the third and fourth quarters of 1989.

30 Press **Page Down** (PgDn) to display the operating expenses table.

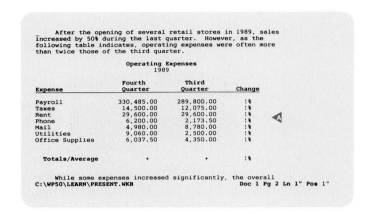

31 Press **Up Arrow** (↑) four times to display the last paragraph on the previous page.

The last paragraph mentions the table, but without using a page number reference.

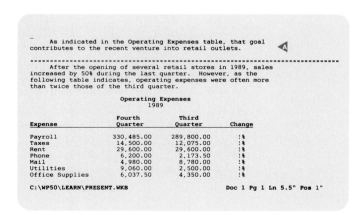

Let's add a page number reference and tie it to the table by using Automatic Reference.

32 Place the cursor on the comma after the "…Operating Expenses table" phrase and then press the **Space Bar**.

33 Type the **(see page)** phrase, press **Left Arrow** (←), and then press the **Space Bar**.

The cursor should now be on the closing parenthesis, with a space separating "page" from the parenthesis.

▲ CURSOR POSITION

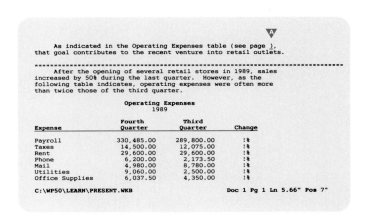

```
                                         ▼
       As indicated in the Operating Expenses table (see page ),
   that goal contributes to the recent venture into retail outlets.

   -----------------------------------------------------------------------
       After the opening of several retail stores in 1989, sales
   increased by 50% during the last quarter.  However, as the
   following table indicates, operating expenses were often more
   than twice those of the third quarter.

                           Operating Expenses
                                  1989

                        Fourth          Third
   Expense              Quarter         Quarter        Change

   Payroll              330,485.00      289,800.00        !%
   Taxes                 14,500.00       12,075.00        !%
   Rent                  29,600.00       29,600.00        !%
   Phone                  6,200.00        2,173.50        !%
   Mail                   4,980.00        8,780.00        !%
   Utilities              9,060.00        2,500.00        !%
   Office Supplies        6,037.50        4,350.00        !%

   C:\WP50\LEARN\PRESENT.WKB                    Doc 1 Pg 1 Ln 5.66" Pos 7"
```

You are now ready to insert a page number that automatically references the operating expenses table.

34 Press **Mark Text** (Alt-F5), select Automatic Reference (1), and then type **3** to mark both the reference and the target at the same time.

A *reference* is the place you want the page number to appear ("see page…"), while a *target* is the item you want to reference (operating expenses table).

The menu on your screen lets you select the type of reference you want to create.

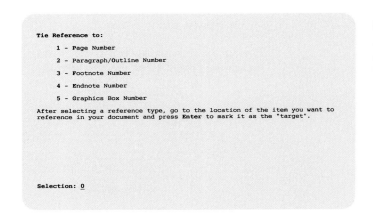

```
Tie Reference to:

      1 - Page Number

      2 - Paragraph/Outline Number

      3 - Footnote Number

      4 - Endnote Number

      5 - Graphics Box Number

After selecting a reference type, go to the location of the item you want to
reference in your document and press Enter to mark it as the "target".




Selection: 0
```

All you need to do for the report is to refer to the page number on which the operating expenses table is located.

35 Select Page Number (1).

You are returned to the document to move the cursor to the item you want referenced.

36 Place the cursor on the "Operating Expenses" title and then press **Enter** to mark the target.

37 Enter **operate** for the target name, and then press **Down Arrow** (↓).

The page number inserted next to "see page" automatically references the table on the next page.

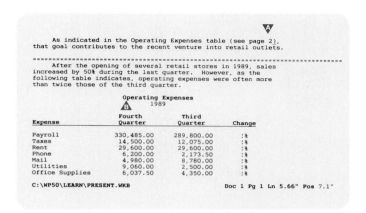

A Reference code displays the page number, while a Target code (inserted at the table title) keeps the number updated if the table moves to a new page. The two codes are tied together because they both contain the "operate" target name that you entered.

For information on creating multiple references to the same target, turn to the WordPerfect reference manual.

38 Press **Exit** (F7), type **y**, and then enter **present** to create a new file for the second part of the report.

39 Type **n** to clear the screen.

Retrieving the Final Part of the Report

The final part of the report contains projections about the future of HALVA International for the next fifty years.

40 Press **Retrieve** (Shift-F10) and enter **future.wkb** to retrieve the last part of the report.

Although the word "problems" in the first paragraph is adequate, another word could possibly be used that gives a better description of the situation.

Using the Thesaurus to Find the Right Word

Fortunately, WordPerfect includes a thesaurus that can help you quickly find just the right word.

41 Place the cursor on the word "problems" in the third line of the first paragraph.

If you are running WordPerfect from a two disk drive system, replace the Workbook diskette with the Thesaurus diskette before continuing.

If you are running WordPerfect from a two disk drive system, replace the Workbook diskette with the Thesaurus diskette before continuing.

42 Press **Thesaurus** (Alt-F1) to display a list of synonyms for the word "problems."

A list of nouns, adjectives, and even antonyms (opposite meaning) appear from which you can select a replacement.

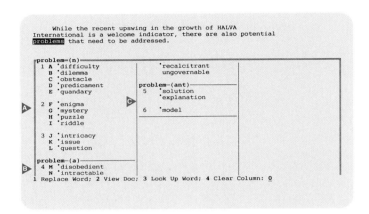

```
        While the recent upswing in the growth of HALVA
   International is a welcome indicator, there are also potential
   problems that need to be addressed.

┌problem─(n)─────────────────
│   1 A ·difficulty              │        ·recalcitrant
│     B ·dilemma                 │         ungovernable
│     C ·obstacle                │
│     D ·predicament             │ problem─(ant)──────────
│     E ·quandary                │   5   ·solution
│                                │       ·explanation
│   2 F ·enigma                  │
│     G ·mystery                 │   6   ·model
│     H ·puzzle                  │
│     I ·riddle                  │
│                                │
│   3 J ·intricacy               │
│     K ·issue                   │
│     L ·question                │
│                                │
│ problem─(a)────────────        │
│   4 M ·disobedient             │
│     N ·intractable             │
 1 Replace Word; 2 View Doc; 3 Look Up Word; 4 Clear Column: 0
```

43 Select Replace Word (1), and then type the letter next to "obstacle" in the list (**c**).

WordPerfect immediately replaces the word "problems" with "obstacle" for you.

44 Type **s** to make the word "obstacle" a plural noun.

The Thesaurus is very powerful and lets you search through levels of lists for just the right word. For details on all the Thesaurus features, turn to the Thesaurus heading in the WordPerfect reference manual.

Comparing Documents

Once you edit the document on your screen, you may want to compare it with the original document on disk. WordPerfect provides a Document Compare feature that compares text automatically for you.

45 Press **Mark Text** (Alt-F5), select Generate (6), and then type **2** to compare the screen and disk documents.

46 Press **Enter** to compare "Future.wkb" to the edited future text on your screen.

WordPerfect begins the comparison, and then displays the document on your screen with the compared text.

```
                        The Next Fifty Years

    While the recent upswing in the growth of HALVA
International is a welcome indicator, there are also potential
obstacles that need to be addressed. there are also potential
problems that need to be addressed.

    However, if these needs are met, the company can look
forward to a bright and exciting future through the decade of the
1990's and beyond.

Expanding Markets

    From oriental rugs to imported jewelry, HALVA International
has always provided a variety of merchandise to its customers.
However, the variety of products has often been limited to those
items that are a known quantity.

    Recently trends indicate, however that there is profit to be
made in areas such as oriental furniture and music boxes.  In
fact, our research indicates that music boxes may become a long-
term, profitable investment.

C:\WP50\LEARN\FUTURE.WKB                       Doc 1 Pg 1 Ln 1" Pos 1"
```

The reverse video and strikethrough text in the illustration may not be displayed on your screen, depending on the type of graphics card you are using (or whether you have a graphics card installed). However, you can see the Redline and Strikeout codes in the Reveal Codes screen.

Notice that the last phrase of the first paragraph ("there are also potential. . .") has been repeated twice.

The first repetition (reverse video) is the phrase with the new word "obstacles" inserted, and is surrounded by Redline codes. The second repetition (strikethrough) is the old phrase from the file on disk, and is surrounded by Strikeout codes.

Whenever WordPerfect compares the screen and file documents, any text that has been changed in the screen document is placed in Redline codes with the original text from the file document placed in Strikeout codes.

Removing the Redline and Strikeout

If you want to remove the redline codes and delete the strikeout text you can use Generate on the Mark Text menu.

47 Press **Mark Text** (Alt-F5), select Generate (6), type **1** to remove the Redline codes (markings) and Strikeout text, and then type **y** to start the process.

48 Press **Home** twice and then **Up Arrow** (↑) to move to the top of the document.

When WordPerfect finishes, the text of the first paragraph should look exactly like it did before you selected Document Compare.

```
                    The Next Fifty Years

      While the recent upswing in the growth of HALVA
 International is a welcome indicator, there are also potential
 obstacles that need to be addressed.

      However, if these needs are met, the company can look
 forward to a bright and exciting future through the decade of the
 1990's and beyond.

 Expanding Markets

      From oriental rugs to imported jewelry, HALVA International
 has always provided a variety of merchandise to its customers.
 However, the variety of products has often been limited to those
 items that are a known quantity.

      Recently trends indicate, however that there is profit to be
 made in areas such as oriental furniture and music boxes.  In
 fact, our research indicates that music boxes may become a long-
 term, profitable investment.

 C:\WP50\LEARN\FUTURE.WKB                     Doc 1 Pg 1 Ln 1" Pos 1"
```

49 Press **Exit** (F7), type **y**, and then enter **future** to create a new file for the final part of the report.

50 Type **n** to clear the document screen.

Defining an Index

After (or before) marking text for a table of contents or index, you need to indicate the place where the table or index should be created (generated) by WordPerfect.

In order to make it easy for you to mark the place, all you need to do is define the style of numbering, and then WordPerfect generates the table or index at the definition code.

For example, let's create a title for the index, and then mark the place to begin generation of the index.

51 Press **Center** (Shift-F6), press **Bold** (F6), and then type **Index** for the title.

52 Press **End** to move past the Bold Off code, and then press **Enter** twice to double space.

53 Press **Mark Text** (Alt-F5), select Define (5), and then select Define Index (3).

You are asked for the filename of a concordance. A concordance is a list of words that you want WordPerfect to include in the index. Instead of marking the words in the report, all you need to do is create a list of the words, and WordPerfect does the rest.

Let's enter a concordance filename, and then create the file after defining the index.

54 Enter **concord** for the filename of the concordance.

The following menu of numbering styles is displayed on your screen.

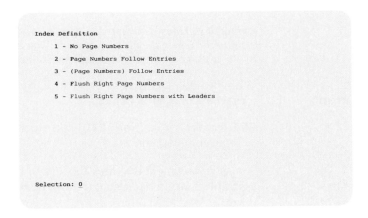

```
Index Definition

    1 - No Page Numbers

    2 - Page Numbers Follow Entries

    3 - (Page Numbers) Follow Entries

    4 - Flush Right Page Numbers

    5 - Flush Right Page Numbers with Leaders




Selection: 0
```

These are the same styles that are available for the table of contents and lists you generate with WordPerfect.

55 Type **2** to have page numbers follow the index headings.

Marking the Index Heading for the Table of Contents

Before saving the index page, the title needs to be marked for the table of contents.

56 Press **Word Left** (Ctrl-←), press **Block** (Alt-F4), and then press **End** to highlight the title.

57 Press **Mark Text** (Alt-F5), select Table of Contents (1), and then type **1** for the level.

58 Press **Exit** (F7), type **y**, enter **index** to create a new file, and then type **n** to clear the screen.

Although you do not need to place the index definition in a separate file, it makes it easier when organizing a master document.

Creating a Concordance File

Now that the index definition is created and the screen cleared, you can quickly create a concordance file.

59 Type **Merchandise** and then press **Enter** to start a new line.

60 Type **Mail Order** and then press **Enter** to start a new line.

61 Press **Exit** (F7), type **y**, enter **concord** for the filename, and then type **n** to clear the screen.

All you need to do is type and save the headings, and WordPerfect does the rest when you generate the index. Just make sure that each word or phrase is followed by a Hard Return.

Although you may be tempted to create a concordance with all the headings you want in the index, the number of words you can have in a concordance is limited by the amount of memory available when generating the index.

Retrieving the Master Document

With the editing completed, and a file created for the index, you are ready to retrieve the master document.

62 Press **Retrieve** (Shift-F10) and enter **master.wkb** for the name of the master document.

A master document is simply the idea of being able to automatically assemble a larger document (report, book, etc.) from several smaller files.

As you can see, the master document on your screen contains commands for retrieving the files you created in this lesson.

▲ SUBDOCUMENT COMMAND

```
                          A Time For Growth
                        HALVA in the 1990's
------------------------------------------------------------------

   Subdoc: TABLE.WKB

------------------------------------------------------------------

▲  Subdoc: PAST

------------------------------------------------------------------

   Subdoc: PRESENT

------------------------------------------------------------------

C:\WP50\LEARN\MASTER.WKB                    Doc 1 Pg 1 Ln 1" Pos 1"
```

Including a Subdocument

Each file is called a *subdocument,* and can be included in the master document by using Mark Text.

63 Press **Home** twice and then **Down Arrow** (↓) to move to the end of the master document.

64 Press **Mark Text** (Alt-F5), select Subdocument (2), and then enter **index** to include the index in the master document.

A comment is displayed on your screen, indicating that the "Index" file will be retrieved when you *expand* the master document.

While a Hard Page break has been used between the subdocument comments to make sure that each retrieved file starts on a new page, page breaks are not necessary if you do not need them.

Placing the Endnotes

Before expanding the master document, you should indicate the place where you want the endnotes created. If you don't, WordPerfect will automatically create them at the end of the document (after the index).

65 Press **Left Arrow** (←) to place the cursor above the index comment.

66 Press **Center** (Shift-F6), press **Bold** (F6), and type **Additional Notes** for the title of the endnotes.

67 Press **Right Arrow** (→) to move past the Bold Off code, and then press **Enter** twice to add extra spacing.

68 Press **Footnote** (Ctrl-F7), select Endnote Placement (3), and then type **n** to have the numbering begin at "A".

A comment is displayed on the screen, and an extra Hard Page break inserted after the comment.

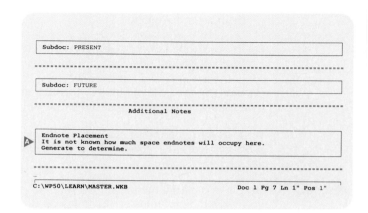

The comment indicates that you need to use Generate to find out how many pages the endnotes will need. However, after generating, the comment will not be replaced with the endnotes. Instead, WordPerfect simply reserves the number of pages needed to print the endnotes.

If you want to see the endnotes before printing, use the Preview screen.

Marking the Endnotes Title for the Table of Contents

The "Additional Notes" title on the endnotes page should be included in the table of contents.

69 Press **Word Left** (Ctrl-←) twice to move the cursor to the beginning of the title.

70 Press **Block** (Alt-F4), and then press **Home** and **Right Arrow** (→) to highlight the title.

71 Press **Mark Text** (Alt-F5), select Table of Contents (1), and then type **1** for the level number.

72 Press **Exit** (F7), type **y**, enter **master** to save the master document in a new file, and then type **n** to clear the screen.

Expanding the Master Document

With the files and master document edited, you are ready to see what WordPerfect can do to help you automate the process of creating reports.

73 Press **Retrieve** (Shift-F10) and enter **master** to retrieve the master document.

74 Press **Mark Text** (Alt-F5), select Generate (6), and then select Expand Master Document (3).

Because Hyphenation is on in the first part of the report, WordPerfect also hyphenates the rest of the report. If you see a message asking for help with hyphenation, simply press **Escape** (Esc) to hyphenate and continue expanding the document.

75 Press **Home** twice and then **Up Arrow** (↑) to move to the beginning of the expanded report.

Notice that comments indicate the beginning and ending of each retrieved file.

▲ BEGINNING OF SUBDOCUMENT

▲ END OF SUBDOCUMENT

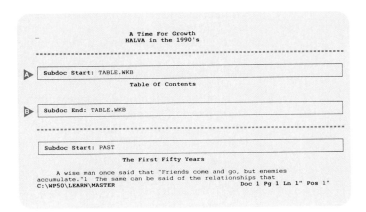

```
                              A Time For Growth
                            HALVA in the 1990's

  ==================================================================

  ┌──────────────────────────────────────────────────────────────┐
▲ │ Subdoc Start: TABLE.WKB                                        │
  └──────────────────────────────────────────────────────────────┘
                            Table Of Contents

  ┌──────────────────────────────────────────────────────────────┐
▲ │ Subdoc End: TABLE.WKB                                          │
  └──────────────────────────────────────────────────────────────┘

  ==================================================================

  ┌──────────────────────────────────────────────────────────────┐
  │ Subdoc Start: PAST                                             │
  └──────────────────────────────────────────────────────────────┘
                          The First Fifty Years

        A wise man once said that "Friends come and go, but enemies
  accumulate."1   The same can be said of the relationships that
  C:\WP50\LEARN\MASTER                              Doc 1 Pg 1 Ln 1" Pos 1"
```

Generating the Table, Endnotes, and Index

Now that the report has been assembled into one document, you can automatically generate the table of contents, endnotes, and index just as easily.

76 Press **Mark Text** (Alt-F5) and select Generate (6).

77 Type **5** and then type **y** to begin generating.

A counter at the bottom of the screen keeps you informed of the progress. When the generating is completed, you are returned to the report.

78 Press **Home** twice and then **Up Arrow** (↑) to return to the beginning of the report.

At this point you may want to use Page Down to scroll through the report a page at a time to see the completed report. The report can also be viewed in the Preview screen or printed (the comments are not displayed or printed). Just remember to select your own printer before printing.

Condensing the Master Document

Returning the master document to its original size (condensing the document) is as simple as expanding the master document.

79 Press **Mark Text** (Alt-F5) and select Generate (6).

80 Select Condense Master Document (4), and then type **n** to delete the expanded subdocuments without saving them.

You can also type "y" if you have edited the text in the master document and want to save a file instead of deleting it.

The master document returns to its original size, and you can edit the document or clear the screen for the next word processing task.

81 Press **Exit** (F7) and type **n** twice to clear the screen.

Summary

During this lesson, you were introduced to the following tasks:

- Changing the footnote/endnote numbering style.
- Comparing documents.
- Condensing a master document.
- Creating a concordance.
- Creating a footnote/endnote.
- Creating a master document.
- Defining an index.
- Expanding a master document.
- Generating tables, indexes, automatic references, etc.
- Hyphenating text.
- Marking a title for the table of contents.
- Marking a word or phrase for the index.
- Referencing text and illustrations.
- Using the thesaurus.

For a complete listing of all tasks introduced in the lessons, turn to *Feature Summary* at the end of the workbook.

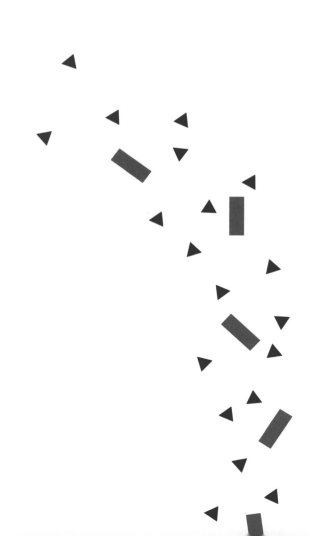

Feature Summary

The following features have been compiled from the summary at the end of each lesson. The features are listed alphabetically with an indication of the lessons in which they are introduced. More than one lesson indicates various ways in which the feature has been used.

Adding a Keystroke to the Keyboard Layout
Lesson 27
1 Press **Setup** (Shift-F1) and select Keyboard Layout (6).
2 Place the reverse video cursor on the name of the keyboard layout, and select Edit (5).
3 Select Create (4) from the keystroke menu, and then press the key you want to assign to the task.
4 Select Description (1) and enter a description of the task.
5 Select Action (2), press **Right Arrow** (→) and type the keystroke(s) you want included.
6 Press **Exit** (F7) four times to return to the document editing screen.

Adding a Record to a Secondary File (^R and ^E)
Lesson 21
1 Place the cursor at the position where you want the new record inserted.
2 Type the information for the first field, and then press **Merge R** (F9) to end the field.
3 Continuing adding fields and ending them with **Merge R** (F9). If a field is empty simply press **Merge R** and continue.
4 When you finish, press **Merge Codes** (Shift-F9) and type **e** to end the record with a ^E and a Hard Page break.

Adding Extra Spacing
Lessons 2 and 3
1 Press **Enter** to add blank lines between blocks of text on the page, or press **Tab** to add extra spacing between items in a line.

Advancing Text from the Left Edge of the Page
Lesson 16
1 Place the cursor at the beginning of the line.
2 Press **Format** (Shift-F8), select Other (4), and then select Advance (1).
3 Select Column (6) and enter the distance from the left edge of the page.
4 Press **Exit** (F7) to save the setting and return to the document screen.

Advancing Text from the Top Edge of the Page
Lessons 13, 16, and 22
1 Place the cursor at the beginning of the line.
2 Press **Format** (Shift-F8), select Other (4), and then select Advance (1).

3 Select Line (3) and enter the distance from the top edge of the page, or select Down (2) and enter the distance from the current cursor position.

4 Press **Exit** (F7) to save the setting and return to the document screen.

Advancing Text Up the Page
Lesson 14

1 Write down the Line (Ln) number of the line to which you want the text moved.

2 Place the cursor at the beginning of the text.

3 Press **Format** (Shift-F8), select Other (4), and then select Advance (1).

4 Select Line (3) and enter the line number you wrote down. Include a "u" with the number (e.g., **25u**).

5 Press **Exit** (F7) to save the setting and return to the document screen.

Aligning Text at the Right Margin (One Line)
Lesson 13

1 Place the cursor at the beginning of the line and press **Flush Right** (Alt-F6).

2 Press **Down Arrow**(↓) after existing text or **Enter** after typed text to end the flush right.

Aligning Text at the Right Margin (Several Lines)
Lesson 13

1 Use **Block** (Alt-F4) to highlight the lines you want flush against the right margin.

2 Press **Flush Right** (Alt-F6) and type **y** to align the text.

Blocking (Highlighting) Part of Your Text
Lesson 9

1 Place the cursor at the beginning (or end) of the text you want to highlight, and then press **Block** (Alt-F4).

2 Move the cursor to the end (or beginning) of the text.

3 Select a feature that works with Block.

Bolding Text
Lesson 3

1 Press **Bold** (F6) to begin bolding.

2 Type the text, and then press **Bold** again to end bolding.

Calculating Math Columns
Lesson 16

1 Place the cursor after the Math On code so that the "Math" message is displayed on the status line.

2 Press **Math/Columns** (Alt-F7) and select Calculate (2).

Calculating Totals
Lesson 28

While Math is on, you can type a plus sign (+), an equal sign (=), or an asterisk (*) in a numeric or total column to calculate a subtotal, total, or grand total. You can also type a "t" or "T" in front of a number to include it as an extra subtotal or total figure.

Canceling a Menu or Message and Returning to Your Document
Lesson 7

1 Press **Cancel** (F1) until you back out of a menu or message and return to your document.

Centering Text Between the Left and Right Margins
Lesson 3

1 Press **Center** (Shift-F6), type the text, and then press **Enter** to end centering and start a new line.

Centering Text Between the Top and Bottom Margins
Lesson 4

1 Move the cursor to the very beginning of the page.

2 Press **Format** (Shift-F8), select Page (2), and then select Center Page Top to Bottom (1).

3 Press **Exit** (F7) to return to your document.

Changing the Footnote/Endnote Numbering Style
Lesson 32

1 Place the cursor at the beginning of the document, or where you want the numbering style to begin changing.

2 Press **Footnote/Endnote** (Ctrl-F7), and then select Footnote (1) or Endnote (2).

3 Select Options (4), and then set the style using the options in the displayed menu.

4 Press **Exit** (F7) to save the settings and return to the document.

Changing the Proportions of a Graphics Figure
Lesson 31

1 Press **Graphics** (Alt-F9) and select Figure (1), Table (2), Text Box (3), or User-Defined (4).

2 Select Edit (2), and then enter the number of the box you want to edit.

3 Select Edit (8) from the graphics editing menu to display the graphics figure.

4 Select Scale (2), and then enter an X percentage value and a Y percentage value.

5 Press **Exit** (F7) twice to return to the document screen.

The X value is the width of the figure, while the Y value is the height of the figure. You can also press Page Up or Page Down to increase or decrease the overall size of the graphics figure.

Clearing and Exiting the Second Document Screen
Lesson 9
1 Press **Exit** (F7), and then type **y** and enter a filename if you want to save the document on the screen.
2 When you see the message "Exit doc 2?", then type **y** to exit the second document screen and return to the first document screen.

Clearing the Screen (Without Saving)
Lesson 1
1 Press **Exit** (F7) and type **n** twice to clear the screen before starting another document.

Comparing Documents
Lesson 32
1 Press **Mark Text** (Alt-F5), select Generate (6), and type **2** to compare the document on your screen with a document on disk.
2 Enter the filename of the document on disk you want to compare.

Condensing a Master Document
Lesson 32
1 Press **Mark Text** (Alt-F5), select Generate (6), and then select Condense Master Document (4) to condense the document on your screen.
2 Type **y** to save the subdocuments (or type **n** for no), and then type **y** when prompted to replace a subdocument or simply select "Replace All Remaining Files" to have WordPerfect do all the replacing automatically.

Copying a File to a Backup Diskette
Lesson 11
1 Insert the backup diskette into drive A.
2 Press **List Files** (F5) and then press **Enter** to display the list of files.
3 Place the cursor on the file you want to copy.
4 Select Copy (8), and then enter **a:** to copy the file to the backup diskette.

Copying a Group of Files to a Backup Diskette
Lesson 1
1 Insert the backup diskette into drive A.
2 Press **List Files** (F5) and then press **Enter** to display the list of files.
3 Move the cursor to each file you want copied and type an asterisk (*) to mark the file.
4 Select Copy (8), type **y**, and then enter **a:** to copy the files to the backup diskette.

Creating a Caption
Lesson 30

1 While in the graphics figure, table, text box, or user-defined definition menu, select Caption (2) to create a caption.

2 Press **Exit** (F7) when you finish to return to the definition menu.

The Graphics Option menu lets you set the numbering style and position of the caption.

Creating a Concordance
Lesson 32

1 Create a list of words you want referenced in the index by typing each word or phrase on a line that ends with a Hard Return.

2 Save the list as a WordPerfect document, and then, when creating the index definition, enter the name of the document.

Creating a Document Summary
Lesson 19

1 Press **Format** (Shift-F8), select Document (3), and then select Summary (4).

2 Select options from the Document Summary screen to enter a descriptive filename, subject, author, etc.

3 Press **Exit** (F7) to save the summary and return to the document screen.

Creating a Footnote/Endnote
Lesson 32

1 Place the cursor next to the word(s) in the document that you want referenced.

2 Press **Footnote** (Ctrl-F7), select Footnote (1) or Endnote (2), and then select Create (1).

3 Type the text of the footnote (or endnote), and then press **Exit** (F7) to return to the document screen.

Creating a Form Type
Lesson 27

1 Press **Print** (Shift-F7), type **s**, place the cursor on the printer for which you want to create a form type, and then select Edit (3).

2 Select Forms (4) from the Edit menu, and then select Add (1) from the form type list.

3 Select a paper type from the displayed menu of types (select Other to name your own type).

4 Use the options on the paper type editing menu to set the size, orientation, location, etc.

5 Press **Exit** (F7) five times to return to the document screen.

Creating a Graphics Figure
Lessons 17 and 30
1 Place the cursor at the beginning of the page or paragraph.
2 Press **Graphics** (Alt-F9), select Figure (1), and then select Create (1).
3 Select Filename (1) and enter the name of the graphics file.
4 Use other options on the menu to set caption, type, position, and size.
5 Press **Exit** (F7) to return to the document screen.

Creating a Header or Footer for Every Page
Lessons 10 and 17
1 Move the cursor to the very beginning of the page where you want the header to start.
2 Press **Format** (Shift-F8), select Page (2), and then select Headers (3) or Footers (4).
3 Select Header A (1) or Footer A (1), and then select Every Page (2).
4 Type the text of the header, including any formats or codes (^B for page numbering).
5 Press **Exit** (F7) twice to save the header and return to your document.

Creating a Horizontal Line
Lessons 17 and 30
1 Place the cursor at the beginning of the page or line.
2 Press **Graphics** (Alt-F9), select Line (5), and then select Horizontal Line (1).
3 Use the Horizontal Line options to set the line position, length, width, and shading (100% = black).
4 Press **Exit** (F7) to return to the document screen.

Creating a Key for Sorting
Lesson 26
1 Press **Merge/Sort** (Ctrl-F9) and select Sort (2).
2 Enter a name for the input file, and then enter a name for the output file.
3 Select Type (7) and then select from Merge, Line, Paragraph.
4 Select Keys (3), and then enter the one or more keys for the sort.
5 Press **Exit** (F7), and then select Perform Action (1) to start the sort.

Creating a Keyboard Layout
Lesson 27
1 Press **Setup** (Shift-F1) and select Keyboard Layout (6).
2 Select Create (4) and enter a name for the keyboard layout file.
3 Use Create (4) and Retrieve (6) on the Keystroke menu to create keystroke tasks or retrieve macros and assign them to keystrokes.
4 Press **Exit** (F7) twice to return to the document screen.

Creating a Master Document
Lesson 32
1 Place the cursor where you want a file inserted.
2 Press **Mark Text** (Alt-F5) and select Sub Document (2).
3 Enter the filename of the sub document you want retrieved when the master document is expanded.
4 Continue using **Mark Text** to insert sub document filenames, and then save the document (it is now a master document).

Creating a Math Formula
Lesson 16
While in the Math Define menu (Alt-F7,2), you can create a formula for a Math column by typing **0** for the Type, and then entering the formula. The formula can contain numbers, column letters (A-X), and the operators available with Math (+,-,*,/,etc.).

Creating a Menu in a Primary File (^O)
Lesson 29
You can use the ^O merge code to create a menu or message for a ^C in a primary file. Insert a ^O (Shift-F9,O), type the menu or message, insert a second ^O, and then insert the ^C. You can only type text, spaces, and tabs between the ^O's.

Creating a Style
Lesson 18
1 Press **Style** (Alt-F8) and select Create (3).
2 Use the options on the Edit menu to enter a name, type, and description for the style.
3 Select Codes (4) and then use the available WordPerfect features to create the style.
4 Press **Exit** (F7) three times to save the style and return to the document screen.

Creating a Vertical Line
Lessons 29 and 30
1 Place the cursor at the beginning of the page or line.
2 Press **Graphics** (Alt-F9), select Line (5), and then select Vertical Line (2).
3 Use the Vertical Line options to set the horizontal and vertical positions, length, width, and shading (100% = black).
4 Press **Exit** (F7) to return to the document screen.

Creating a Vertical Line Between Columns
Lesson 30
1 Place the cursor at the beginning of the first column on the page.
2 Press **Graphics** (Alt-F9), select Line (5), and then select Vertical Line (1).

3 Select Horizontal Position (1), select Between Columns (3), and then enter the column number for the first of the two columns.

4 Use the Vertical Line options to set the vertical position, length, width, and shading (100% = black).

5 Press **Exit** (F7) to return to the document screen.

Creating an Outline
Lesson 31

1 Press **Date/Outline** (Shift-F5) and select Outline (4).

2 Press **Enter** to insert an automatic paragraph number and press **Tab** to move to number to the correct level.

3 Type the text for the number.

4 Continue using **Enter**, **Tab**, and typing text for each item in the outline.

5 Press **Date/Outline** (Shift-F5) and select Outline (4) to return to normal editing.

To indent after inserting a paragraph number, press the Space Bar and the tab or ♦Indent.

Creating and Editing Comments
Lesson 16

1 Press **Text In/Out** (Ctrl-F5) and select Comment (5).

2 Select Create (1) or Edit (2) to create a comment or edit the first comment above the cursor in the document.

3 Edit the comment as you would a normal document, using **Bold** (F6) and **Underline** (F8) to emphasize text.

4 Press **Exit** (F7) to save the comment and return to the document screen.

Defining a Simple Macro
Lessons 23 and 24

1 Press **Macro Define** (Ctrl-F10), and then hold down **Alt** and type a letter, or enter a filename to name the macro.

2 Press **Enter** to bypass assigning a description.

3 Perform the task you want recorded in the macro file.

4 Press **Macro Define** (Ctrl-F10) to end defining the macro and save the macro file.

If you are starting a merge with the macro, the macro automatically ends once the merge has started. You do not need to press the Macro Define key a second time to end the macro definition.

Defining an Index
Lesson 32
1 Place the cursor at the top of a new page, type an index heading, and then press **Enter** twice to double space.

2 Press **Mark Text** (Alt-F5), select Define (5), and then select Define Index (3).

3 Enter a concordance name (or press **Enter** to continue), and then select a numbering style for the index.

Defining an Outline or Paragraph Numbering Style
Lessons 29 and 31
1 Place the cursor above the outline or paragraph numbering.

2 Press **Date/Outline** (Shift-F5) and select Define (6).

3 Select a preset style (2 through 5) or select User-Defined (6) to create your own style.

4 Press **Exit** (F7) twice to return to the document screen.

Defining Math Columns
Lessons 16 and 28
1 Use the Line Format menu (Shift-F8,1,8) to set a tab for each Math column.

2 Press **Math/Columns** (Alt-F7) and select Math Define (2).

3 Set the type, negative number display, and number of digits for each tabbed column.

4 Press **Exit** (F7) to return to the Math/Columns menu.

5 Select Math On (1) to turn on the defined columns.

Defining Newspaper and Parallel Columns
Lessons 19 and 27
1 Place the cursor at the point where you want columns to begin.

2 Press **Math/Columns** (Alt-F7) and select Column Define (4).

3 Select Type (1), and then select Newspaper (1), Parallel (2), or Parallel with Block Protect (3).

4 Select Number of Columns (2) and enter the number of columns you want across the page (up to 24).

5 Select Distance Between Columns (3) and Margins (4) if you want to adjust the displayed settings.

6 Press **Exit** (F7) to save the definition and return to the Math/Columns menu.

7 Select Columns On/Off (3) to start typing in columns.

Defining Tabbed Columns
Lesson 15
1 Place the cursor at the beginning of the columns.
2 Press **Format** (Shift-F8), select Line (1), and then select Tab Set (8).
3 Press **Delete to End of Line** (Ctrl-End) and then set a tab for each column you want defined.
4 Press **Exit** (F7) twice to save the tab settings and return to the document screen.

Deleting a File
Lesson 11
1 Press **List Files** (F5) and then press **Enter** to display the list of files.
2 Place the cursor on the file you want deleted.
3 Select Delete (2) and then type **y** to delete the file.

Deleting a Group of Files
Lesson 11
1 Press **List Files** (F5) and then press **Enter** to display the list of files.
2 Move the cursor to each file you want deleted and type an asterisk (*) to mark the file.
3 Select Delete (2) and then type **y** twice to delete the files.

Displaying a Document Summary
Lesson 19
You can display a document summary while in List Files by using Look (6) to display the document contents. The document summary can also be displayed for editing while the document is on the screen by using Summary on the Format Document menu.

Displaying a Keyboard Template
Lesson 7
1 Press **Help** (F3) twice to display a keyboard template of WordPerfect features.

or

If you are already using Help, simply press **Help** (F3) once to display the keyboard template.

2 Press **Enter** (or the **Space Bar**) to return to your document.

Displaying a List of Features and Keystrokes
Lesson 7
1 Press **Help** (F3) and then type a letter of the alphabet to display a list of features beginning with that letter.
2 Press **Enter** (or the **Space Bar**) to return to your document.

Displaying a List of Filenames
Lesson 2
1 Press **List Files** (F5) and then press **Enter** to display the list.
2 Press **Exit** (F7) to return to your document.

Displaying a Page of Reference Information for a Feature
Lesson 7
1 Press **Help** (F3) and then press the keystrokes for a feature to display a page of reference information about the feature.
2 Press **Enter** (or the **Space Bar**) to return to your document.

Displaying Another Directory from the List Files Screen
Lesson 11
1 Place the cursor on the "<CURRENT>" directory in the list.
2 Press **Enter**, type the name of the directory (e.g., **a:**), and then press **Enter** again.

Editing a Header
Lesson 14
1 Press **Format** (Shift-F8), select Page (2), and then select Headers (3).
2 Select Header A (1) or Header B (2), and then select Edit (5).
3 Edit the header using the normal editing and formatting keys.
4 Press **Exit** (F7) three times to save the editing changes and return to the document screen.

Editing a Macro
Lesson 24
1 Press **Macro Define** (Ctrl-F10) and enter the name of the macro you want to edit.
2 Select Edit (2) to edit the macro, and then select Action (2) to place the cursor in the macro editing window.
3 Insert keystrokes by pressing the normal keys for the features; insert editing keystrokes (Home, Arrow, Enter) by pressing **Macro Define** (Ctrl-F10) before typing the keys.
4 Press Exit (F7) twice to save the edited macro.

Editing a Style
Lesson 18
1 Press **Style** (Alt-F8) and place the reverse video cursor on the style you want to edit.
2 Select Edit (4) and then select Codes (4) to display and edit the contents of the style.
3 Press **Exit** (F7) three times to save the changes and return to the document screen.

Editing in the Reveal Codes Screen
Lesson 5
1 Press **Reveal Codes** (Alt-F3) to display the text in your document with all the WordPerfect codes.
2 Edit and format the document as you normally would in the document screen.
3 Press **Reveal Codes** (Alt-F3) to exit the Reveal Codes screen.

Editing Text in a Graphics Box
Lesson 30
1 Press **Graphics** (Alt-F9) and select Figure (1), Table (2), Text Box (3), or User-Defined (4).
2 Select Edit (2) and enter the number of the box you want to edit.
3 Select Edit (8) to display the contents of the box.
4 Edit the text using formatting, font, and other editing features.
5 Press **Exit** (F7) twice to return to the document screen.

Editing the Graphics Figure Options
Lesson 31
1 Place the cursor to the right of the existing graphics option code.
2 Press **Graphics** (Alt-F9), and select Figure (1), Table (2), Text Box (3), or User-Defined (4).
3 Select Options (4) and then make the changes to the displayed menu.
4 Press **Exit** (F7) to save the settings and insert a new option code.
5 Press **Left Arrow** (←) and then press **Backspace** (and type **y** if necessary) to delete the original option code.

Editing Two Documents
Lesson 9
1 Press **Switch** (Shift-F3) to open up a second WordPerfect screen in which you can edit another document.

Ending or Canceling a Merge
Lesson 23
1 End or cancel a merge by pressing **Merge Codes** (Shift-F9) and typing **e**.

Erasing a Block of Text
Lessons 22 and 25
1 Place the cursor at the beginning of the text you want to delete, press **Block** (Alt-F4), and then move the cursor to the end of the text.
2 Press **Backspace** and type **y** to delete the text from your document.

Erasing a Line of Text
Lesson 8
1 Place the cursor at the beginning of the line, and then press **Delete to End of Line** (Ctrl-End).

Erasing a Page of Text
Lesson 14
1 Place the cursor at the beginning of the page, press **Delete to End of Page** (Ctrl-PgDn), and then type **y** to delete the text on the page.

Erasing a Word
Lesson 8
1 Place the cursor in the word, and then press **Delete Word** (Ctrl-Backspace).

Erasing Characters
Lesson 8
1 Press **Backspace** to erase the character to the left of the cursor, or press **Delete** (Del) to erase the character at the cursor.

Hold down either key to erase several characters at the same time.

Erasing Codes in the Document Screen
Lesson 10
1 Press **Backspace** or **Delete** (Del) to erase a code.
2 Type **y** (for yes) if WordPerfect asks if you want the code erased.

Erasing Codes in the Reveal Codes Screen
Lesson 5
1 Press **Backspace** or **Delete** (Del) to erase WordPerfect codes (such as a tab) while in the Reveal Codes screen.

Exiting WordPerfect
Lesson 11
1 Press **Exit** (F7) and then type **n** or type **y** when asked if you want to save the document on your screen.
2 Type **y** when asked if you want to exit WordPerfect.

Expanding a Master Document
Lesson 32
1 Press **Retrieve** (Shift-F10) and then enter the filename of the master document to retrieve it to your screen.
2 Press **Mark Text** (Alt-F5), select Generate (6), and then select Expand Master Document (3).

A master document needs to be expanded in order to print the text in the subdocument. If you print without expanding, only the text on your screen (not the comments) are printed.

Formatting with Styles
Lesson 18
1 Press **Style** (Alt-F8) and place the cursor on the style you want to use for formatting.

2 Select On (1) to insert the style in the document.

3 After typing the text for a paired style, press **Enter** to insert a Hard Return and a new pair of style codes, or press **Style** (Alt-F8) and select Off (2) to turn off the paired style.

You can also use Block with paired styles to place style on and off codes around existing text.

Generating Tables, Indexes, Automatic References, etc.
Lesson 32
1 Press **Mark Text** (Alt-F5), select Generate (6), and then type **5** to generate all defined tables, lists, indexes, and automatic references.

2 Type **y** to begin generating (all old tables, etc., are replaced), or type **n** to return to your document.

Hyphenating Text
Lesson 32
1 Place the cursor at the beginning of your document, or at the place in your document where you want WordPerfect to begin hyphenating.

2 Press **Format** (Shift-F8), select Line (1), and then select Hyphenation (1).

3 Select Manual (2) to have WordPerfect stop to let you do the hyphenating, or select Automatic (3) to have WordPerfect do the hyphenating for you.

4 Press **Exit** (F7) to return to your document.

If you want to turn Hyphenation off before the end of the document, move the cursor to the place where you want hyphenating to end and then turn off hyphenation with the Line Format menu.

Ignoring Merge Codes in a Secondary File (^V)
Lesson 29
You can place a pair of ^V merge codes (Shift-F9,V) around a merge code in a secondary file to have WordPerfect ignore the code during a merge.

Indenting a Paragraph with a Hanging Indent
Lesson 13
1 Place the cursor at the beginning of the first line in the paragraph.

2 Press →**Indent** (F4) to indent the entire paragraph, and then press ←**Margin Release** (Shift-Tab) to release the first line back to the left margin.

3 Type the text of the paragraph, pressing **Enter** to end the last line.

Indenting All the Lines of a Paragraph
Lesson 13
1 Place the cursor at the beginning of the first line in the paragraph.
2 Press ◆**Indent** (F4) to indent all the lines in the paragraph at the next tab stop.

Indenting Single Lines of Text
Lesson 13
1 Press **Tab** at the beginning of a line to move the line to the next tab stop. The lines should end with a Hard Return (Enter).

Indenting the First Line of a Paragraph
Lesson 13
1 Press **Tab** to indent the first line of a paragraph.

Inserting a Date
Lessons 3 and 6
1 Press **Date/Outline** (Shift-F5).
2 Select Date Text (1) to insert the current date as text or select Date Code (2) to insert a code that updates the date automatically whenever the document is retrieved or printed.

Inserting a Field in a Primary File (^F)
Lessons 21 and 24.
1 Insert a ^F into a primary file by pressing **Merge Codes** (Shift-F9), typing **f**, and then entering the field number.

Inserting a Paragraph Number
Lesson 29
1 Press **Date/Outline** (Shift-F5) and select Paragraph Number (5).
2 Enter a level number to have the paragraph number fixed at that level, or press **Enter** to have the paragraph number automatically update as you move from level to level.

You can also use Outline to insert paragraph numbers automatically.

Inserting Merge Codes into a Document
Lesson 21
1 Place the cursor at the position in the primary or secondary file where you want the merge code inserted.
2 Press **Merge Codes** (Shift-F9) and then type the letter of the merge code. For the ^F merge code, you will also need to enter the field number.

You can also insert a merge code into a primary or secondary file by holding down Control (Ctrl) and typing the letter of the merge code. However, if you are inserting a merge code such as ^R, ^E, or ^F, you will also need to insert a Hard Return, Hard Page break, or field number for the merge to work correctly.

Inserting Text/Codes from the Keyboard During a Merge (^C)
Lesson 23

1 Press **Merge Codes** (Shift-F9) and type **c** to insert a ^C code into a primary file that pauses during a merge for input from the keyboard.

When the merge pauses, press Merge R (F9) to continue the merge.

Inserting the Current Date in a Primary File (^D)
Lessons 21 and 23

1 Press **Merge Codes** (Shift-F9) and then type **d** to place a ^D code into a primary file that inserts the current date during a merge.

Looking into a File on Disk
Lesson 4

1 Press **List Files** (F5) and then press **Enter**.
2 Move the cursor to the filename of a WordPerfect document.
3 Select Look (6) or press **Enter** to display the contents of the file.
4 Press **Exit** (F7) twice to return to the WordPerfect editing screen.

Marking a Title for the Table of Contents
Lesson 32

1 Highlight the title you want included in the table of contents with **Block** (Alt-F4).
2 Press **Mark Text** (Alt-F5), and then select Table of Contents (1).
3 Type the level number to mark the title for the table of contents.

Marking a Word or Phrase for the Index
Lesson 32

1 Highlight the word or phrase you want referenced in the index with **Block** (Alt-F4).
2 Press **Mark Text** (Alt-F5) and select Index (3).
3 Press **Enter** to use the displayed word or phrase as a heading, or enter a heading of your own.
4 Enter a subheading, or press **Enter** if no word or phrase appears to bypass creating a subheading.

Marking and Unmarking Files in the List Files Screen
Lesson 11

While in the List Files screen (F5), you can mark or unmark a file by placing the cursor on the file and typing an asterisk (*). You can then use options such as Delete (2) or Copy (3) for a group of files.

Merging a Primary and Secondary File
Lessons 20, 22, 24, and 25
1 Clear the screen by pressing **Exit** (F7) and then typing **n** twice (if you do not want to save the document on your screen).
2 Press **Merge/Sort** (Ctrl-F9) and then select Merge (1).
3 Enter the name of the primary file, and then enter the name of the secondary file to start the merge.

Merging a Primary File Only
Lessons 23 and 25
1 Clear the screen by pressing **Exit** (F7) and then typing **n** twice (if you do not want to save the document on your screen).
2 Press **Merge/Sort** (Ctrl-F9) and then select Merge (1).
3 Enter the name of the primary file, and then press **Enter** for the name of the secondary file to start the merge.

Moving a Block of Text
Lesson 9
1 Place the cursor at the beginning of the text you want to move.
2 Press **Block** (Alt-F4) and then highlight the text by moving the cursor.
3 Press **Move** (Ctrl-F4), select Block (1), and then select Move (1) or Copy (2).
4 Place the cursor at the location where you want the text to be retrieved.
5 Press **Enter** to retrieve the highlighted text.

Moving a Sentence, Paragraph, or Page
Lessons 4 and 9
1 Place the cursor in the sentence, paragraph, or page you want to move.
2 Press **Move** (Ctrl-F4), select Sentence (1), Paragraph (2), or Page (3), and then select Move (1) or Copy (2).
3 Place the cursor at the location where you want the text retrieved.
4 Press **Enter** to retrieve the text.

Moving Between Text Columns
Lesson 30
You can move from one text column to the next by pressing **Go To** (Ctrl-Home) and then **Left Arrow** (←) or **Right Arrow** (→). Press **Go To** twice and then **Left Arrow** or **Right Arrow** to move across the page to the first or last column.

Moving the Cursor
Lessons 2 and 5
You can use the arrow keys to move through the text on your screen a character or line at a time without changing the text. Press **End** to move the cursor to the end of the current line.

Moving the Cursor a Page at a Time
Lessons 4 and 8
1 Press **Page Up** (PgUp) or **Page Down** (PgDn) to move to the very beginning of the previous or next page.

Moving the Cursor a Screen at a Time
Lesson 8
1 Press **Home** and then **Up Arrow** (↑) or **Down Arrow** (↓) to move a screen at a time through your document.

Moving the Cursor to the Beginning or End of a Document
Lesson 8
1 Press **Home** twice and then press **Up Arrow** (↑) or **Down Arrow** (↓) to move to the very beginning or very end of your document. Press **Home** three times and **Up Arrow** (↑) to move to the very beginning of the document (before any codes).

Moving the Cursor to the Top or Bottom of a Page
Lesson 21
1 Press **Go To** (Ctrl-Home) twice and then press **Up Arrow** (↑) or **Down Arrow** (↓) to move to the top or bottom of the current page.

Numbering Lines
Lesson 29
1 Place the cursor at the beginning of a page or the document.
2 Press **Format** (Shift-F8), select Line (1), select Line Numbering (5), and then type **y**.
3 Set the numbering and position of the numbers from the displayed Page Numbering menu, and then press **Exit** (F7) to return to the document screen.

Numbering Pages
Lesson 8
1 Place the cursor at the very beginning of the page on which you want numbering to start.
2 Press **Format** (Shift-F8), select Page (2), and then select Page Numbering (7).
3 Select the position of the number on the page, and then press **Exit** (F7) to return to the document screen.

Numbering Pages in a Header
Lesson 10
1 Include page numbering in a header by holding down **Ctrl** and typing **b** to insert a ^B code while creating the header.

Opening (and Closing) a Window
Lesson 20
1 Press **Screen** (Ctrl-F3), select Window (1), and then enter the number of lines you want in the window. Entering "12" splits most screens in half.

2 Use **Switch** (Shift-F3) to move the cursor from one half of the screen to the other.

3 Press **Screen**, select Window (1), and then enter a number of lines larger than what can be displayed on your screen to close the window. Entering "0" will close the window for all monitors.

Opening the Second Document Screen
Lesson 9
1 Press **Switch** (Shift-F3) to open a second document editing screen.

Previewing a Document
Lessons 4, 30, and 31
1 Press **Print** (Shift-F7) and then select View Document (6).

2 Select 100% (1), 200% (2), Full Page (3), or Facing Pages (4) to change the display of the Preview screen.

3 Use **Page Up** (PgUp), **Page Down** (PgDn), **Home**, or the arrow keys to scroll through the document.

4 Press **Exit** (F7) to return to the document screen, or press **Cancel** (F1) and select Full Document (1) to print the document.

Printing a Document
Lesson 1
1 Press **Print** (Shift-F7) and select Full Document (1) to print the document on your screen.

Printing a List of Files
Lesson 11
1 Press **Print** (Shift-F7) while in the List Files screen (F5), to print a list of all the files in the directory or on the diskette.

Printing a Page
Lesson 21
1 Press **Print** (Shift-F7) and select Page (2) to print the page on which the cursor is positioned.

Redlining Text
Lesson 29
1 Press **Font** (Ctrl-F8), select Appearance (2), and then select Redline (8).

2 Type the text you want added to the document.

3 Press **Font** (Ctrl-F8) and select Normal (3) to return to typing normal text.

You can also redline existing text by highlighting the text with Block before selecting Font.

Referencing Text and Illustrations
Lesson 32
1 Place the cursor at the point where you want the automatic page reference number to be displayed and printed.

2 Press **Mark Text** (Alt-F5), select Automatic Reference (1), and then select Mark Both Reference and Target (3).

3 Select a reference type (page number, paragraph/outline number, etc.).

4 Move the cursor to the item in the document that you want referenced (the target), and then press **Enter** to mark the item.

Removing Redline Markings and Strikeout Text
Lesson 29
1 Press **Mark Text** (Alt-F5) and select Generate (6).

2 Type **1** and then type **y** to remove all redline markings (codes) and strikeout text from the document.

Repeating a Character
Lesson 3
1 Press **Escape** (Esc), type the repeat value, and then type the character you want repeated.

or

Hold down the key to repeat the character.

Repeating a WordPerfect Feature
Lesson 9
1 Press **Escape** (Esc), type the repeat value, and then press the keys for the feature you want to repeat.

Many of the editing features such as the arrow keys, Backspace, Delete, and Delete Word can be repeated. Check the WordPerfect reference manual for a complete list of features that can be assigned a repeat value.

Replacing a Document and Clearing the Screen
Lesson 4
1 Press **Exit** (F7) and type **y** to save the document on your screen.
2 Press **Enter** and type **y** to replace the original file on disk with the document on your screen.
3 Type **n** to stay in WordPerfect and clear the screen.

Replacing Text and Codes
Lessons 24 and 25
1 Place the cursor at the beginning of the document.
2 Press **Replace** (Alt-F2) and type **y** to have WordPerfect stop for confirmation at each replacement, or type **n** to have the replacing done without stopping.
3 Type the text and/or press the keystrokes for the text and/or codes you want WordPerfect to replace.
4 Press **◆Search** (F2), and type the new text and/or codes you want inserted.
5 Press **◆Search** (F2) to begin the replacing.

Restarting Paragraph Numbering
Lesson 29
1 Place the cursor above the first paragraph number where you want numbering to restart.
2 Press **Date/Outline** (Shift-F5) and select Define (6).
3 Select Starting Paragraph Number (1) and enter the number at which you want numbering to begin.
4 Press **Exit** (F7) to return to the document screen.

Restoring Deleted Text
Lesson 8
1 Press **Cancel** (F1) to display the deleted text.
2 Select Restore (1) to insert the deleted text back into your document, or select Previous Deletion (2) until the deleted text is displayed and then select Restore (1).

Retrieving a File (List Files)
Lesson 4
1 Press **List Files** (F5) and then press **Enter** to display a list of files.
2 Place the cursor on a filename.
3 Select Retrieve (1) and then type **y** to retrieve the file.

Retrieving a File (Retrieve)
Lesson 6
1 Press **Retrieve** (Shift-F10), type the name of the file, and then press **Enter**.

Retrieving a Style List
Lesson 18
1 Press **Style** (Alt-F8) and select Retrieve (7).
2 Enter the filename of the style list.

If you have indicated a style list for the Style Library in the Setup menu, then that style list is automatically retrieved when you press Style.

Rewriting (Formatting) the Text on Your Screen
Lesson 13
1 Press **Screen** (Ctrl-F3) and select Rewrite (0) or press **Enter** to format the text on your screen.

This feature is useful if you have Automatic Format & Rewrite turned off, or if the text on your screen is not displayed correctly.

Saving a Document and Clearing the Screen
Lesson 2
1 Press **Exit** (F7) and type **y** to save the document.
2 Type a name for the file and press **Enter**, or press **Enter** and type **y** to use the displayed filename.
3 Type **n** to stay in WordPerfect and clear the screen.

Saving a Document While Editing
Lesson 8
1 Press **Save** (F10) and then press **Enter** to use the same filename.
2 Type **y** to replace the original document with the one on your screen, and then continue editing.

Searching for a Filename in the List Files Screen
Lesson 11
1 Press ◆**Search** (F2) or select Name Search (N) and begin typing the name of the file.
2 When the cursor moves to the filename, press **Enter** to return to normal cursor movement.

Searching for a Word in a File
Lesson 19
1 Press **List Files** (F5) and then press **Enter** to display the files.
2 Select Word Search (9), and then select Document Summary (1), First Page (2), or Entire Document (3).
3 Enter the word you want to find in the files.
4 After search is completed, press **Tab** to move from marked file to marked file, and then use Look (6) to display the contents of the marked files.

You can also use Search while in the Look screen to search for lines that contain the word you want to find.

Searching for Text or Codes
Lessons 10 and 28
1 Press ◆**Search** (F2) or ◆**Search** (Shift-F2) to search forward or back through the document.
2 Type the word(s) you want to find and/or press the keystrokes for a feature code.
3 Press ◆**Search** (F2) to start the search.

Selecting a Base Font
Lesson 31
1 Press **Font** (Ctrl-F8) and select Base Font (4).
2 Highlight the font you want to use, and then press **Enter** to select the font.

Selecting a Font Attribute
Lesson 17
1 Press **Font** (Ctrl-F8) and select Size (1) or Appearance (2).
2 Select an attribute from the Size or Appearance menus.
3 Type the text you want printed in the font attribute.
4 Press **Font** (Ctrl-F8) and select Normal (3), or simply press **Right Arrow** (→), to return to typing normal text.

You can also use Block before selecting Font to assign an attribute to existing text.

Selecting a Paper Size and Type
Lesson 22
1 Place the cursor at the beginning of the document.
2 Press **Format** (Shift-F8), select Page (2), and then select Paper Size/Type (7).
3 Select the paper size from the displayed menu, or select Other (O) and enter your own width and height.
4 Select the paper type from the displayed menu, or select Other (8) to enter a type you have created.
5 Press **Exit** (F7) to return to the document screen.

Selecting a Printer
Lessons 8 and 13
1 Press **Print** (Shift-F7), and type **s** to choose the Select Printer option.
2 Highlight the name of the printer you want to select, and then press **Enter**.
3 Press **Exit** (F7) to return to the document screen.

Selecting Records from a Secondary Merge File (Global)
Lesson 26
1 Select Select (4) from the Sort menu.

2 Type **g=** and then type the word or number that you want to use to select the records.

3 Add any other words or numbers to the selection process by using "g=" and linking the global keys together with the and (*) or the or (+) symbols.

4 Press **Exit** (F7) to save the select statement, and then select Perform Action (1) to begin record selection.

Sending a "Go" to the Printer
Lesson 22
1 Press **Print** (Shift-F7) and then select Control Printer (4) if WordPerfect "beeps" after selecting Full Document or Page from the Print menu.

2 Check the message at the top of the Control Printer menu, take any corrective action, and then select Go (4) to start printing.

Setting a New Page Number
Lesson 14
1 Place the cursor at the beginning of the page on which you want the numbering to begin.

2 Press **Format** (Shift-F8), select Page (2), and then select New Page Number (6).

3 Enter the number at which you want page number to start.

4 Press **Exit** (F7) to save the setting and return to the document screen.

Setting a Tab Stop
Lessons 5 and 15
1 Place the cursor at the beginning of the document, or at the beginning of the line where you want the tab stop to begin.

2 Press **Format** (Shift-F8), select Line (1), and then select Tab Set (8).

3 Press **Delete to End of Line** (Ctrl-End) to erase all previous tab stop settings.

4 Type the position of the tab stop and press **Enter**, or move the cursor to the place in the tab ruler where you want the tab stop and type **l**.

5 Press **Exit** (F7) twice to save the tab stop and return to the WordPerfect editing screen.

Setting Left and Right Margins
Lesson 22
1 Place the cursor at the beginning of the page where you want the new margins to begin.

2 Press **Format** (Shift-F8), select Line (1), and then select Margins Left/Right (7).

3 Enter the left margin setting, and then enter the right margin setting.

4 Press **Exit** (F7) to return to the document screen.

Setting Line Spacing
Lesson 18
1 Place the cursor at the beginning of the line or page where you want the new spacing to begin.
2 Press **Format** (Shift-F8), select Line (1), and then select Line Spacing (6).
3 Enter a number by which to multiply the current line height (2 = double spacing, 3 = triple spacing).
4 Press **Exit** (F7) to return to the document screen.

Setting Options for a Graphics Figure
Lessons 17 and 30
1 Place the cursor on the graphics figure code, or set the options before creating the graphics figure.
2 Press **Graphics** (Alt-F9), select Figure (1), and then select Options (4).
3 Use the Figure Options menu to set items such as the box border, spacing between the box and text, shading, etc.
4 Press **Exit** (F7) to return to the document screen.

Setting the Units of Measure
Lesson 19
1 Press **Setup** (Shift-F1) and select Units of Measure (8).
2 Select Display and Entry (1), and then enter the units you want to use in menus and messages.
3 Select Status Line Display (2), and then enter the units you want displayed on the status line.
4 Press **Exit** (F7) to return to the document screen.

Setting Top and Bottom Margins
Lessons 17 and 22
1 Place the cursor at the beginning of the page where you want the new margins to begin.
2 Press **Format** (Shift-F8), select Page (2), and then select Margins Top/Bottom (5).
3 Enter the top margin setting, and then enter the bottom margin setting.
4 Press **Exit** (F7) to return to the document screen.

Sorting a List from the Screen to a File (and vice versa)
Lesson 26
1 Press **Merge/Sort** (Ctrl-F9) and then select Sort (2).
2 Enter the name of a file you want to sort, or press **Enter** to sort the text on your screen.
3 Enter the name of the file in which you want the sorted records saved, or press **Enter** to save the to the screen.
4 After selecting the correct settings and entering the key(s), select Perform Action (1) to sort the records and save them to the indicated file or to the screen.

Sorting a List of Items (alphabetically)
Lesson 10

1 Move the cursor to the beginning of the first word in the list.

2 Press **Block** (Alt-F4), and then move the cursor to the end of the last word in the list.

3 Press **Merge/Sort** (Ctrl-F9) and then select Perform Action (1).

Sorting in Descending Order
Lesson 26

1 Select Order (6) from the Sort menu, and then select Descending (2).

2 Select Perform Action (1) to begin sorting the records.

Spell-Checking a Document
Lesson 6

1 Press **Spell** (Ctrl-F3), and then select Document (3).

2 When WordPerfect stops at a word, select the correct spelling, or select an option from the menu to skip or edit the word.

3 Press **Exit** (F7) when spell-checking is completed to return to your document.

Starting a Macro from a Primary File (^G)
Lesson 23

1 Place the cursor at the end of the primary file.

2 Press **Merge Codes** (Shift-F10) and type **g** to insert a ^G.

3 Type the name of the macro (filename).

4 Press **Merge Codes** and type **g** to insert a second ^G after the name of the macro.

Starting a Macro with Alt
Lesson 23

1 Hold down **Alt** and type the letter you used when naming the macro with **Alt**.

Starting a Macro with Macro
Lesson 31

1 Press **Macro** (Alt-F10) and enter the filename you entered when defining the macro.

Starting a New Page
Lesson 8

1 Place the cursor at the beginning of the first line you want on the new page.

2 Press **Hard Page** (Ctrl-Enter) to insert the hard page break.

Striking Out Text
Lesson 29
1 Press **Block** (Alt-F4) and highlight the text you want to remove from the document.

2 Press **Font** (Ctrl-F8), select Appearance (2), and then select Strikeout (9).

Switching Between Document Screens
Lesson 9
1 Press **Switch** (Shift-F3) to switch back and forth between the two document screens.

Typing Over Existing Text
Lesson 4
1 Press **Insert** (Ins) to begin typing over text. A "Typeover" message appears on the status line.

2 When you finish, press **Insert** again to return to inserting text.

Typing Text in Tabbed Columns
Lesson 15
1 Press **Tab** or ♦**Indent** (F4) to move to the next tab stop when typing information in tabbed columns.

The ♦Indent key can only be used for the last column if you want to type more than one line of text.

Typing Text to the Right of the Center Position
Lesson 23
1 Place the cursor at the beginning of an empty line.

2 Press **Center** (Shift-F6) and then press **Enter** or **Down Arrow** (↓) to move the cursor to the next line.

3 Press **Left Arrow** (←) to move to the right of the Center codes, and then type the text you want to the right of the center position.

Typing Uppercase Letters
Lesson 2
1 Press **Caps Lock** to type all uppercase (capital) letters.

2 When you finish, press **Caps Lock** again to return to typing lowercase letters.

Underlining Spaces and Tabs
Lesson 14
1 Place the cursor at the beginning of the document, page, or line in which you want to underline both spaces and tabs.

2 Press **Format** (Shift-F8), select Other (4), and then select Underline (7).

3 Type **y** twice to have WordPerfect underline spaces and tabs, and then press **Exit** (F7) to return to the document screen.

Underlining Text
Lesson 5

1 Press **Underline** (F8), type the text, and press **Underline** again.

or

Block the text (Alt-F4) and press **Underline**.

Using the Thesaurus
Lesson 32

1 Place the cursor on the word you want to replace, and then select **Thesaurus** (Alt-F1).

2 Select Replace Word (1) and type the letter next to the new word you want to use.

or

Press **Cancel** (F1) if you cannot find the word you want.

Index

Y

Y Value 341

Z

ZIP code 233